Contemporary
Japanese
Architects

Volume II

Philip Jodidio

Contemporary **Japanese** Architects

Volume II

TASCHEN

KÖLN LISBOA LONDON NEW YORK PARIS TOKYO

Acknowledgements | Danksagung | Remerciements

The author wishes to thank Masakazu Bokura for
his kind assistance in the preparation of this book.

Der Autor dankt Masakazu Bokura für seine freundliche
Unterstützung bei der Entstehung des Buches.

L'auteur tient à remercier Masakazu Bokura pour son
soutien sur ce projet de livre.

Page 2 | Seite 2
Arata Isozaki, Saitama Arena, Saitama, Japan. A 1995 computer drawing
of an as yet unbuilt structure.

Arata Isozaki, Saitama Arena, Saitama, Japan. Eine 1995 entstandene
Computerzeichnung eines bislang nicht realisierten Gebäudes.

Arata Isozaki, Saitama Arena, Saitama, Japan. Dessin par ordinateur,
1995, d'une structure encore non-réalisée.
© Arata Isozaki

© 1997 Benedikt Taschen Verlag GmbH
Hohenzollernring 53, D-50672 Köln

Edited by Silvia Kinkel, Cologne
Design: Sylvie Chesnay, Paris; Samantha Finn, Mark Thomson, London
Cover Design: Angelika Taschen, Cologne; Mark Thomson, London
French translation: Jacques Bosser, Paris
German translation: Franca Fritz, Heinrich Koop, Cologne

Printed in Italy
ISBN 3-8228-8434-0

Contents | Inhalt | Sommaire

6 The Sun Also Rises
Japanese Architects in the 1990s

Und wieder geht die Sonne auf
Japanische Architekten in den 90er Jahren

Le soleil se lève aussi
Architectes japonais des années 90

66 Tadao Ando
82 Masakazu Bokura
90 Hiroshi Hara
102 Itsuko Hasegawa
108 Arata Isozaki
126 Toyo Ito
132 Fumihiko Maki
148 Kazuyo Sejima
158 Shin Takamatsu
164 Shoei Yoh

170 Biographies | Biographien
174 Bibliography | Bibliographie
175 Index
176 Credits | Fotonachweis |
Crédits photographiques

The Sun Also Rises
Japanese Architects in the 1990s

Und wieder geht die Sonne auf
Japanische Architekten in den 90er Jahren

Le soleil se lève aussi
Architectes japonais des années 90

A city with no end

In 1996, at the Hara Museum of Contemporary Art in Tokyo, the artist Kimio Tsuchiya (b. 1955) installed a work called "Urban Ruin," which carried a strong symbolic message about the fragility of the built environment. His work consisted entirely of ashes, molded into three-dimensional shapes on the floor, like an urban landscape. He described this piece as a reaction to the Great Hanshin Earthquake of 1995, which killed more than 5,000 people in Kobe. As the curator of the show, Kazuko Aono, wrote: "Terrible events such as this remind us of the power of nature, as well as undermine our arrogant trust in technology and the blind faith we place in our capacity to ensure our own safety. Indeed, it was not just the concrete infrastructure that was fragile."[1] The architect Masakazu Bokura draws another conclusion from Kimio Tsuchiya's "Urban Ruin." "In Western thought," he says, "the permanence of existence is emphasized, whereas Eastern philosophy and religion accept its ephemeral nature."

Indeed, many powerful forces play on contemporary Japanese architecture, not the least of which is the constant threat of earthquakes. The visitor who arrives in Tokyo for the first time is overwhelmed by the spectacle of a city like no other on earth. In its metropolitan area, Tokyo counts no fewer than 26.8 million inhabitants, making it far larger than the next largest urban area in the world, São Paulo, Brazil (16.4 million residents). The crowding of Japan, especially in the eastern coastal areas, is considerable. With a land area of 374,744 square kilometers, Japan is slightly smaller than California, and yet has a population of 125,506,000 (July 1995 estimate). Particularly for the Western visitor, Tokyo at first glance is an almost infinite jumble of unsightly electrical wires and small, ugly buildings. Aside from esthetic considerations, there are two good reasons for the unusual appearance of Tokyo, and indeed of other large Japanese cities. One is that it is forbidden for any two buildings to share a structural wall. A tiny passageway between walls naturally limits the danger that the collapse of one building during an earthquake will cause a chain reaction. The second is the so-called "Sunshine Law," which requires that any new build-

Page 6: Kimio Tsuchiya, "Urban Ruin," ashes from demolished house, 50 x 900 x 600 cm, installation at the Hara Museum of Contemporary Art, Tokyo, Japan, 1996. A testimony to the fragility of architecture and of life. Right: View of Tokyo, looking toward Mount Fuji. An almost endless panorama of small buildings.

Seite 6: Kimio Tsuchiya, »Urban Ruin«, Asche von zerstörten Häusern, 50 x 900 x 600 cm, Installation im Hara Museum of Contemporary Art, Tokio, Japan, 1996. Ein Zeugnis der Vergänglichkeit der Architektur und des Lebens. Rechts: Ansicht von Tokio mit Blick auf den Fudschijama. Ein nahezu endloses Panorama kleiner Gebäude.

Page 6: Kimo Tsuchiya, «Ruine urbaine», installation, cendres de maisons détruites, 50 x 900 x 600 cm, Musée Hara d'art contemporain, Tokyo, Japon, 1996. Un témoignage de la fragilité de l'architecture et de la vie. A droîte: Vue de Tokyo, vers le Mont Fuji: une mer de bâtiments bas qui s'étale presque à l'infini.

Die unendliche Stadt

1996 installierte der Künstler Kimio Tsuchiya (geb. 1955) im Hara Museum of Contemporary Art in Tokio eine Arbeit unter dem Titel »Urban Ruin«, mit der er eine Botschaft über die Vergänglichkeit der bebauten Umgebung vermitteln wollte. Seine Installation bestand ausschließlich aus Asche, die auf dem Boden zu räumlichen Gebilden geformt war und einer urbanen Landschaft ähnelte. Tsuchiya beschrieb seine Arbeit als eine Reaktion auf das große Hanshin-Erdbeben von 1995, bei dem in Kobe mehr als 5000 Menschen ums Leben kamen. Der Kurator der Ausstellung, Kazuko Aono, schrieb dazu: »Schreckliche Ereignisse wie dieses rufen uns nicht nur die Macht der Natur ins Gedächtnis, sie untergraben auch unser arrogantes Vertrauen in die Technik und den blinden Glauben in unsere Fähigkeit, uns selbst schützen zu können. Denn es waren nicht nur unsere Betonbauten, die sich als vergänglich erwiesen.«[1] Der Architekt Masakazu Bokura zieht aus der Betrachtung von »Urban Ruin« eine weitere Schlußfolgerung: »In der westlichen Auffassung«, so Bokura, »wird die Dauerhaftigkeit der Existenz betont, wogegen die östlichen Philosophien und Religionen deren Vergänglichkeit akzeptieren.«

Tatsächlich wirkt eine ganze Reihe von Kräften auf die zeitgenössische japanische Architektur ein, von denen die konstante Bedrohung durch Erdbeben nicht die geringste sein dürfte. Wer zum ersten Mal Tokio besucht, wird überwältigt vom Schauspiel einer Stadt, die auf der Welt ihresgleichen sucht. In Tokio wohnen 26,8 Millionen Menschen, was die Stadt zum größten urbanen Ballungsraum der Welt macht (São Paulo, die nächstgrößte Stadt, zählt 16,4 Millionen Einwohner). Die Bevölkerungsdichte Japans, vor allem in den östlichen Küstenregionen, ist bemerkenswert. Mit einer Landfläche von 374 744 km² ist Japan etwas kleiner als Kalifornien; dennoch leben hier 125 506 000 Menschen. Vor allem für westliche Besucher präsentiert sich Tokio auf den ersten Blick als nahezu endloses Chaos von unansehnlichen Oberleitungen und kleinen, häßlichen Gebäuden. Von ästhetischen Erwägungen einmal abgesehen, gibt es jedoch zwei gute Gründe für das ungewöhnliche Erscheinungsbild Tokios

La ville sans fin

En 1996, l'artiste Kimio Tschuiya (né en 1955) met en place au musée d'art contemporain de Hara à Tokyo une installation intitulée «Ruine urbaine». Chargée d'un puissant message symbolique sur la fragilité de notre environnement construit, l'œuvre est entièrement composée de cendres, moulées selon des formes variées, réparties sur le sol comme un paysage urbain. Cette œuvre est la réaction de l'artiste face au tremblement de terre *Hanshin* qui avait fait plus de 5000 victimes à Kobe en 1995. Commissaire de l'exposition, Kazuko Aono écrit à son sujet: «Des événements aussi terribles que celui-ci nous rappellent la puissance de la nature. Ils remettent en question la confiance arrogante que nous avons dans la technologie, comme notre foi aveugle en notre soi-disant capacité à assurer notre propre sécurité. En fait, les infrastructures de béton n'ont pas été les seules à se révéler fragiles.»[1] L'architecte Masakazu Bokura tire une autre conclusion de cette «Ruine Urbaine»: «Dans la pensée occidentale,» dit-il, «l'accent est mis sur la permanence de l'existence, alors que la philosophie et la religion orientales en acceptent la nature éphémère.»

Il est certain que l'architecture japonaise se trouve confrontée à de fortes presssions, la moindre n'étant pas la menace quotidienne des tremblements de terre. Le visiteur qui arrive à Tokyo pour la première fois est subjugué par le spectacle de cette ville sans équivalent aucun. Cette métropole ne compte pas moins de 26,8 millions d'habitants, ce qui en fait la première zone urbaine du monde, loin devant São Paulo, au Brésil, et ses 16,4 millions de résidents. La surpopulation du Japon, en particulier sur les côtes orientales est considérable. Avec une surface de 374 744 kilomètres carrés, le pays est légèrement moins étendu que la Californie, mais il possède une population de 125 506 000 habitants (estimation de juillet 1995). Pour notre visiteur occidental, à première vue Tokyo semble une sorte d'infini désordre de câbles électriques et de bâtiments aussi petits que laids. Toute considération esthétique mise à part, deux raisons expliquent cet étrange aspect de la capitale nippone, ainsi que de toutes les villes japonaises. La première est l'interdiction

ing not deprive its neighbors of more than a certain amount of their light. This rather humane measure results in the odd positions of many structures in their lots.

Successive disasters, some natural, and some very much man-made, have shaped the contemporary face of Tokyo. The first of these in the 20th century was the Great Kanto Earthquake of 1923, measuring 7.9 on the Richter scale, which may have killed 200,000 and left 64% of the remaining population homeless. The second, even more radical in its destruction, was the American firebombing of the city between March and May of 1945. More people died in these months than in the instantaneous devastation of Hiroshima. By September 1945, the population, which had exceeded 6,900,000 in 1942, had dropped through death and emigration to 2,777,000. Incendiary devices, dropped on a city constituted mostly of wooden structures, were particularly efficient. For this reason, it can be said that the largest city on earth has been built almost entirely since 1945. At the outset, this construction went forward with limited means. As in war-torn Europe, it was essential to build cheaply and fast. In more recent times, an implacable commercial logic, which has little to do with the canons of esthetics, has been the dominant influence. In a sense, this tidal wave of bad architecture is the second man-made disaster of Tokyo's 20th century history. It has swept before it much of the beauty of a centuries-old tradition.

Today, Tokyo is very much a capital of bad taste when it comes not only to architecture but also to a strident urban decor whose range and breadth baffles the Western imagination. Massive elevated roadways and train tracks cut off far more light and air at street level than the "Sunshine Law" preserves. Signs of every description, including giant video screens, jostle each other for the attention of hurried pedestrians, while forlorn rows of imitation plastic sushi and spaghetti announce the presence of their "real" counterparts inside at almost every restaurant's door. Yet for ten days in April, this huge gray city celebrates the thousands of cherry trees that temporarily transform it into a moving feast for the eyes. Contradiction, or what the Westerner perceives as contradiction, is omnipresent in Japan. Even more than the

und anderer japanischer Großstädte. Zum einen dürfen zwei Gebäude keine gemeinsame tragende Wand haben: Ein winziger Durchgang zwischen den Hauswänden soll verhindern, daß beim Einsturz eines Gebäudes während eines Erdbebens eine Kettenreaktion entsteht. Das zweite ist das sogenannte »Sonnenschein-Gesetz«, das besagt, daß neue Bauten ihren Nachbargebäuden nur eine bestimmte Menge des ihnen zustehenden Lichts rauben dürfen. Diese im Grunde sehr humane Regelung führt dazu, daß viele Häuser in äußerst ungewöhnlichen Positionen auf ihren Grundstücken stehen.

Das heutige Stadtbild Tokios wurde durch eine Reihe von Katastrophen geprägt, die nur zum Teil natürlichen, zum Großteil aber menschlichen Ursprungs sind. Der erste dieser Schicksalsschläge war das große Kanto-Erdbeben von 1923. Dieses Beben mit einer Stärke von 7,9 tötete 200 000 Menschen und machte 64 % der Überlebenden zu Obdachlosen. Die zweite, noch radikalere Verwüstung hinterließen die amerikanischen Bombenangriffe auf Tokio: Zwischen März und Mai 1945 starben mehr Menschen als bei der plötzlichen Zerstörung Hiroshimas. Von 1942 bis September 1945 schrumpfte die Zahl der Einwohner Tokios von 6,9 auf 2,777 Millionen. Der Abwurf von Brandbomben auf eine Stadt, die hauptsächlich aus Holzbauten bestand, hatte verheerende Auswirkungen. Daher läßt sich behaupten, daß die größte Stadt der Welt beinahe vollständig nach 1945 erbaut wurde. Zu Beginn standen für den Wiederaufbau nur begrenzte Mittel zur Verfügung. Wie im Nachkriegseuropa galt es auch hier, so schnell und billig wie möglich zu bauen. Dagegen wurde die Baubranche in den letzten Jahren von einer unnachgiebigen kommerziellen Logik beherrscht, die nur selten auf ästhetische Grundsätze Rücksicht nahm. In gewisser Weise stellt diese »Flutwelle« schlechter Architektur die zweite von Menschenhand geschaffene Katastrophe dar, die Tokio im 20. Jahrhundert traf und viel von der Schönheit einer jahrhundertealten Tradition mit sich riß.

Heute ist Tokio nicht nur in architektonischer Hinsicht eine Hauptstadt des schlechten Geschmacks; es existiert darüber hinaus auch ein schrilles städtisches Dekor, dessen Bandbreite

légale pour deux constructions voisines de partager un mur structurel mitoyen. La seconde est la réglementation appelée «Loi du Soleil», selon laquelle aucun bâtiment nouveau ne peut priver ses voisins de plus d'une certaine quantité de la lumière dont ils jouissaient auparavant. Cette mesure d'esprit humaniste explique l'étrange implantation de certaines constructions.

Des désastres successifs, certains naturels, d'autres indéniablement dus à l'homme, ont contribué à dessiner le visage actuel de Tokyo. Au XXe siècle, le premier est le grand tremblement de terre *Kanto* de 1923 (7,9 sur l'échelle de Richter) qui a peut-être tué 200 000 personnes et laissé 64 % de la population sans abri. Le second, encore plus radical dans ses destructions, est le bombardement de la ville par les Américains, de mars à mai 1945. Plus de personnes moururent au cours de ces quelques mois que de la bombe d'Hiroshima. En septembre 1945, la population qui avait dépassé 6 900 000 personnes en 1942, était retombée à 2 777 000 habitants. Lâchées sur une ville essentiellement construite en bois, les bombes incendiaires furent particulièrement destructrices. Pour cette raison on peut dire que la plus grande ville du monde a pour l'essentiel été construite après 1945. Au départ, la reconstruction se fit avec des moyens limités. Comme dans l'Europe de l'après-guerre, il était essentiel de construire vite et à moindre frais. Plus récemment, une logique commerciale implacable, sans rapport avec les canons de l'esthétique, a exercé une influence dominante. C'est en ce sens que la vague de fond de mauvaise architecture est le second désastre provoqué par l'homme dont Tokyo ait souffert au XXe siècle. Elle a balayé devant elle une bonne part de la beauté léguée par des siècles de tradition.

Aujourd'hui, Tokyo est devenue une sorte de capitale du mauvais goût, qu'il s'agisse d'architecture ou de décor urbain agressif, dont la diversité et la force ne cessent de surprendre l'Occidental. D'énormes rocades ou des voies de chemin de fer surélevées bloquent bien davantage la lumière au niveau de la rue que ce tout ce que peut tenter de préserver la «Loi du Soleil». Des panneaux publicitaires de toutes sortes, y compris des écrans vidéo géants, luttent les uns contre les autres pour attirer

Two night views of Tokyo, showing the overlapping road system and the proliferation of neon signs. A different type of urban organization.

Zwei Nachtansichten von Tokio, die das Gewirr einander überlappender Straßen und unzähliger greller Neonlichter zeigen – eine eigene Form urbaner Organisation.

Deux vues nocturnes de Tokyo: superposition du système routier, et prolifération d'enseignes au néon pour un type d'organisation urbaine original.

A view of the Shokintei Tea Pavilion, Katsura Palace, Kyoto, Japan, early 17th century. The "modernity" of the blue and white pattern on the sliding doors (fusuma) is a testimony to the rapport between Japanese tradition and contemporary architecture.

Ansicht des Shokintei-Teepavillon im Katsura-Palast, Kioto, Japan, frühes 17. Jahrhundert. Die moderne Ausstrahlung der blauweißen Schiebetüren (fusuma) zeigt die enge Verbindung von japanischer Tradition und zeitgenössischer Architektur.

Le pavillon de thé Shokintei, Palais de Katsura, Kyoto, Japon, début XVIIe siècle. La «modernité» du motif bleu et blanc des portes coulissantes (fusuma) témoigne des rapports entre tradition japonaise et architecture contemporaine.

United States, this is the capital of kitsch. And yet, Japan harbors places of exceptional beauty and subtlety, and a variety of architectural talents equaled by few countries. It is by looking back in a constructive way at their own tradition that Japanese architects have found their identity in the modern world. The pure simplicity of many Japanese gardens like that of Ryoan-ji in Kyoto, or palaces, such as the early 17th century Imperial residence of Katsura, is not as much in fundamental opposition with modernity as is most traditional Western architecture.

In a schematic way, it can be said that contemporary Japanese architects have reacted in two distinct ways to the peculiarities of their environment, both in philosophical terms, and in terms of their choice of building materials. Their first reaction against an earth that is likely to tremble at any moment is to make buildings as stable as possible. Particularly since 1981, strict laws have

weit über die westliche Vorstellungskraft hinausgeht. Gewaltige Stadtautobahnen und Hochbahnen rauben den Häusern mehr Licht, als das »Sonnenschein-Gesetz« je bewahren könnte. Schilder aller Art, darunter riesige Videobildschirme, wetteifern miteinander um die Aufmerksamkeit der vorbeihastenden Passanten, während vor nahezu jedem Restaurant Kunststoff-Sushi und -Spaghetti die Existenz ihrer »realen« Gegenstücke im Inneren ankündigen. Auf der anderen Seite feiert diese Stadt jedes Jahr im April zehn Tage lang Tausende von Kirschbäumen, die Tokio vorübergehend in ein Fest für das Auge verwandeln. Widersprüche – oder was dem Besucher aus dem Westen widersprüchlich erscheint – sind in Japan allgegenwärtig. Es ist das Mutterland des Kitsches, und übertrifft darin sogar noch die Vereinigten Staaten. Dennoch findet man in Japan Plätze von außergewöhnlicher Schönheit sowie eine solche Vielzahl architektonischer Talente wie in kaum einem anderen Land. Durch die konstruktive Auseinandersetzung mit der eigenen Tradition gelang es den japanischen Architekten, ihre Identität in der modernen Welt zu finden. Die schlichte Schönheit japanischer Gärten (wie des Ryoan-ji in Kioto) und Paläste (wie die aus dem frühen 17. Jahrhundert stammende Kaiserliche Residenz in Katsura) steht in einem viel geringeren Gegensatz zur Moderne als vergleichbare traditionelle Bauwerke der westlichen Architektur.

Als Faustregel könnte man behaupten, daß die modernen japanischen Architekten in zwei deutlich unterschiedlichen Ansätzen auf die Besonderheiten ihrer Umgebung reagiert haben und zwar in philosophischer Hinsicht wie auch durch die Wahl der Baumaterialien. Ihre erste Reaktion auf eine Erde, die jeden Moment beginnen könnte zu beben, besteht darin, so stabil wie möglich zu bauen. Seit 1981 regelt eine strenge Gesetzgebung die Standfestigkeit von Häusern und öffentlichen Bauten. Diese Tatsache kann als teilweise Erklärung dafür gelten, warum viele moderne japanische Bauwerke besonders massiv wirken – sie scheinen fest auf dem Erdboden zu sitzen, als ob sie nur darauf warten, ihre Stärke mit den Kräften der Natur zu messen. Erhöhte Straßen, Brücken oder die Stahlskelette neuer Gebäude weisen eine bauliche Dichte auf, die ebenfalls das Erscheinungs-

l'attention des piétons pressés, tandis qu'aux portes des restaurants, de sinistres étalages d'imitations plastiques de sushi et de spaghetti signalent l'existence de leur contrepartie «réelle» à l'intérieur. Cependant, chaque année en avril pendant dix jours, cette immense ville grise célèbre les milliers de cerisiers qui la transforment brièvement en une fête pour le regard. Au Japon la contradiction, du moins ce que l'Occidental perçoit comme tel, est omniprésente. Plus que n'importe où aux Etats-Unis, nous sommes ici dans la capitale du kitsch. Pourtant, le pays peut aussi se flatter de lieux d'une beauté d'une subtilité exceptionnelles, d'une réelle richesse de talents architecturaux. C'est en décidant de porter un nouveau regard constructif sur leur propre tradition que les architectes japonais ont trouvé leur identité face au monde moderne. La simplicité épurée de nombreux jardins comme celui du Ryoan-ji, à Kyoto, ou de palais comme la résidence impériale de Katsura datant du début du XVIIe siècle, n'est pas aussi fondamentalement opposée à la modernité que leurs équivalents traditionnels occidentaux.

De façon schématique, on peut dire que les architectes japonais contemporains ont réagi de deux façons distinctes aux spécificités de leur environnement, aussi bien en terme de philosophie que dans le choix de leurs matériaux. Leur première réaction, face à un sol susceptible de bouger à chaque instant, est de concevoir des constructions aussi stables que possible. Depuis 1981 en particulier, des lois strictes gouvernent la solidité des bâtiments et des équipements publics. Cette législation, plus souvent qu'une approche esthétique, explique que certaines constructions japonaises modernes semblent inhabituellement massives, s'appuyant sur le sol comme si elles rassemblaient leurs forces, prêtes à réagir à toute catastrophe naturelle. Les rocades surélevées, les ponts ou les squelettes d'acier des nouveaux bâtiments présentent une densité minimale obligatoire qui contribue à leur aspect final. Une seconde direction presque contradictoire de cette architecture contemporaine tend vers une légèreté aérienne qui trouve sans doute ses racines dans les constructions traditionnelles en bois. Telles des bateaux, ces structures semblent vouloir échapper à la tempête menaçante,

governed the solidity of buildings and public works. This fact, together with an allied esthetic approach, can often explain why certain modern structures in Japan seem to be unusually massive, sitting on the earth as though they are waiting to pit their strength against natural upheavals. Elevated roadways, bridges or the steel skeletons of new buildings have an obligatory density here, which may tend to define their final appearance. A second, almost contradictory direction in contemporary architecture tends toward an airy lightness, which may trace its origin back to traditional wooden buildings. Like ships, these structures seem to hope to ride out the impending storm by floating on the land or even in the air. Just as a love for kitsch and a profound respect for the subtle beauties of tradition exist side by side in Japan, so does the dichotomy of lightness and weight inform its architecture.

The Bubble bursts

After economic growth averaging 10 % a year in the 1960s and 5 % a year in the 1970s and 1980s, the formidable Japanese economic machine practically ground to a halt in 1992 and 1993, partially because of contradictory domestic policies intended to wring speculative excesses from the stock and real estate markets. The "Bubble" years that preceded this time of reckoning saw the price of land in Japan reach incredible heights. In the late 1980s it had been said that the land of the Imperial Palace in central Tokyo had a theoretical market value as high as that of the whole of Manhattan. In the speculative climate that reigned, banks saw no objection to lending large sums at very low interest rates to finance purchase and construction of often extravagant buildings. In the boom years, Japan became an enormous laboratory for the development of contemporary architecture. Naturally, a majority of the new structures were without considerable esthetic merit, but in other cases, talented young architects were given a chance to make their dreams, or those of their clients, come true. Building an unusual structure, such as "La Flamme," Philippe Starck's 1989 restaurant for the Asahi Breweries (Sumida-ku, Tokyo), was considered a perfectly reasonable

bild dieser Bauten prägt. Dagegen tendiert die zweite Richtung der zeitgenössischen japanischen Architektur zu einer graziösen Leichtigkeit, deren Ursprünge wahrscheinlich auf die traditionellen Holzbauten zurückgehen. Diese Bauwerke scheinen wie Schiffe die drohenden Stürme überstehen zu wollen, indem sie auf dem Land oder sogar in der Luft treiben. Und ebenso wie die Liebe zum Kitsch und der tief empfundene Respekt für die zarte Schönheit der Tradition in Japan Seite an Seite existieren können, prägt die Dichotomie von Leichtigkeit und Schwere die japanische Architektur.

Die Seifenblase platzt

Nachdem die Wirtschaft in den 60er Jahren jährlich um etwa 10 % und in den 70er und 80er Jahren um 5 % pro Jahr gewachsen war, kam die gewaltige japanische Wirtschaftsmaschinerie 1992 und 1993 praktisch völlig zum Erliegen. Dies war u.a. den widersprüchlichen innenpolitischen Entscheidungen zu verdanken, mit denen die spekulativen Exzesse auf dem Aktien- und Immobilienmarkt eingeschränkt werden sollten. In den Jahren der sogenannten »Seifenblasenökonomie«, die dieser Zeit des Haushaltens vorausgingen, erreichten die Grundstückspreise in Japan unglaubliche Höhen. Gegen Ende der 80er Jahre wurde behauptet, das Grundstück des Kaiserlichen Palastes in Tokio besäße einen theoretischen Marktwert, der dem von ganz Manhattan entspräche. In diesem spekulativen Klima verliehen die Banken zu niedrigen Zinssätzen große Geldsummen, mit denen der Kauf oder Bau häufig extravaganter Gebäude finanziert werden sollte. Während der Boomjahre entwickelte sich Japan zu einem riesigen Forschungslabor der modernen Architektur. Naturgemäß besaß ein Großteil der neuen Bauten keinen bemerkenswerten ästhetischen Wert, aber in einigen Fällen erhielten talentierte junge Architekten die Chance, ihre Träume – oder die ihrer Kunden – zu verwirklichen. Der Bau eines ungewöhnlichen Gebäudes wie etwa »La Flamme« – ein Restaurant, das Philippe Starck 1989 für die Asahi-Brauerei (Sumida-ku, Tokio) schuf – wurde als durchaus sinnvolle Werbemaßnahme einer großen Firma betrachtet. Der japanische Wunsch nach

Top: One of the fifteen stones of the Ryoan-ji garden, conceived by the painter and garden designer Soami, Kyoto, Japan, 1473. A model of the universe.
Bottom: Kenzo Tange, National Gymnasiums for Tokyo Olympics, Tokyo, Japan, 1961–64. A starting point for contemporary Japanese architecture.

Oben: Einer der 15 Steine im Ryoan-ji-Garten, nach einem Entwurf des Malers und Gartenarchitekten Soami, Kioto, Japan, 1473. Ein Modell des Universums.
Unten: Kenzo Tange, National Gymnasiums for Tokyo Olympics, Tokio, Japan, 1961–64. Der Beginn der zeitgenössischen japanischen Architektur.

En haut: L'un des 15 rochers du jardin zen du Ryoan-ji, conçu par le peintre et créateur de jardins Soami, Kyoto, Japon, 1473. Une représentation de l'univers.
En bas: Kenzo Tange, Gymnases des Jeux Olympiques de Tokyo, Tokyo, Japon, 1961–64. Un des points de départ de l'architecture japonaise contemporaine.

en flottant sur le sol ou même dans l'air. De même que coexistent au Japon un amour du kitsch et un profond respect pour les beautés subtiles de la tradition, la dichotomie entre le poids et la légèreté nourrit son architecture actuelle.

Quand la bulle explosa

Après une croissance économique moyenne de 10% au cours des années 60 et de 5% dans les années 70 et 80, la formidable machine économique japonaise allait marquer un arrêt brutal en 1992 et 1993, en partie à cause de mesures politiques internes contradictoires qui tentaient de juguler les excès spéculatifs des marchés boursiers et ceux de l'immobilier. Les années de la «bulle financière» qui précèdent cette période de remise en cause virent le prix des terrains atteindre des sommets incroyables. A la fin des années 80, on disait par exemple que la valeur du terrain du Palais, impérial au centre de Tokyo, était théoriquement égale à celle de tout Manhattan. Dans ce climat spéculatif, les banques ne voyaient aucune objection à prêter de fortes sommes à très faible taux d'intérêt pour financer l'acquisition et la construction de bâtiments souvent extravagants. Au cours de ce boom, le Japon se transforma en un énorme laboratoire d'expérimentation pour l'architecture contemporaine. Naturellement, une majorité de ces nouvelles constructions ne présentait guère de mérites esthétiques, mais, dans certains cas, de talentueux jeunes architectes se virent offrir la chance de réaliser leurs rêves, ou ceux de leurs clients. Construire une structure surprenante comme le restaurant «La Flamme» de Philippe Starck en 1989, pour les Brasseries Asahi (Sumida-ku, Tokyo) pouvait alors sembler une action de relations publiques parfaitement raisonnable pour une grande entreprise. La soif japonaise d'architecture nouvelle alla même jusqu'à faire appel à des architectes étrangers comme les Français Philippe Starck et Christian de Portzamparc, les Américains Steven Holl et Peter Eisenman, l'Italien Aldo Rossi et beaucoup d'autres. Le jeune architecte japonais Makoto Sei Watanabe reflétait tout à fait l'esprit du temps en dessinant en 1988–90, son école d'art Aoyama à Tokyo, qui semble sortir tout droit d'une bande dessinée. C'était

public relations gesture for a large company. The Japanese thirst for new architecture even included a call to foreigners such as the Frenchmen Starck and Christian de Portzamparc, Steven Holl and Peter Eisenman from the United States, the Italian Aldo Rossi, and many others. The young Japanese architect Makoto Sei Watanabe was very much in the spirit of the times with his 1988–90 Aoyama Art School in Tokyo, which looked like something out of a Power Rangers cartoon. This was also the period when Japanese millionaires or corporations were astonishing the art world by paying record prices for Impressionist and Post-Impressionist paintings at auction in New York or London. A wave of museum building swept across the archipelago, and the clients, both private and public, often had the good sense to call on talented architects. Despite the excessive nature of the real estate speculation that characterized this period and the economic havoc that was to wreak afterwards, it might be said that the "Bubble" years were a fruitful time for contemporary architecture in Japan. Money and clients were available in abundance, and the high quality of Japanese construction made it possible for some of the most innovative and interesting architecture in the world to be built. Naturally though, this euphoria had to come to an end. As Arata Isozaki, one of the leading figures of the profession explains, "The recession started in 1991. It was called the bursting of the bubble here. At first private activity sponsored by private developers stopped. The result was that there were to be no more crazy little buildings. The taxes kept coming in for public authorities though, so they had money for new projects. After the private side dropped out, the public side remained a good client for architects. In 1995, the public authorities began to complain about these projects. But then, many people in the administration believe that the only way to get Japan out of the recession is to promote construction. Housing is benefiting from this trend. There are no longer many cultural projects. There was a wave of art museum construction which began in the bubble years, and then theaters and concert halls were built. It seems to me that this cycle has ended. Lately there has been a fashion for sports arenas, for example."[2] Arata

neuer Architektur war so stark, daß sogar Ausländer wie die Franzosen Philippe Starck und Christian de Portzamparc, die Amerikaner Steven Holl und Peter Eisenman, der Italiener Aldo Rossi und andere ins Land geholt wurden. Die 1988–90 von dem jungen japanischen Architekten Makoto Sei Watanabe erbaute Aoyama Art School in Tokio, die wie ein Gebilde aus einem »Power Rangers«-Comic wirkt, lag genau im damaligen Trend der Zeit. Zur gleichen Zeit verblüfften japanische Millionäre oder Unternehmen die Kunstwelt, indem sie auf Auktionen in London oder New York Rekordpreise für impressionistische und nach-impressionistische Gemälde zahlten. Eine Welle von Museums-gebäuden überspülte das Inselreich – wobei öffentliche wie private Auftraggeber so vernünftig waren, auf die Fähigkeiten talentierter Architekten zurückzugreifen. Trotz der exzessiven Grundstücksspekulationen dieser Ära, und trotz der wirtschaftlichen Verwüstung, die sie hinterließen, erwiesen sich die »Seifenblasen«-Jahre für die zeitgenössische japanische Architektur als besonders fruchtbar. Geld und Auftraggeber waren im Überfluß vorhanden, und der hohe Qualitätsstandard der japanischen Bauindustrie ermöglichte den Bau einiger der innovativsten und interessantesten architektonischen Werke dieser Zeit. Der Architekt Arata Isozaki erklärt: »Die Rezession begann 1991, und hier sprach man davon, daß die Seifenblase platzte. Zuerst blieben die Aufträge von privaten Bauunternehmern aus; also wurden keine verrückten kleinen Häuser mehr gebaut. Aber da die Behörden nach wie vor Steuergelder einnahmen, konnten sie auch Geld für neue Projekte ausgeben. Nachdem der private Sektor ausfiel, blieb also die öffentliche Hand weiterhin ein attraktiver Auftraggeber. Erst 1995 begannen sich die Behörden über diese Projekte zu beklagen. Andererseits glauben viele Leute in der Regierung, daß die Förderung des Baugewerbes der einzige Weg sei, um Japan aus der Rezession herauszuführen. Der Wohnungsbau profitiert von diesem Trend; dafür findet man kaum noch kulturelle Projekte. Es gab eine Welle von Museums-bauten, die in den »Seifenblasenjahren« begann, und danach folgten Theater und Konzerthallen. Es erscheint mir, daß sich dieser Kreis geschlossen hat. In letzter Zeit sind Sportarenen

aussi la période où milliardaires et grandes entreprises japonais étonnaient le monde de l'art en payant des sommes record pour des tableaux impressionnistes et postimpressionnistes, dans les ventres aux enchères de New York ou de Londres. Une vague d'édification de musées s'abattit sur l'archipel, dont les promoteurs, qu'ils soient privés ou publics, eurent souvent le bon sens de faire appel à des architectes de talent. Malgré la nature excessive de la spéculation immobilière qui caractérise cette période et la récession économique qui allait en résulter, on peut dire que les années d'effervescence furent une période fructueuse pour l'architecture contemporaine au Japon. L'argent et les clients se trouvaient en abondance, et la haute qualité de la construction permit certaines des réalisations les plus innovantes et les plus intéressantes du monde. Naturellement, cette euphorie devait connaître une fin. Comme l'explique Arata Isozaki, l'une des principales figures de la profession: «La récession a commencé en 1991. On a parlé ici d'éclatement de la «bulle». D'abord, l'activité financée par les promoteurs privés s'arrêta. On ne vit plus apparaître de ces nouveaux «petits immeubles délirants» qui avaient marqué la période précédente. Les impôts continuaient néanmoins à rentrer et les autorités publiques continuaient à pouvoir financer de nouveaux projets. Le secteur public restait donc un bon client pour les architectes. En 1995, certains hommes politiques commencèrent à critiquer ces projets. Mais de nombreux responsables de l'administration persistèrent à penser que la meilleure façon de faire sortir le Japon de la récession était de promouvoir la construction. Si le logement bénéficia de cette tendance, les projets culturels furent moins fréquents. A la vague de construction de musées des années de la «bulle», succéda celle de théâtres et de salles de concert. Il semble que ce cycle soit terminé. Récemment, par exemple, la mode était aux équipements sportifs.»[2] Arata Isozaki, dont les considérables talents architecturaux s'accompagnent d'un solide sens de l'humour, explique par deux facteurs le nouveau climat économique et architectural: «Plus de petits bâtiments délirants», et «Plus de *gaijins*». *Gaijin* étant le terme assez péjoratif qui désigne les étrangers, pas toujours appréciés par une popu-

Isozaki, whose considerable architectural talents are matched by a keen sense of humor, in fact lays out two simple rules for understanding the impact on architecture of the new economic climate. The first of these is."No more crazy little buildings;" and the second, "No more gaijins". Gaijin is of course the rather derogatory Japanese word for foreigners, who are not universally appreciated by the comparatively homogeneous population. With less available work, the prestigious Japanese commissions are logically given to known architects, but foreigners such as the Argentine-American Cesar Pelli have in fact continued to build there. Pelli completed two large buildings in Japan in 1995; the thirty-story NTT Shinjuku Headquarters Office (Tokyo), and the thirty-six-story Sea Hawk Hotel and Resort, in Fukuoka. One of the largest commissions ever given to a foreign architect in Japan, the massive Tokyo International Forum, was completed in 1996. This $1.6 billion project occupying the 3 hectare site of the former Tokyo City Hall near the Tokyo JR Railroad Station was won by Rafael Viñoly, an Argentine architect established in New York since 1979, in a 1989 competition. The jury for this project, which was the first open international design competition staged in Japan, included I.M. Pei, Vittorio Gregotti, Arthur Erickson and Fumihiko Maki. The complex includes an exhibition hall with a capacity of 5,000 persons, and a boat shaped atrium soaring to a height of 60 meters under a 200 meter cantilevered truss. Though completed recently, the Tokyo International Forum was very definitely a project born of the euphoric bubble years.

In 1994, the Japanese economy began a modest recovery with 0.6 % economic growth, but somehow, the assurance which had presided over the triumph of the 1980s had been lost, replaced by new doubts. As Lionel Barber wrote in *The Financial Times*, "...Even a partial view of Japanese society points to far-reaching political and economic change... The reality is that Japan is becoming a 'normal' country. Just as Americans and Europeans suffer from job insecurity and economic dislocation, so the Japanese are struggling to adapt to global competition. Unemployment is edging upwards. The population is aging. For the

wieder groß in Mode.«[2] Arata Isozaki, dessen architektonisches Talent nur von seinem beißenden Humor übertroffen wird, erklärt in zwei einfachen Sätzen, wie sich das neue wirtschaftliche Klima auf die Architektur auswirkt. Die erste Regel lautet: »Keine verrückten kleinen Häuser mehr«, und die zweite: »Keine gaijin mehr«. Gaijin ist die ziemlich abfällige japanische Bezeichnung für Ausländer, die von der vergleichsweise homogenen Bevölkerung nicht überall gern gesehen werden. Wenn die Auftragslage schlecht ist, werden prestigeträchtige japanische Projekte natürlich an bekannte einheimische Architekten vergeben, aber man findet auch Ausländer wie den argentinisch-amerikanischen Architekten Cesar Pelli, die nach wie vor in Japan bauen. Pelli schloß 1995 die Arbeiten an zwei Großbauten ab, dem 30 Stockwerke hohen NTT Shinjuku Headquarters Office in Tokio und dem 36 Stockwerke hohen Sea Hawk Hotel and Resort in Fukuoka. 1996 wurde eines der größten japanischen Bauprojekte fertiggestellt, das je ein ausländischer Architekt entwerfen durfte: das gewaltige Tokyo International Forum. Den 1989 ausgeschriebenen Wettbewerb für dieses 1,6 Milliarden-Dollar-Projekt auf dem 3 Hektar großen Gelände der ehemaligen Tokyo City Hall gewann Rafael Viñoly, ein seit 1979 in New York lebender argentinischer Architekt. In der Jury dieses ersten offenen internationalen Architekturwettbewerbs in Japan saßen unter anderem I.M. Pei, Vittorio Gregotti, Arthur Erickson und Fumihiko Maki. Der Komplex umfaßt eine Halle für 5000 Personen und ein bootförmiges Atrium, das sich unter einem 200 Meter langen auskragenden Dachbinder zu einer Höhe von 60 Metern erhebt. Obwohl erst kürzlich fertiggestellt, sollte man das Tokyo International Forum unbedingt als Produkt der euphorischen »Seifenblasenjahre« betrachten.

1994 erlebte die japanische Wirtschaft einen leichten Aufschwung, aber die Zuversicht, die die Triumphe der 80er Jahre begleitet hatte, war verloren. Lionel Barber schrieb in der »Financial Times«: »...Selbst bei einem begrenzten Einblick in die japanische Gesellschaft deutet vieles auf weitreichende politische und wirtschaftliche Veränderungen hin... Tatsache ist, daß sich Japan zu einem ›ganz gewöhnlichen‹ Land entwickelt. Ebenso

lation relativement homogène. Le travail disponible se faisant rare, les commandes prestigieuses sont logiquement confiées à des architectes nationaux reconnus, mais des étrangers comme l'argentino-américain Cesar Pelli ont néanmoins continué à y construire. Pelli a ainsi achevé deux grands immeubles en 1995, les 30 étages du siège social de NTT dans le quartier de Shinjuku (Tokyo), et les 36 étages de l'hôtel et complexe touristique Sea Hawk à Fukuoka. Une des plus importantes commandes jamais confiée à un architecte étranger, le massif Forum international de Tokyo, a été achevé en 1996. Ce bâtiment de 1,6 milliard de $ élevé sur les 3 hectares de l'ancien hôtel de ville de Tokyo, près de la gare de Tokyo JR, a été remporté sur concours en 1989 par Rafael Viñoly, architecte argentin établi à New York depuis 1979. Le jury de ce premier concours international d'architecture organisé au Japon, comprenait I.M. Pei, Vittorio Gregotti, Arthur Erickson, et Fumihiko Maki. Le complexe comprend un hall d'exposition capable d'accueillir 5000 visiteurs, et un atrium en forme de bateau s'élevant à une hauteur de 60 m sous une charpente d'une portée de 200 m. Bien qu'achevé récemment, ce Forum international est un de ces projets qui portent encore la marque de l'euphorie des années de la «bulle».

En 1994, l'économie japonaise a connu un modeste réveil avec une croissance de 0,6%. Mais, d'une certaine façon, l'assurance qui avait présidé au triomphe des années 80 avait fait place à des doutes nouveaux. Comme l'écrivit Lionel Barber dans «The Financial Times», «... Même une vue partielle de la société japonaise révèle des changements politiques et économiques profonds... La réalité est que le Japon est en train de devenir un pays ‹normal›. De même que les Américains et les Européens souffrent d'insécurité dans le travail et de la dislocation de leurs économies, les Japonais se battent maintenant pour s'adapter à la concurrence internationale. Le chômage est orienté à la hausse. La population vieillit. Pour la première fois depuis 1945, le public Japonais éprouve des doutes sur les perspectives de croissance. Le terme à la mode est: une prospérité stagnante... Une partie de ce pessimisme est exagéré, l'héritage de presque

Two images taken shortly after the Great Hanshin Earthquake, in January 1995, show the extent of the devastation in Kobe.

Zwei Bilder, die kurz nach dem Großen Hanshin-Erdbeben im Januar 1995 aufgenommen wurden, zeigen das Ausmaß der Verwüstung in Kobe.

Deux images de Kobe prises après le tremblement de terre Hanshin en janvier 1995, montrant la gravité des dommages.

first time since 1945, the Japanese public is having doubts about the prospects for growth. The fashionable term is: stagnant prosperity. Some of this pessimism is exaggerated, the legacy of nearly five years of zero growth following the collapse of the bubble economy... The crash has been a searing experience."[3]

Any hope that 1995 would mark a return to business as usual was disrupted on January 17 at 5:46 a.m. local time, when an earthquake measuring 7.2 on the Richter scale devastated a large part of the port city of Kobe. Historically, this area was thought to be less prone to seismic activity than Tokyo and other areas of Japan, but in 1916, a magnitude 6.1 earthquake occurred at almost the same epicentral location, the Island of Awaji, and an event probably exceeding magnitude 7 was recorded there in 1596. Devastated by twenty-five aerial attacks in the final year of World War II, Kobe had become Japan's second port after Yokohama, and the sixth largest port in the world, with approximately 1.5 million inhabitants. The Great Hanshin Earthquake, as it has been named, affected areas located primarily along the coastline and the numerous watercourses in the general area of Kobe and the valley between Kobe and Osaka, causing extensive ground failures. In twenty seconds, 5,480 persons were killed, 310,000 left homeless, and 192,706 buildings destroyed. Images of a long section of the Hanshin Expressway with fifteen of its huge reinforced concrete pillars lying on their side flashed around the world. A perceived slowness in official rescue efforts contributed to the strong impression that, far from being invincible, Japan was extremely vulnerable. The architect Tadao Ando demonstrated the depth of feeling in his country for the victims of Kobe by contributing the $100,000 he received with the 1995 Pritzker Prize to a foundation for orphans of the earthquake. A visit to Kobe fourteen months after the Great Hanshin Earthquake confirms, if anything, that few nations could have carried out such massive construction efforts in such a short period of time. The elevated roadways have been rebuilt, ruins cleared, and the casual visitor might even wonder if such devastation had actually occurred so recently.

The natural calamity of the Great Hanshin Earthquake was

wie die Amerikaner und Europäer unter unsicheren Arbeitsmarktverhältnissen und wirtschaftlichen Problemen zu leiden haben, müssen auch die Japaner kämpfen, um sich im weltweiten Wettbewerb zu behaupten. Die Arbeitslosenzahlen steigen; die Bevölkerung altert. Zum ersten Male seit 1945 hat die japanische Öffentlichkeit Zweifel an den Wachstumsaussichten. Das Modewort lautet: Stagnierende Konjunktur. Ein Teil dieses Pessimismus ist übertrieben – das Erbe von nahezu fünf Jahren Nullwachstum, die auf den Zusammenbruch der ›Seifenblasenökonomie‹ folgten... Der Börsenkrach war eine einschneidende Erfahrung.«[3]

Jede Hoffnung, daß 1995 eine Rückkehr zu alten Verhältnissen bringen würde, wurde am 17. Januar um 5.46 Uhr Ortszeit zerstört, als ein Erdbeben der Stärke 7,2 die Hafenstadt Kobe verwüstete. Historisch betrachtet, ist dieses Gebiet seltener seismischer Aktivität ausgesetzt als Tokio oder andere Regionen Japans; aber schon 1916 war beinahe vom gleichen Epizentrum – der Insel Awaji – ein Erdbeben der Stärke 6,1 ausgegangen, und historische Quellen berichten von einem Beben, das 1596 an ähnlicher Stelle stattfand und die Stärke 7 überschritten haben soll. Kobe, das im letzten Jahr des Zweiten Weltkriegs durch 25 Bombenangriffe völlig verwüstet wurde, hatte sich zum zweitgrößten Hafen Japans und zum sechstgrößten Hafen der Welt entwickelt, und die Stadt zählte etwa 1,5 Millionen Einwohner. Das sogenannte »Große Hanshin-Erdbeben« betraf hauptsächlich die Küstenregion sowie die zahlreichen Wasserläufe in Kobe und dem Tal zwischen Kobe und Osaka, wo an vielen Stellen der Erdboden einbrach. Innerhalb von zwanzig Sekunden starben 5480 Menschen, wurden 310 000 Menschen obdachlos und 192 706 Gebäude zerstört. Die Bilder des Hanshin Expressway, einer erhöhten Schnellstraße, die auf mehreren 100 Metern zur Seite gekippt war, weil 15 ihrer riesigen Betonpfeiler einfach umfielen, gingen um die Welt. Von seiten der Regierung spürbar zu langsam eingeleitete Hilfsmaßnahmen verstärkten den Eindruck der japanischen Öffentlichkeit, daß Japan nicht unbesiegbar, sondern äußerst verwundbar sei. Der Architekt Tadao Ando demonstrierte das tiefe Mitgefühl seines

cinq années de croissance zéro succèdant à l'éclatement de l'économie de la ‹bulle›... La catastrophe a laissé des traces.»[3]

Tout espoir de voir 1995 marquer le retour à une situation normale a été anéanti le 17 janvier à 5 H 46 lorsqu'un tremblement de terre de 7,2 sur l'échelle de Richter a dévasté une grande partie de la cité portuaire de Kobe. Historiquement, cette zone était considérée comme moins sensible à l'activité sismique que Tokyo ou d'autres régions du Japon, quoiqu'en 1916, un tremblement de terre de 6,1 se soit déjà produit avec pratiquement le même épicentre, l'île d'Awaji, et qu'un autre, de magnitude probablement supérieur à 7, y ait été enregistré en 1596. Détruite par 25 bombardements aériens en 1945, Kobe était devenue le second port japonais après Yokohama et le sixième port mondial, avec une population d'environ 1,5 million d'habitants. Le grand tremblement de terre *Hanshin*, selon le nom qui lui a été donné, a essentiellement affecté des zones situées le long de la côte, les nombreuses voies d'eau de Kobe, et la vallée entre Kobe et Osaka, provoquant de vastes effondrements de terrain. En vingt secondes, 5480 personnes ont été tuées, 310 000 laissées sans abri, et 192 706 constructions détruites. Les images d'une longue section de la voie express de Hanshin, avec ses 15 énormes piliers de béton armé gisant sur le sol, ont fait le tour du monde. La lenteur évidente des secours officiels a contribué à donner l'impression que loin d'être invincible, le Japon était extrêmement vulnérable.

L'architecte Tadao Ando a donné l'exemple de la profonde affliction de ce pays pour les victimes de Kobe en offrant les 100 000 $ du Prix Pritzker 1995 qu'il venait de recevoir, au bénéfice de la fondation d'un orphelinat pour les enfants des victimes de la catastrophe. 14 mois plus tard, une visite à Kobe confirme pour le moins que peu de pays auraient été capables de se lancer dans un tel effort de reconstruction en un laps de temps aussi court. Les voies surélevées ont été reconstruites, les ruines dégagées, et un visiteur peu attentif pourrait même se demander si une telle dévastation s'est vraiment produite il y a aussi peu de temps.

not the only upsetting event for the Japanese in 1995. The all-important dollar/yen parity shifted strongly to the disadvantage of Japan, and a bizarre cult, Aum Shinrikyo, whose goals include an opposition to the United States and to modern society, was blamed for sarin gas attacks in the Tokyo subways. On March 20, 1995, eleven persons were killed in one of these attacks and 3,800 injured. Again the apparent inability of public officials to immediately solve this case worked to shatter the image of absolute safety that the Japanese cherish. Confidence in the very stability of Japanese society was further eroded, despite the fact that the forty-one year old leader of the sect, Shoko Asahara, was eventually arrested. The critic Yoshitake Doi links this succession of events, and particularly the bursting of the bubble economy, to a significant mishap in the world of Japanese architecture.4 In 1995, the newly elected governor of Tokyo, Yukio Aoshima, decided to cancel the World City Exposition in which Toyo Ito, Kazuhiro Ishii, Kengo Kuma, Kazuyo Sejima and others were to take part. Intended as a forceful demonstration of the position of Tokyo as a world capital, this exhibition, which would also have shown how much confidence Japan places in its own talented architects, became a victim of greater forces.

Foreign influences and the new Japan

When Commodore Perry viewed the city of Edo during his 1853–54 expedition, he described it as an "extensive plain with a magnificent background of mountains and wooded country." The far-reaching consequences of the Perry Expedition have often been analyzed, but it should be recalled that as early as 1872, the Meiji government called on the British architect and planner Thomas Waters to rebuild the sector to the southeast of the Imperial Palace, destroyed in that year by fire. Along a broad avenue, Waters laid out neoclassical buildings along what became known as the Ginza. Another Englishman, Josiah Conder (1852–1920), built numerous heavy Second Empire style masonry buildings, such as the National Museum in Ueno Park (1882), which became the symbols of the Japanese establishment until the Ministry of the Cabinet decided to call on the

Landes für die Opfer von Kobe, indem er die 100 000 Dollar Preisgeld für den Pritzker Preis 1995 in eine Stiftung für Erdbeben-Waisen einbrachte. Ein Besuch in Kobe, 14 Monate nach dem Großen Hanshin-Erdbeben, bestätigt, daß nur wenige Nationen in der Lage gewesen wären, in so kurzer Zeit derart gewaltige Baumaßnahmen durchzuführen. Die erhöhten Schnellstraßen wurden wieder aufgebaut, die Ruinen geräumt, und ein zufälliger Besucher könnte sich sogar fragen, ob hier wirklich vor so kurzer Zeit eine derartige Verwüstung herrschte.

Diese Naturkatastrophe war jedoch nicht das einzige Ereignis, das Japan 1995 erschütterte. Der das Wirtschaftsleben beherrschende Dollar-Yen-Kurs verschob sich stark zuungunsten Japans, und die Aum Shinrikyo-Sekte, die sich den Widerstand gegen die Vereinigten Staaten und gegen die moderne japanische Gesellschaft zum Ziel gesetzt hatte, wurde für die Saringas-Anschläge auf die Tokioter U-Bahn verantwortlich gemacht. Am 20. März 1995 starben bei einem dieser Attentate 11 Menschen, und 3800 wurden verletzt. Auch diesmal erschütterte die offensichtliche Unfähigkeit der verantwortlichen Stellen das Bild der absoluten Sicherheit, das die Japaner so sehr schätzen. Der Glaube an die Stabilität der japanischen Gesellschaft wurde noch weiter untergraben – trotz der Tatsache, daß man den Anführer der Aum-Sekte, Shoko Asahara, festnehmen konnte. Für den Kritiker Yoshitake Doi stehen die oben genannten Ereignisse in direktem Zusammenhang mit einer vielsagenden Panne in der Welt der japanischen Architektur.4 1995 entschied der neugewählte Gouverneur von Tokio, Yukio Aoshima, die für März 1996 geplante World City Exposition abzusagen, an der unter anderem Toyo Ito, Kazuhiro Ishii, Kengo Kuma und Kazuyo Sejima teilnehmen sollten. Die ursprünglich als Demonstration der Kraft Tokios geplante Ausstellung – die darüber hinaus zeigen sollte, wie viel Vertrauen Japan in seine eigenen talentierten Architekten setzt – wurde das Opfer höherer Mächte.

Ausländische Einflüsse und das Neue Japan

Als Commodore Perry 1853–54 auf seiner Expedition die Stadt Edo besuchte, beschrieb er sie als eine »ausgedehnte Ebene vor

Cette calamité naturelle n'a pas été le seul événement grave qu'ait connu le Japon en 1995. Le rapport entre le dollar et le yen, si important pour l'économie nippone, s'est détérioré au détriment du Japon, et une secte bizarre, Aum Shinrikyo, qui, entre autres objectifs, s'oppose à la société moderne et aux Etats-Unis, a été responsable d'attentats au gaz sarin dans le métro de Tokyo. Le 20 mars 1995, onze personnes ont été tuées dans un de ces attentats et 3800 atteintes. Là encore, l'incapacité évidente des pouvoirs publics à résoudre immédiatement ce problème a contribué à saper l'image de sécurité absolue que chérissent tant les Japonais. La confiance dans la stabilité même de la société s'est vue une fois encore érodée, malgré l'arrestation du chef de la secte, Shoko Asahara, 41 ans. Le critique Yoshitake Doi relie cette succession d'événements, et particulièrement l'explosion de l'économie de la «bulle», à un avatar significatif de l'architecture japonaise.4 En 1995, Yukio Aoshima, le gouverneur de Tokyo nouvellement élu, a décidé d'annuler l'Exposition des Villes du Monde à laquelle devaient prendre part, entre autres, Toyo Ito, Kazuhiro Ishii, Kengo Kuma, Kazuyo Sejima. Victime de forces plus puissantes qu'elle, cette manifestation se voulait une puissante démonstration de la position de Tokyo capitale mondiale. De plus, elle aurait dû illustrer la confiance que les Japonais placent dans leurs propres grands architectes.

Influences étrangères et nouveau Japon

Le Commodore Perry visitant la ville de Edo lors de son expédition de 1853–54, la décrit comme «une vaste plaine, sur un fond superbe de montagnes et de forêts.» Si les conséquences historiques de l'expédition Perry ont souvent été analysées, il faut toutefois rappeler que dès 1872, le gouvernement Meiji fait appel à l'architecte et urbaniste britannique Thomas Waters pour reconstruire un quartier au sud-est du palais impérial, détruit par un incendie cette même année. Le long d'une large avenue qui allait devenir Ginza, Waters élève des immeubles néoclassiques. Un autre Britannique, Josiah Conder (1852–1920) construit de nombreux édifices lourds de style Napoléon III, comme le Musée National du Parc Ueno (1882), qui deviennent

Makoto Sei Watanabe, Aoyama Art School, Tokyo, Japan, 1988–90. A product of a visually chaotic urban environment.

Makoto Sei Watanabe, Aoyama Art School, Tokio, Japan, 1988–90. Das Produkt einer visuell chaotischen urbanen Umgebung.

Makoto Sei Watanabe, Ecole d'art Aoyama, Tokyo, Japon, 1988–90. Le produit d'un environnement urbain visuellement chaotique.

Josiah Conder, National Museum of Art, Ueno Park, Tokyo, Japan, 1882. An early mixture of Western and Oriental forms.

Josiah Conder, National Museum of Art, Ueno Park, Tokio, Japan, 1882. Eine frühe Mischung westlicher und orientalischer Formen.

Josiah Conder, Musée national d'art, Parc Ueno, Tokyo, Japon, 1882. Un des premiers exemples de mariage entre formes orientales et occidentales.

Germans Hermann Ende (1829–1907) and Wilhelm Böckmann (1832–1902). Their plan for a Prussian-style building for the Japanese Diet capped with a pagoda-like form met with concerted opposition, and calls for a resolution to the conflict between indigenous and Western architectural styles.[5]

"There was sixty to seventy feet of soft mud below the upper depth of eight feet of surface soil on the site. That mud seemed a merciful provision – a good cushion to relieve the terrible shocks. Why not float the building upon it ? A battleship floats on salt water..."[6] This is how another foreign architect in Japan, Frank Lloyd Wright, described his plans for the Imperial Hotel in Tokyo (1916–22). Demolished in 1967, this eccentric structure famously survived the devastating earthquake of 1923, adding to Wright's reputation, not least of all in Japan.

Wright was of course not the only Western architect to have exerted an influence on the development of modern Japanese architecture. Le Corbusier, for example, who continues to fascinate many contemporary architects, made his presence felt through projects such as the National Museum of Western Art in Ueno Park in Tokyo (1959), and through the work of such figures as Kunio Maekawa, who worked in Le Corbusier's atelier in France from 1928 to 1930 before establishing his own office in Tokyo in 1935. Maekawa completed the 1979 addition to the

einem großartigen Hintergrund aus Gebirgen und Wäldern«. Die weitreichenden Konsequenzen der Perry-Expedition sind ausführlich analysiert worden, aber bereits 1872 erteilte die Meiji-Regierung dem britischen Architekten und Stadtplaner Thomas Waters den Auftrag, einen Stadtteil im Südosten des Kaiserlichen Palastes wiederaufzubauen, der im selben Jahr von einem Feuer zerstört worden war. Entlang eines breiten Boulevards entwarf Waters klassizistische Bauten in einem Viertel, das später als Ginza bekannt wurde. Ein weiterer Engländer, Josiah Conder (1852–1920), schuf zahlreiche Steinbauten im wuchtigen Second Empire Style, darunter auch das National Museum im Ueno-Park (1882). Diese Bauten entwickelten sich zu Symbolen des japanischen Establishments, bis das Kabinettsministerium die deutschen Baumeister Hermann Ende (1829–1907) und Wilhelm Böckmann (1832–1902) als Architekten gewann. Ihr Plan, für den Diet (das japanische Unterhaus) ein Gebäude im preußischen Stil zu entwerfen, das von einer pagodenähnlichen Form gekrönt werden sollte, traf jedoch auf Widerstand und auf die Forderung nach einer Lösung des Konflikts zwischen einheimischen und westlichen Architekturstilen.[5]

»Das Baugelände bestand aus einer oberen Schicht von etwa zweieinhalb Metern Erde, unter der eine Schicht von 20 bis 25 Metern weichen Lehms lag. Dieser Lehm erschien uns wie... ein gutes Kissen, um die schrecklichen Erdstöße aufzufangen. Warum das Bauwerk nicht darauf schwimmen lassen? Ein Schlachtschiff schwimmt auf Salzwasser...«[6] So beschrieb Frank Lloyd Wright seine Pläne für das Imperial Hotel in Tokio (1916–22). Dieses 1967 abgerissene, exzentrische Bauwerk war berühmt dafür, das Erdbeben des Jahres 1923 schadlos überstanden zu haben, was nicht nur in Japan zu Wrights Reputation beitrug.

Wright war natürlich nicht der einzige westliche Architekt, der Einfluß auf die Entwicklung der modernen japanischen Architektur nahm. Le Corbusier beeinflußte die japanische Architekturszene unmittelbar durch Projekte wie das National Museum of Western Art im Ueno-Park in Tokio (1959) sowie mittelbar durch die Bauten Kunio Maekawas, der von 1928 bis 1930 in

les symboles de l'establishment japonais, jusqu'à ce que le ministre du Cabinet décide de faire appel aux allemands Hermann Ende (1829–1907) et Wilhelm Böckmann (1832–1902). Leur plan de style prussien pour le parlement japonais, surmonté d'une sorte de toit en pagode rencontra une vive opposition, et souleva le problème du conflit entre les styles architecturaux locaux et occidentaux.[5]

«Il y avait une couche de 20 à 25 m de boue sous la croûte de surface de 2,50 m. Cette boue semblait une cadeau de la Providence, comme un coussin qui allait absorber les terribles chocs. Pourquoi ne pas faire flotter le bâtiment là-dessus? Un bateau de guerre flotte bien sur l'eau salée ...»[6] C'est ainsi qu'un autre architecte étranger, Frank Lloyd Wright, décrit ses plans pour l'Imperial Hotel de Tokyo (1916–22). Démolie en 1967, cette construction excentrique survécut au tremblement de terre dévastateur de 1923, ce qui ajouta à la réputation de Wright, en particulier au Japon.

Bien sûr, Wright n'est pas le seul architecte occidental a avoir exercé son influence sur le développement de l'architecture japonaise moderne. Le Corbusier, par exemple, qui continue à fasciner de nombreux architectes actuels, fit sentir sa présence dans des projets comme le Musée national d'art occidental du Parc Ueno à Tokyo (1959), et dans l'œuvre de praticiens comme Kunio Maekawa qui travailla dans l'atelier de Le Corbusier en France, de 1928 à 1930, avant de créer sa propre agence à Tokyo en 1935. Maekawa acheva d'ailleurs l'extension de 1979 du Musée national d'art occidental en réaffirmant symboliquement l'importance de Le Corbusier (1887–1965) au Japon.

Le 4 novembre 1935, l'architecte allemand Bruno Taut (1880–1938) écrivait dans son journal: «Je peux honnêtement prétendre être le découvreur de Katsura.» Cette affirmation, sur une résidence impériale du XVIIe siècle, située près de Kyoto, est d'importance considérable pour l'évolution de l'architecture contemporaine. Alors que les Japonais avaient absorbé de diverses façons les influences occidentales auxquelles ils avaient été soumis depuis l'expédition Perry, ils en étaient venus à rejeter de nombreux aspects de leurs propres traditions. Ainsi la

National Museum of Western Art, symbolically reaffirming the importance of Le Corbusier (1887–1965) in Japan.

On November 4, 1935, the German architect Bruno Taut (1880–1938) wrote in his journal, "I can truly claim to be the discoverer of Katsura." This affirmation, concerning the 17th century imperial residence located near Kyoto, is of considerable importance for the evolution of contemporary Japanese architecture. Whereas the Japanese had in various ways absorbed the Western influences to which they were subjected after the Perry Expedition, they had come to reject many aspects of their own tradition. Thus the rise of fascism in Japan was accompanied by a certain rejection, of Western-inspired modernity in favor of an architecture called *Teikan yoshiki* or the "Imperial roof style," which featured heavy cubic structures capped by equally heavy "Japanese" roofs. Having arrived in Japan in May 1933, Taut spent three and a half years writing about Katsura, linking its elegant simplicity to the goals of the modern movement and calling it an "eternal monument." As Arata Isozaki points out, other Western architects, such as the German Gustav Prattz, had visited Katsura even before Taut, and had integrated its lessons into "the renewal of world architecture."[7]

The rediscovery of the fundamental links between the purity of Japanese tradition and modernism itself occurred only after the trauma of II World War partially because the very idea of calling on tradition had been misappropriated by a largely discredited political ideology in Japan.

The post-war discovery of Japanese tradition by the Japanese themselves was aided by figures such as Sofu Teshigahara, creator of the Sogetsu school of *ikebana*, whom *Time Magazine* called the "Picasso of Flowers" in 1955, and by the architect Kenzo Tange. Born in 1913, Tange had worked in the 1930s in the office of Kunio Maekawa, but his national Gymnasiums for the 1964 Tokyo Olympics announced the emergence of an indigenous modernity on a par in terms of quality and inventiveness with that of the West. Author of the Hiroshima Peace Park and Museum, a moving testimony to the horrific impact of the atomic bomb, Tange today remains the elder statesman of

Le Corbusiers Atelier in Frankreich arbeitete, bevor er 1935 sein eigenes Büro in Tokio eröffnete. Maekawa schloß 1979 die Arbeiten zu einem Anbau des National Museum of Western Art ab und bestätigte damit symbolisch die Bedeutung Le Corbusiers in Japan.

Am 4. November 1935 schrieb der deutsche Architekt Bruno Taut (1880–1938) in sein Tagebuch: »Ich kann wahrlich von mir behaupten, der Entdecker von Katsura zu sein.« Diese Aussage bezog sich auf die in der Nähe von Kioto liegende kaiserliche Residenz aus dem 17. Jahrhundert und war von erheblicher Bedeutung für die Entwicklung der zeitgenössischen japanischen Architektur. Während die Japaner in der Zeit nach der Perry-Expedition die westlichen Einflüsse auf verschiedenste Weise absorbierten, verdrängten sie zugleich viele Aspekte ihrer eigenen Tradition. Daher wurde der Aufstieg des Faschismus in Japan von einer gewissen Ablehnung der westlich inspirierten Moderne begleitet. Statt dessen bevorzugte man einen Architekturstil namens *Teikan yoshiki* oder »Kaiserlicher Dachstil«, bei dem massive, kubische Bauten von entsprechend schweren »japanischen« Dächern bekrönt wurden. Nach seiner Ankunft in Japan im Mai 1933 schrieb Taut dreieinhalb Jahre an einem Buch über Katsura, in dem er dessen elegante Schlichtheit mit den Zielen der Moderne verglich und die Anlage als »Monument der Ewigkeit« bezeichnete. Laut Arata Isozaki hatten vor Taut aber auch schon andere westliche Architekten wie der Deutsche Gustav Prattz Katsura besucht und dessen Lehren in die »Erneuerung der Weltarchitektur« integriert.[7] Die Wiederentdeckung intensiver Beziehungen zwischen der Reinheit der japanischen Tradition und der Moderne fand allerdings erst nach dem Zweiten Weltkrieg statt – unter anderem deshalb, weil das Konzept der Rückbesinnung auf die Tradition zuvor von einer zweifelhaften politischen Ideologie mißbraucht worden war.

Die Entdeckung der japanischen Tradition durch die Japaner wurde nach dem Zweiten Weltkrieg von Persönlichkeiten wie Sofu Teshigahara und dem Architekten Kenzo Tange eingeleitet. Teshigahara, den das amerikanische »Time Magazine« 1955 als »Picasso der Blumen« bezeichnete, war der Gründer der Soget-

montée du fascisme s'accompagna-t-elle d'un certain rejet d'une modernité à l'occidentale en faveur d'une architecture appelée *Teikan yoshiki*, ou «style de toit impérial», faite de lourdes constructions cubiques surmontées de toits «à la japonaise» tout aussi pesants. Arrivé au Japon en mai 1933, Taut passa trois ans et demi à écrire sur Katsura, faisant le lien entre son élégante simplicité et les objectifs du mouvement moderne. Il le qualifie de «monument éternel». Comme le fait remarquer Arata Isozaki, d'autres architectes occidentaux, tel l'Allemand Gustav Prattz avaient déjà visité Katsura, et en avaient intégré les leçons dans «le renouvellement de l'architecture mondiale».[7] La redécouverte des liens fondamentaux entre la pureté de la tradition japonaise et le modernisme ne se produisit qu'après le traumatisme de la seconde guerre mondiale, en partie parce que l'idée même de retour à la tradition avait été récupérée par une idéologie politique largement discréditée.

Cette redécouverte de leurs traditions par les Japonais eux-mêmes fut aidée par des personnages comme Sofu Teshigahara, créateur de l'école d'*ikebana* Sogetsu, que «Time Magazine» a surnommé le «Picasso des fleurs» en 1955, et par l'architecte Kenzo Tange. Né en 1913, Tange avait travaillé au cours des années 30 dans l'agence de Kunio Maekawa. Toutefois, son Hall des sports pour les Jeux Olympiques de Tokyo de 1964 annonçait déjà une modernité nippone de qualité et d'inventivité égales à celles de l'Occident. Concepteur du Parc et du Musée de la Paix d'Hiroshima, témoignages émouvants du terrible impact de la bombe atomique, Tange est aujourd'hui considéré comme le vieux sage de l'architecture japonaise ayant récemment achevé le nouvel hôtel de ville de Tokyo, et les tours voisines du parc de Shinjuku. Lorsqu'on lui demande quelles leçons philosophiques peuvent être tirées de son hôtel de ville pour Tokyo, – deux tours jumelles de 243 m de haut qui occupent trois îlots du quartier de Shinjuku (1991), et symboles pour certains des excès de la bulle financière – l'homme qui, en un certain sens, a inventé l'architecture contemporaine de son pays répond: «Jusqu'en 1960, le Japon a pour objectif l'industrialisation, puis se dessine une orientation nouvelle vers une société

Kenzo Tange, Tokyo City Hall, Tokyo, Japan, 1986–91 (left), and Shinjuku Park Tower, Tokyo, 1986–94 (right), in the Shinjuku area, proof of the wealth of Japan and the continuing presence of Kenzo Tange.

Kenzo Tange, Tokyo City Hall, Tokio, Japan, 1986–91 (links), und Shinjuku Park Tower, Tokio, 1986–94 (rechts). Im Shinjuku-Bezirk liegt dieser Beweis für den Reichtum Japans und die ungebrochene Präsenz Kenzo Tanges.

Kenzo Tange, Hôtel de ville de Tokyo, Tokyo, Japon, 1986–91 (à gauche), et Tour du Parc Shinjuku, Tokyo, 1986–94 (à droite), dans le quartier de Shinjuku qui illustrent la richesse japonaise et la présence continue de Kenzo Tange.

Japanese architecture, having recently completed the new Tokyo City Hall and nearby Shinjuku Park Towers. When asked what lessons, in philosophical, terms can be learned from building the Tokyo City Hall, a 243 meter tall double tower which occupies three full blocks in the Shinjuku area (1991), considered by some to be a symbol of the excesses of the bubble years, the man who in some sense invented Japanese contemporary architecture replied: "Until about 1960, Japan was pursuing industrialization, but after that Japan became an information oriented society in which more importance was put on communication as opposed to manufacturing. Today Japan is still progressing in that direction. So I considered what architecture ought to look like in an information oriented society. During the process of industrialization, Japan pursued functionalism, and the philosophy of architecture was oriented towards function, which generated rationalism. Today, rather than physical, material production, intangible streams of data are highly valued. In this new society, a human being cannot memorize or even grasp all of the information that

su-Schule für *Ikebana*. Der 1913 geborene Tange hatte in den 30er Jahren im Büro von Kunio Maekawa gearbeitet, aber seine Sportstadien für die Olympiade 1964 in Tokio kündeten vom Aufkommen einer einheimischen Moderne, die sich in Qualität und Einfallsreichtum mit der des Westens messen konnte. Als Schöpfer des Hiroshima Peace Park and Museum, einem bewegenden Zeugnis der schrecklichen Auswirkungen der Atombombe, gilt Tange heute als der große alte Mann der japanischen Architektur. Erst kürzlich schloß er die Bauarbeiten zur neuen Tokyo City Hall und den nahegelegenen Shinjuku Park Towers ab. Auf die Frage, welche philosophischen Lehren man aus dem Bau der Tokyo City Hall (1991) ziehen kann – einem 243 Meter hohen Doppelturm, der im Bezirk Shinjuku die Fläche von drei Häuserblocks einnimmt und von manchen als Symbol der exzessiven »Seifenblasenjahre« betrachtet wird –, antwortet der Mann, der als Begründer der modernen japanischen Architektur gelten kann: »Bis etwa 1960 betrieb Japan die Industrialisierung. In den Jahren danach entwickelte es sich zu einer Informationsgesellschaft, in der mehr Wert auf Kommunikation als auf Herstellung gelegt wurde. Daher habe ich überlegt, wie Architektur in einer solchen Gesellschaft aussehen sollte. Während der Industrialisierung war Japan vom Funktionalismus geprägt; die Philosophie der Architektur orientierte sich an der Funktion, was wiederum den Rationalismus förderte. Heute sind es keine greifbaren Produkte mehr, die unser Leben bestimmen, sondern immaterielle Datenströme. In dieser neuen Gesellschaft ist der Mensch nicht mehr in der Lage, alle verfügbaren Informationen zu erfassen oder im Gedächtnis zu behalten. Das leistet nur noch der Computer. Für die Kommunikation ist die reibungslose Übertragung von Informationen lebenswichtig, und Tokio hat sich zu einem der größten Kommunikationszentren der Welt entwickelt. Bis in die 60er Jahre hinein war Raum ein Ort zur Herstellung von Produkten, aber heute ist Raum ein Schauplatz für Kommunikation zwischen diesen Objekten und ein Ort, an dem materielle Objekte organisch zu einem Ganzen verbunden werden. Es ist viel einfacher geworden, von Tokio aus die Welt zu sehen. Anstelle der unabhängigen Wahrnehmung einzelner For-

de l'information, qui accorde une importance plus grande à la communication qu'à la fabrication d'objets. Aujourd'hui, le Japon progresse toujours dans cette orientation. J'en suis donc venu à réfléchir à ce que l'architecture devait devenir dans une société orientée dans ce sens. Au cours de son processus d'industrialisation, le Japon visait le fonctionnalisme, et la philosophie de l'architecture était donc orientée vers la fonction, qui générait le rationalisme. Aujourd'hui, on attache plus de valeur à la circulation de flux de données, qu'à une production physique, matérielle. Dans cette nouvelle société, un être humain ne peut simplement pas mémoriser ni même saisir la totalité de l'information à laquelle il a accès. Seul l'ordinateur peut le faire. Pour la communication, la transmission sans problème de l'information est devenue essentielle. Tokyo est devenu l'un des grands centres de communication du monde. Jusqu'aux années 60, l'espace était le lieu où les objets étaient produits. Aujourd'hui, c'est un lieu de communication entre ces objets, où les objets fabriqués sont organiquement connectés en un tout. Il est devenu plus facile de voir le monde à partir de Tokyo. Plutôt que de concevoir chaque forme indépendamment, le lien entre ces différents types d'architecture est maintenant d'une plus grande importance.»[8] Malgré son âge, Kenzo Tange demeure une personnalité avec laquelle l'architecture japonaise doit compter, bien qu'il ne fasse plus partie, même de loin, de l'avant-garde. Le fait que son agence soit appelée à concevoir d'énormes bâtiments officiels ou pour de grandes entreprises peut s'analyser comme le fruit d'un long parcours de réussites.

De façon plus subtile et plus poétique, les grandes figures de l'art japonais montrent à quel point une authentique symbiose entre modernité et tradition a pu s'installer depuis la seconde guerre mondiale. L'une d'entre elles est le sculpteur Isamu Noguchi (1904–88). Né à San Francisco d'un mère américaine, il a trouvé un lieu de paix et de créativité à Mure, sur l'île de Shikoku. Les sculptures de la dernière période de sa vie, dont beaucoup sont restées autour de son atelier de Mure nous offrent le témoignage silencieux de la profondeur de sa recherche artistique et peut-être celui de la présence d'une modernité différente

he has access to. Only the computer can do that. For communication, the smooth transmission of information has become essential. Tokyo has become one of the great centers for communication in the world. Until the 1960s, space was the place where products were produced, but today space is a venue for communication between those objects, and space is a place where manufactured objects are organically connected into a whole. It has become easier to see the world from Tokyo. Rather than conceiving each form independently, the linkage between these different types of architecture is now of greater importance."[8] Despite his age, Kenzo Tange obviously remains a force to be reckoned with in the world of Japanese architecture, though he is no longer anywhere near what might be called the cutting edge. The fact that his office is called on to design enormous corporate or official structures can be considered the fruit of his long years of success.

In much more subtle and poetic ways, figures of the Japanese art world symbolize the extent to which a true symbiosis between modernity and tradition has been found since World War II. One of these is the great sculptor Isamu Noguchi (1904–88), who found a place of peace and creativity in Mure on the island of Shikoku in Japan, having been born in San Francisco of an American mother. The sculptures of his later life, many of which remain on the grounds of his atelier in Mure, now bear silent testimony to the depth of his search for art, and perhaps to the presence in Japan of a different, more powerful modernity. "We are the past," he said. "We go toward the past because that is where memory is. If we go toward the future, there is no memory." Noguchi designed a monument to the dead, which he proposed for the Peace Park in Hiroshima in agreement with Kenzo Tange, but his ambiguous situation as a half-American Japanese caused his project to be rejected. It was at the suggestion of Sofu Teshigahara that he did finally create two bridges in the city where the first wartime use of the atomic weapon occurred.

Teshigahara's son Hiroshi at first rejected his father's return to tradition, but later became in his turn the director of the Sogetsu

men ist die Verbindung verschiedener Architekturtypen heute von wesentlich größerer Bedeutung.«[8] Offensichtlich bleibt Kenzo Tange trotz seines Alters eine feste Größe in der Welt der japanischen Architektur, obwohl er nicht länger als »Speerspitze« der Architekturentwicklung gesehen werden muß. Die Tatsache, daß sein Büro Aufträge für riesige Firmen- oder Verwaltungsgebäude erhält, ist das Ergebnis langjähriger erfolgreicher Arbeit.

Auf subtilere und poetischere Weise symbolisieren Persönlichkeiten der japanischen Kunstszene die Symbiose zwischen Moderne und Tradition nach dem Zweiten Weltkrieg. Einer dieser Künstler ist der Bildhauer Isamu Noguchi (1904–88). Der in San Francisco geborene Sohn einer amerikanischen Mutter fand in Mure auf der japanischen Insel Shikoku einen Ort des Friedens und der Kreativität. Die Skulpturen seines Spätwerks, von denen viele immer noch auf dem Gelände seines Ateliers stehen, legen ein stilles Zeugnis seiner intensiven Suche nach der Kunst ab und weisen zugleich auf die Präsenz einer andersartigen, machtvollen Moderne in Japan hin. »Wir sind die Vergangenheit«, sagte Noguchi, »Wir gehen in die Vergangenheit, weil dort die Erinnerung ist. In der Zukunft gibt es keine Erinnerung.« Noguchi entwarf ein Denkmal für die Toten, das er im Einverständnis mit Kenzo Tange im Peace Park von Hiroshima aufstellen wollte – was jedoch aufgrund seiner halb-amerikanischen Herkunft abgelehnt wurde. Erst auf Anregung Sofu Teshigaharas erhielt er den Auftrag für zwei Brücken in der Stadt, in der der erste Kriegseinsatz einer Atombombe stattfand.

Teshigaharas Sohn Hiroshi lehnte zunächst die Rückbesinnung seines Vaters auf die Tradition ab, übernahm aber später seinerseits den Direktorenposten an der Sogetsu-Schule. Er ist heute als der Schöpfer spektakulärer Bambus-Environments bekannt, die er u.a. 1992 in Numazu, etwa 100 km südwestlich von Tokio gestaltete. Zu diesem Zweck bat er die Architekten Arata Isozaki, Tadao Ando und Kiyonori Kikutake, Teehäuser zu entwerfen, die eine Verbindung zwischen der offensichtlich radikalen Modernität zeitgenössischer japanischer Architektur und den jahrhundertealten Traditionen des Landes schaffen sollten.

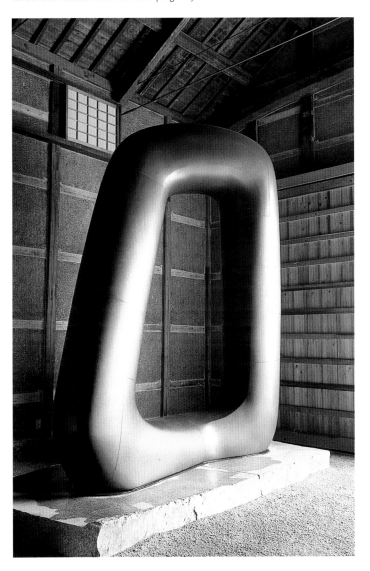

et forte. «Nous sommes le passé,» disait-il. «Nous allons vers le passé parce que c'est là que se trouve la mémoire. Si nous allons vers le futur, il n'y plus de mémoire.» Noguchi avait conçu un monument aux morts pour le Parc de la Paix d'Hiroshima, en accord avec Kenzo Tange, mais sa situation ambiguë de Japonais à demi américain fit rejeter son projet. C'est à la suggestion de Sofu Teshigahara qu'il créa finalement deux ponts pour la ville victime de la première bombe atomique stratégique.

Hiroshi, le fils de Teshigahara, avait quant à lui initialement rejeté le retour de son père vers la tradition. Mais il a fini par prendre à son tour la direction de l'école Sogetsu. Teshigahara est aujourd'hui célèbre pour ses spectaculaires environnements de bambous, comme celui qu'il a conçu à Numazu à 100 kilomètres au sud-ouest de Tokyo, en 1992. Là, il a demandé aux architectes Arata Isozaki, Tadao Ando et Kiyonori Kikutake de créer des maisons de thé qui forment un lien entre la modernité apparemment radicale de l'architecture contemporaine et les traditions profondes de ce pays.

Si Kenzo Tange a exercé une première influence formatrice sur des architectes comme Kisho Kurokawa ou Arata Isozaki, d'autres qui appartiennent plus ou moins à la même génération ont joué un rôle central dans l'émergence de créateurs de talent. Kazuo Shinohara (né en 1925) fait certainement partie de ce dernier groupe. Il enseigne à l'Institut de Technologie de Tokyo depuis 1953. L'essentiel de sa production personnelle consiste en maisons individuelles. Après avoir étudié en profondeur l'espace traditionnel et la structure formelle des maisons japonaises, dans les années 80, il a évolué vers des bâtiments d'une originalité spectaculaire comme son Hall du Centenaire, pour l'Institut de Technologie de Tokyo (1985–87). Conçu comme une «machine flottant dans l'air», ce grand bâtiment est surmonté d'un volume argenté en demi-cylindre suspendu à 20 m au dessus du sol. L'approche théorique de l'architecte fait référence à « l'efficacité terrifiante» de machines apparemment maladroites comme le Lunar Landing Module (LEM, module d'alunissage) ou le chasseur F-14. Selon lui, l'organisation apparemment chaotique des villes japonaises contemporaines représente une

school. Teshigahara is known today as the creator of spectacular bamboo environments, such as that which he created in Numazu 100 kilometers to the southwest of Tokyo in 1992. There, he asked the architects Arata Isozaki, Tadao Ando and Kiyonori Kikutake to create tea houses which formed a link between the apparently radical modernity of contemporary Japanese architecture and the country's profound traditions.

Though Kenzo Tange did exert an early formative influence on architects such as Kisho Kurokawa or Arata Isozaki, others who are more or less of his generation have played a central role in the continued emergence of talented creators. One of these is certainly Kazuo Shinohara (born in 1925). Shinohara has taught at the Tokyo Institute of Technology since 1953. Most of his personal production was in the form of individual houses. Having studied traditional space and the form of the Japanese house extensively, Shinohara evolved in the 1980s toward a capacity to design spectacularly original buildings, like his Centennial Hall for the Tokyo Institute of Technology (1985–87). Conceived like a "machine floating in the air," this large structure is topped by a silver, semi-cylindrical volume suspended 20 meters above the ground. Shinohara's theoretical approach makes reference to the "terrifying efficiency" of apparently awkward machines like the Lunar Landing Module (LEM) or the F-14 fighter aircraft. He also postulates that the seemingly chaotic organization of contemporary Japanese cities represents an evolution toward a different and higher form of order, which Western cities have not yet attained. Indeed, any visitor who has more than a passing acquaintance with public transport in Japan realizes that it is possible to move through a city like Tokyo with surprising ease, despite the excessive congestion of automobile traffic. In this area, Shinohara's thought approaches the findings of "chaos theory" in mathematics. Whereas the boldness of Kenzo Tange launched a generation of creative Japanese architects, born for the most part in the 1930s, Shinohara has had a considerable influence on figures such as Toyo Ito and Itsuko Hasegawa, both born in 1941.

Obwohl Kenzo Tange einen prägenden Einfluß auf Architekten wie Kisho Kurokawa oder Arata Isozaki ausübte, spielten andere Baumeister seiner Generation eine zentrale Rolle bei der kontinuierlichen Förderung junger Talente. Zu ihnen gehört der 1925 geborene Kazuo Shinohara, der seit 1953 am Tokyo Institute of Technology lehrt. Die meisten seiner eigenen Arbeiten entstanden in Form individueller Wohnhäuser. Nach ausgiebigen Studien des traditionellen Raums und der Form japanischer Häuser entwickelte Shinohara in den 80er Jahren die Fähigkeit zum Bau aufsehenerregender, eigenständiger Bauten wie der Centennial Hall des Tokyo Institute of Technology (1985–87). Die als eine »in der Luft schwebende Maschine« bezeichnete Halle wird von einem silbernen, halb-zylindrischen Baukörper gekrönt, der etwa 20 Meter über dem Boden aufgehängt ist. Shinoharas theoretischer Ansatz nimmt Bezug auf die »schreckenerregende Effizienz« augenscheinlich sperriger Maschinen wie der Mondfähre (LEM) oder des amerikanischen F-14 Jagdflugzeugs. Darüber hinaus postuliert Shinohara, daß die scheinbar chaotische Organisation der modernen japanischen Großstädte eine Entwicklung zu einer andersartigen und höheren Ordnungsebene darstellt, die westliche Großstädte bisher noch nicht erreicht haben. In diesem Bereich kommen Shinoharas Ansätze den Erkenntnissen der »Chaostheorie« sehr nahe. Während die Kühnheit Kenzo Tanges eine Generation um 1930 geborener, kreativer japanischer Architekten beeinflußte, übte Shinohara einen bedeutenden Einfluß auf Persönlichkeiten wie Toyo Ito und Itsuko Hasegawa aus, die beide 1941 zur Welt kamen.

Masters of the Universe

Es ist eine bekannte Tatsache, daß man in Japan stärker als im Westen das Vorrecht des Alters respektiert. Dennoch hat kürzlich sogar das politische System Japans – das zuvor seine Führer rein auf der Grundlage des Senioritätsprinzips auszuwählen schien – die Vorzüge jüngerer Führungskräfte erkannt: Morihiro Hosokawa, der 1993 zum japanischen Ministerpräsidenten gewählt wurde, war mit nur 56 Jahren für japanische politische Verhältnisse fast noch ein Kind. In der Architektur spielt die Erfahrung eine große

évolution vers un ordre différent et plus élevé, que les cités occidentales n'ont pas encore atteint. En fait, chaque visiteur qui
comprend un peu le système des transports publics locaux, réalise qu'il est étonnement facile de se déplacer dans une ville
comme Tokyo, malgré la congestion permanente de la circulation
automobile. Dans ce domaine, la pensée de Shinohara se rapproche de la théorie mathématique du chaos. Alors que l'audace
d'un Kenzo Tange a permis l'éclosion d'une génération d'architectes créatifs, nés pour la plupart dans les années 30, Shinohara
exerce une influence considérable sur des praticiens plus jeunes,
comme Toyo Ito et Itsuko Hasegawa, tous deux nés en 1941.

Les maîtres de l'univers

Il est certain que le Japonais continue de respecter davantage les
privilèges de l'âge que les sociétés occidentales. Et pourtant,
même le système politique qui semblait toujours choisir ses responsables sur une stricte base d'antériorité sans grande considération pour les mérites personnels, a commencé à comprendre qu'il aurait intérêt à faire appel à des leaders plus jeunes.
Lorsqu'il devint premier ministre en 1993 à 56 ans, Morihiro
Hosokawa était pratiquement considéré comme un jeune
homme. L'architecture est naturellement un domaine dans
lequel l'expérience continue à jouer un grand rôle, en particulier
en période de difficultés économiques. Lorsque les commandes
se font plus rares, les clients, tant publics que privés, ont tendance à s'adresser à des noms connus. En dehors des anciens,
comme Tange, la scène architecturale japonaise du milieu des
années 90 est dominée par quatre personnalités nées entre 1928
et 1936: Fumihiko Maki (1928), Arata Isozaki (1931), Kisho Kurokawa (1934) et Hiroshi Hara (1936). Ce constat néglige naturellement un certain nombre d'architectes moins créatifs et d'autres
plus jeunes comme Tadao Ando et Toyo Ito, qui font l'objet du
chapitre suivant.

Fumihiko Maki est à de multiples égards le plus raffiné et le
plus sophistiqué des maîtres actuels. Né à Tokyo, il fait ses
études à l'université de la ville, à la Cranbrook Academy of Art, et
à l'Harvard Graduate School of Design (Master en architecture

Fumihiko Maki, Tepia, Minato-ku, Tokyo, Japan, 1989.
An ample budget provided by the Ministry of International Trade and Industry permitted the architect to create a building that approaches technical and esthetic perfection.

Fumihiko Maki, Tepia, Minato-ku, Tokio, Japan, 1989.
Ein großzügiges Budget des Ministeriums für Außenhandel und Industrie ermöglichte dem Architekten die Gestaltung eines Bauwerks von großer technischer und ästhetischer Perfektion.

Fumihiko Maki, Tepia, Minato-ku, Tokyo, Japon, 1989.
Un important budget financé par le ministère du commerce international et de l'industrie a permis la construction de ce bâtiment qui atteint à la perfection technique et esthétique.

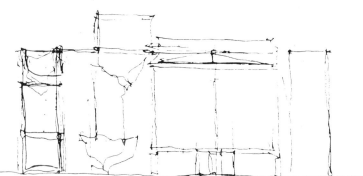

Masters of the Universe

It is true that the Japanese still tend to respect the privileges of age more than Western societies. Yet recently, even the political system, which formerly seemed to choose its leaders strictly on the basis of seniority with little concern for individual merit, has seen the virtues of calling on younger leaders. At just fifty-six years of age Morihiro Hosokawa was a virtual youngster when he became Prime Minister of Japan in 1993. Architecture is naturally an area in which experience continues to count, particularly in a period of economic difficulties. With fewer jobs available, the clients, both public and private, tend to look toward well-known figures. Aside from even older figures like Tange, the Japanese architectural scene in the mid-1990s is dominated by four men born between 1928 and 1936. They are Fumihiko Maki (born in 1928); Arata Isozaki (1931); Kisho Kurokawa (1934); and Hiroshi Hara (1936). This affirmation naturally sets aside a number of architects who deal in less inventive work, and slightly younger masters such as Tadao Ando and Toyo Ito, who are the subject of the next chapter.

Fumihiko Maki is in many ways the most refined and sophisticated of the current leaders of Japanese architecture. Born in Tokyo, he was educated at the University of Tokyo, the Cranbrook Academy of Art and the Harvard Graduate School of Design (M. Arch. 1954). He worked for Skidmore, Owings and Merrill in

Rolle: Bei einer schlechten Lage auf dem Arbeitsmarkt geben sowohl öffentliche wie private Auftraggeber bekannten Namen den Vorzug. Abgesehen von Tange wird die japanische Architekturszene Mitte der 90er Jahre von vier zwischen 1928 und 1936 geborenen Männern dominiert – Fumihiko Maki (geb. 1928), Arata Isozaki (1931), Kisho Kurokawa (1934) und Hiroshi Hara (1936). Diese Aussage läßt allerdings einige Architekten außer acht, die sich mit weniger innovativen Arbeiten beschäftigen, sowie etwas jüngere Baumeister wie Tadao Ando und Toyo Ito.

Fumihiko Maki ist in vieler Hinsicht der subtilste und anspruchsvollste der heutigen Wortführer der japanischen Architektur. Er wurde in Tokio geboren und an der University of Tokyo, der Cranbrook Academy of Art sowie an der Harvard Graduate School of Design ausgebildet (M. Arch. 1954). Maki arbeitete für Skidmore, Owings and Merrill in New York sowie für Sert Jackson and Associates in Cambridge, Massachusetts, bevor er 1965 in Tokio Maki and Associates gründete. Der Gewinner des Pritzker Preises 1993 ist vor allem bekannt für Bauten wie das 1989 entstandene Tepia im Minato-ku-Bezirk von Tokio oder das 1984 fertiggestellte Fujisawa Municipal Gymnasium in der Präfektur Kanagawa. Tepia gehört zu den perfektesten Ausdrucksformen der zeitgenössischen japanischen Architektur. Dieser 13 810 m² große Pavillon für Wissenschaft und High-Tech liegt unmittelbar neben dem Meiji Memorial Park in Tokio. Sein Besitzer, das japanische Ministerium für Außenhandel und Industrie (MITI), verfolgte 1989 offensichtlich die Absicht, ein möglichst deutliches Statement über die weltweit führenden Fähigkeiten der japanischen Industrie und Architektur abzugeben. Maki selbst sagte dazu: »Der hohe technologische und handwerkliche Standard des japanischen Bauwesens hat diesen Entwurf und seine Details erst möglich gemacht. Dennoch wird, aller Wahrscheinlichkeit nach, ein gleichbleibendes technologisches und handwerkliches Niveau nicht bis in alle Ewigkeit aufrechterhalten werden können. Aus diesem Grund ist Tepia ein Zeugnis der heutigen japanischen Industriegesellschaft.«

So wie im Falle von Tepia kunstvoll perforierte Aluminiumgitter Erinnerungen an den traditionellen japanischen Wandschirm

en 1954). Il travaille pour Skidmore, Owings et Merrill à New York, puis pour Sert Jackson and Associates à Cambridge, Massachusetts avant de créer Maki et Associés à Tokyo en 1965. Lauréat du Prix Pritzker 1993, il est surtout célèbre pour des réalisations comme l'immeuble Tepia du quartier de Minato-ku à Tokyo (1989), ou son gymnase municipal de Fujisawa dans la préfecture de Kanagawa (1984). Tepia est l'une des expressions les plus parfaites de l'architecture contemporaine japonaise. Ce pavillon pour les sciences et la haute technologie de 13 810 m² est situé tout près du Parc du souvenir Meiji à Tokyo. Son propriétaire, le ministère du commerce international et de l'industrie (MITI) cherchait, en 1989, à mettre en evidence la capacité de l'industrie et de l'architecture japonaises à diriger le monde. Comme le déclara Maki lui-même: «Ce sont les standards élevés de technologie et de réalisation, préservés par le système japonais de construction, qui ont rendu ce projet possible jusque dans ses moindres détails. Il est fort probable, qu'un niveau équivalent de technologie et de soin de réalisation ne durera pas indéfiniment. Aussi, Tepia, constitue-t-il en un sens un témoignage sur la société japonaise d'aujourd'hui.»

De même que pour l'immeuble Tepia les panneaux d'aluminium perforé sophistiqués rappellent les paravents traditionnels japonais ou *shoji*, les formes du gymnase métropolitain, tout proche, réussissent à marier le passé et le futur. Avec une surface au sol totale de 43 971 m², cet ensemble occupe un terrain de 4 hectares dans le Parc Meiji. Il contient un stade principal de 10 000 places, et une piscine intérieure qui peut accueillir 900 spectateurs. Fumihiko Maki fait remarquer que: «La vue sur le parc et la ville au loin, s'ouvre au fur et à mesure que l'on se déplace entre les masses dynamiques des constructions et des éléments sculpturaux. Cette expérience de modification du paysage n'est pas sans rapport de principe avec le *kaiyushiki*, ou jardin traditionnel japonais.»

Maki travaille actuellement sur la vaste extension de son Centre de Congrès Nippon de Makuhari Masse (Chiba, Chiba) qui devrait être achevé en 1997, ainsi qu'à un petit théâtre flottant pour un festival d'été qui s'est tenu en 1996 dans la ville

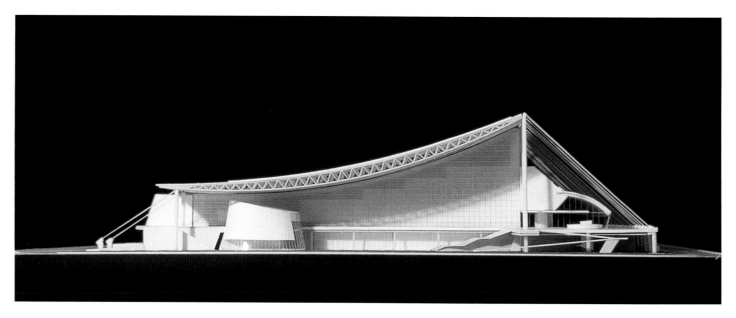

Fumihiko Maki, Nippon Convention Center Makuhari Messe, Phase II, Chiba, Chiba, Japan, 1996–97, exploring the technical limits of new materials for a large extension of this convention complex located near Tokyo.

Fumihiko Maki, Nippon Convention Center Makuhari Messe, Phase II, Chiba, Chiba, Japan, 1996–97. Mit dem großen Erweiterungsbau des Convention Center in der Nähe von Tokio erforscht der Architekt die technischen Grenzen neuer Materialien.

Fumihiko Maki, Centre Nippon de Congrès de la foire de Makuhari, Phase II, Chiba, Chiba, Japon, 1996–97. Exploration des limites techniques des matériaux nouveaux pour cette vaste extension d'un centre de congrès, près de Tokyo.

New York and Sert Jackson and Associates in Cambridge, Massachusetts before creating Maki and Associates in Tokyo in 1965. Winner of the 1993 Pritzker Prize, Fumihiko Maki is best known for buildings like his 1989 Tepia in the Minato-ku area of Tokyo or his 1984 Fujisawa Municipal Gymnasium in Kanagawa Prefecture. Tepia is one of the most perfect expressions of contemporary Japanese architecture. With a total floor area of 13,810 m², this pavilion for science and high-technology is located next to Meiji Memorial Park in Tokyo. Its owner, the Ministry of International Trade and Industry (MITI) was obviously intent in 1989 on making the clearest statement possible about the capacity of Japanese industry and architecture to lead the world. As Maki himself has said, "The high standard of technology and craftsmanship maintained by Japan's system of building and construction has made this design and its details possible. In all likelihood, an equivalent level of technology and craftsmanship may not endure indefinitely: thus, Tepia is in a sense, a testimony to Japanese society of today."

Just as sophisticated perforated aluminum panels play a role in Tepia that recalls the traditional Japanese screen or *shoji*, so the forms of the nearby Tokyo Metropolitan Gymnasium succeed in blending the past and the future. With a total floor area of 43,971 m², this complex occupies a 4 hectare site in Meiji Park. It has a main arena with a capacity of 10,000, and an indoor swimming pool with seating for 900. Fumihiko Maki points out that "Continually changing views of the park and city beyond open up as one moves between the dynamic building masses and sculptural elements. The experience of changing scenery is not unrelated to the compositional principles of the traditional Japanese stroll gardens known as *kaiyushiki*."

Maki's current work includes the large Phase II extension of his own Nippon Convention Center Makuhari Messe (Chiba, Chiba), due to be completed in 1997, as well as a small floating theater for a 1996 summer festival in the Dutch city of Groningen. As a teacher and a member of many prestigious juries, like that of the Aga Khan Award, or the Pritzker Prize, Maki has had a considerable influence on the evolution of con-

oder *shoji* wachrufen, so gelingt es den Formen des ganz in der Nähe gelegenen Tokyo Metropolitan Gymnasium, Vergangenheit und Zukunft miteinander zu verschmelzen. Mit einer Fläche von 43 971 m² nimmt dieser Komplex ein 4 Hektar großes Gelände im Meiji-Park ein. Er verfügt über eine Mehrzweckhalle mit 10 000 Plätzen sowie über ein Hallenbad mit einer Kapazität von 900 Zuschauern. Maki erklärt: »Wenn man sich zwischen den dynamischen Baumassen und den skulpturalen Elementen hin und her bewegt, öffnen sich ständig wechselnde Ausblicke auf den benachbarten Park und die Stadt. Die Erfahrung einer sich verändernden Szenerie ist den Prinzipien des *kaiyushiki*, des traditionellen japanischen Wandelgartens nicht unähnlich.«

Zu Makis aktuellen Projekten gehören die große Phase II-Erweiterung seines eigenen Nippon Convention Center Makuhari Messe (Chiba, Chiba), die 1997 fertiggestellt werden soll sowie ein kleines schwimmendes Theater für das Groninger Sommerfestival 1996. Als Dozent und Mitglied vieler renommierter Jurys, wie etwa des Aga Khan Award oder des Pritzker Preises, übte Maki erheblichen Einfluß auf die Entwicklung der zeitgenössischen japanischen Architektur aus. Sein Kommentar zum aktuellen Zustand seines, von den wirtschaftlichen Problemen der Zeit nach der »Seifenblasenökonomie« geprägten Berufsstandes, ist besonders aufschlußreich: »Natürlich ist der Kuchen ein Stück kleiner geworden«, so Maki, »aber das bedeutet nur, daß die Stücke für alle ein bißchen kleiner ausfallen. Dies gibt uns die Zeit, an Details zu arbeiten, denen wir in der Vergangenheit nicht genügend Aufmerksamkeit schenken konnten. Die Situation in Japan unterscheidet sich von der der Vereinigten Staaten insofern, als dort die Auftraggeber konservativer geworden sind. In Japan haben große Firmen meist keinen Präsidenten mit einer ausgeprägten Vorliebe für einen bestimmten Architekturstil.« Nach Makis Ansicht tendieren die japanischen privaten und öffentlichen Auftraggeber weniger zu einer konservativen Haltung als zu einem stärkeren Kostenbewußtsein. Dennoch hat dies nicht dazu geführt, daß er bei der Qualität seiner häufig exquisiten Materialien nennenswerte Abstriche machen mußte. »Die Hersteller übernahmen einen Teil der wirtschaftlichen Bela-

néerlandaise de Groningue. Enseignant et membre de nombreux jurys prestigieux, comme celui du Prix Aga Khan, ou du Prix Pritzker, Maki exerce une influence considérable sur l'évolution de l'architecture de son pays. Son commentaire sur l'état actuel de la profession, influencé par les difficultés économiques des années de crise, est particulièrement éclairant: «Naturellement, la taille du gâteau s'est rétrécie, »dit-il, «mais cela signifie seulement que la part de chacun d'entre nous est un peu plus petite. Nous avons ainsi plus de temps à consacrer aux détails, ce que nous ne pouvions pas toujours faire dans le passé. La situation au Japon est différente de celle des Etats-Unis, où il est vrai que les clients sont devenus plus conservateurs. Ici, par exemple, les présidents directeurs généraux des grandes entreprises ne manifestent guère de goût pour un style architectural particulier.» Il pense que les clients japonais, privés ou publics, sont devenus plus attentifs aux coûts que conservateurs, ce qui ne l'a pas conduit pour autant à diminuer substantiellement la qualité des matériaux souvent très sophistiqués qu'il utilise. «Les fabricants ont pris en charge une partie du poids de la crise en abaissant leurs coûts. Il est vrai, cependant, qu'aujourd'hui je peux être amené à utiliser des matériaux moins cher que par le passé,» poursuit-il. Il reconnaît que les architectes plus jeunes peuvent rencontrer plus de difficultés pour trouver des clients que jadis. «De nombreux architectes plus jeunes reviennent aux origines du mouvement moderniste. C'est une sorte de néo-modernisme qui peut s'assimiler à un type de conservatisme,» conclut-il.[9]

Trois ans seulement plus jeune que Maki, Arata Isozaki est, à de nombreux égards, le plus influents des architectes japonais actuels. Parce que son style a considérablement évolué au cours des années, il est parfois difficile d'identifier les différents bâtiments qu'il a conçus. Cependant au cours des 15 dernières années, il a construit à plusieurs reprises hors du Japon, en particulier le Museum of Contemporary Art de Los Angeles (MoCA, 1981–86), ou le Centre japonais d'art et de technologie de Cracovie en Pologne (1991–94). Né sur l'île de Kyushu, Isozaki y a beaucoup construit, présidant à des initiatives originales comme l'Artpolis '92 à Kumamoto, où il a fait sélectionner des archi-

temporary Japanese architecture. His commentary on the current state of his profession, as it has been influenced by the economic difficulties of the post-bubble years, is particularly enlightening. "Naturally, the size of the pie has gotten smaller," he says, "but that just means that everybody's piece is a little smaller. It gives us the time to work on details which we might not have had in the past. The situation in Japan is different than that of the United States, where it is true that clients have become more conservative. Here large corporations, for example, do not typically have a Chief Executive Officer with a marked taste for a specific kind of architecture." Rather than becoming more conservative, he says that Japanese clients, whether corporate or public, have become more cost-conscious. Nor has this really led him to substantially downgrade the quality of the often very sophisticated materials that he uses. "Manufacturers have borne part of the burden of the economic situation by bringing down their costs. It is true, however, that today I may use some less expensive materials than I would have in the past," continues Fumihiko Maki. He acknowledges that younger architects may have a more difficult time getting commissions today than they did in the past. As he says, "Many younger architects have looked back to the origins of the modern movement. This is a kind of neo-modernism, which might be attributed to an attitude that leans toward conservatism," he concludes.9

Just three years younger than Fumihiko Maki, Arata Isozaki is in many ways the most influential of living Japanese architects. Because his style has evolved considerably over the years, persons outside of the world of architecture may have had some difficulty in identifying specific structures that he has built. In the past fifteen years, however, he has built outside of Japan on numerous occasions, most notably in the case of the Los Angeles Museum of Contemporary Art (MoCA, 1981–86), or the Center for Japanese Art and Technology in Cracow, Poland (1991–94). A native of the island of Kyushu, Isozaki has built extensively there, presiding over such original initiatives as Kumamoto Artpolis '92, where he helped to select architects such as Toyo Ito and Kazuo Shinohara for projects in this south-

stung, indem sie ihre Kosten senkten. Dennoch ist es richtig, daß ich heute weniger teure Materialien verwende als vor einigen Jahren«, fährt Maki fort. Er bestätigt, daß jüngere Architekten es heute wesentlich schwerer haben als früher, Bauaufträge zu erhalten. »Viele jüngere Architekten haben sich auf die Ursprünge der Moderne zurückbesonnen. Auf diese Weise entsteht eine Neo-Moderne, deren Haltung man mit einer Art von Konservatismus gleichsetzen kann.«9

Arata Isozaki, nur drei Jahre jünger als Fumihiko Maki, ist in vieler Hinsicht der einflußreichste zeitgenössische japanische Architekt. Da sich sein Stil im Lauf der Jahre beträchtlich weiterentwickelt hat, fällt es einigen Betrachtern schwer, die von ihm entworfenen Bauwerke zu identifizieren. Allerdings realisierte Isozaki in den letzten 15 Jahren zahlreiche Projekte außerhalb Japans, von denen das Los Angeles Museum of Contemporary Art (MoCA, 1981–86) und das Zentrum für japanische Kunst und Technologie in Krakau (1991–94) zu den bekanntesten zählen. Der auf Kyushu geborene Isozaki baute sehr häufig auf seiner Heimatinsel; außerdem übernahm er den Vorsitz vieler origineller Projekte wie etwa der Kumamoto Artpolis '92, wo er Architekten wie Toyo Ito und Kazuo Shinohara auswählte, die Projekte in dieser südjapanischen Präfektur realisieren sollten. Im Falle des aktuellen Gifu Kitagata Apartment Reconstruction Project entschied er sich ausschließlich für junge Architektinnen – Kazuyo Sejima, die erst 33 Jahre alte Akiko Takahashi, Christine Hawley, Partnerin von Peter Cook in London, Elizabeth Diller von Diller & Scofidio (eine in Lodz geborene New Yorkerin) sowie die Landschaftsarchitektin Martha Schwarz. Isozaki ist eine eindrucksvolle Persönlichkeit mit einem beißenden Humor, der über die große Zahl der von ihm entworfenen Gebäude hinaus einen deutlichen Einfluß auf die allgemeine Richtung der zeitgenössischen japanischen Architektur ausübt. Während er noch behauptet, daß es in Japan »keine gaijin mehr« geben solle, bemüht er sich bereits um Architektinnen wie Hawley, Diller und Schwarz. Isozaki, der im Gegensatz zu vielen seiner Kollegen fließend Englisch spricht, kann sicherlich als Mitglied der internationalen Architekturelite angesehen werden; gleichzeitig nimmt er, zusam-

tectes comme Toyo Ito et Kazuyo Shinohara sur des projets pour cette ville de préfecture. Dans le cadre du projet actuel de reconstruction d'immeubles d'appartements de Gifu Kitagata, il n'a sélectionné que de jeunes architectes femmes, Kazuyo Sejima, Akiko Takahashi (âgée de 33 ans seulement), Christine Hawley, l'associée de Peter Cook à Londres, Elizabeth Diller de Diller & Scofidio, New yorkaise née à Lodz, Pologne, en 1954, et l'architecte paysager Martha Schwarz. Personnage impressionnant, au sens de l'humour un peu pervers, Isozaki, en-dehors du grand nombre de bâtiments qu'il a édifié, exerce une influence sensible sur le cours de l'architecture nippone dans son ensemble. Alors qu'il déclare qu'il n'y aura «plus de *gaijins*», il fait personnellement appel à des architectes étrangers. Parlant couramment l'anglais, à la différence de beaucoup de ses confrères, il fait clairement partie de l'élite architecturale internationale. De plus, il s'implique avec son épouse le sculpteur Aiko Miyawaki dans l'évolution de l'art de notre temps. Un récent projet à Kyushu, le Centre de Congrès et la B-con Plaza de Oita (Oita, Oita) se compose d'un hall de congrès en forme d'arène de 35 300 m² qui peut recevoir 8000 personnes. Son étonnante tour de 100 m de haut est une section d'une sphère imaginaire, d'un kilomètre de diamètre, dont le centre serait au niveau de la mer dans le parc de Beppu. Parmi ses autres projets à l'étranger, figure une autre importante réalisation, le Columbus Ohio Center of Science and Industry (COSI). Leslie Wexner, le propriétaire milliardaire de la chaîne de magasins de vêtements «The Limited», qui avait commandé à Peter Eisenman le Wexner Center, édifié dans la même ville, dirige et finance la phase d'étude de ce bâtiment public, en tant qu'administrateur du Centre. Avec sa grande façade incurvée, ce nouveau projet rappelle fortement le Centre de Congrès de Nara et le Centre Domus de La Corogne (Espagne) reproduits plus loin.

Dans un commentaire révélateur sur ces trois réalisations, Arata Isozaki explique que «ce sont d'une certaine façon des bâtiments frères. J'ai commencé à utiliser cette forme à Nara, dans sa totalité. Dans les deux autres cas, les formes incurvées ne sont pas achevées. A La Corogne, une seule face est incurvée,

Arata Isozaki, Art Tower Mito, Mito, Japan, 1986–90. This largely symbolic 100 meter high tower and the accompanying cultural center with concert halls, a theater and exhibition galleries is one of Isozaki's best-known works.

Arata Isozaki, Art Tower Mito, Mito, Japan, 1986–90. Dieser symbolhafte, 100 Meter hohe Turm und das benachbarte Kulturzentrum mit Konzertsälen, einem Theater und Ausstellungsräumen zählen zu Isozakis bekanntesten Werken.

Arata Isozaki, Tour d'art de Mito, Mito, Japon, 1986–90. Une des œuvres d'Isozaki les plus connues, cette tour symbolique de 100 m de haut se dresse dans un centre culturel réunissant salles de concert, théâtre, et galeries d'exposition.

Arata Isozaki, Columbus Ohio Center of Science and Industry (COSI), Columbus, Ohio, with its large arc reminiscent of Isozaki's Nara and La Coruña projects.

Arata Isozaki, Columbus Ohio Center of Science and Industry (COSI), Columbus, Ohio, dessen gewaltiger Bogen an Isozakis Projekte in Nara und La Coruña erinnert.

Arata Isozaki, Columbus Ohio Center of Science and Industry (COSI), Columbus, Ohio dont le mur en forme d'arc rappelle les projets d'Isozaki pour Nara et La Corogne.

ern prefecture. In the case of the current Gifu Kitagata Apartment Reconstruction Project he has selected only young female designers: Kazuyo Sejima; Akiko Takahashi, who is just thirty-three years old; Christine Hawley, who is Peter Cook's partner in London; Elizabeth Diller of Diller & Scofidio, who is a New Yorker born in Lodz, Poland in 1954; and the landscape architect Martha Schwarz. A striking man with a wicked sense of humor, Isozaki, beyond the large number of buildings for which he is responsible, also clearly has an influence on the course of contemporary Japanese architecture as a whole. Just as he declares that there are to be "no more *gaijins*" in Japan, so he personally calls on figures like Hawley, Diller and Schwarz. A fluent English speaker, unlike many of his colleagues, Isozaki is very definitely a member of the international architectural elite, participating too, with his wife the sculptor Aiko Miyawaki, in the evolution of the art world. A recent Kyushu project, his 1991–95 B-con Plaza/Oita Convention Center (Oita, Oita) is a 35,300 m² arena style convention hall with a capacity of 8,000 persons. Its astonishing 100 meter high tower is a portion cut out of an imaginary sphere with a diameter of one kilometer and a center at sea level in the Beppu Park site. Amongst his current foreign projects is another large structure, the Columbus Ohio Center of Science and Industry (COSI). Leslie Wexner, the millionaire owner of The Limited clothing retail stores, who commissioned Peter Eisenman's Wexner Center in the same city, is conducting and financing the

men mit seiner Frau, der Bildhauerin Aiko Miyawaki, regen Anteil an der Evolution der Kunstwelt. Sein B-con Plaza/Oita Convention Center (Oita, Oita, 1991–95) umfaßt eine 35 300 m² große Halle mit einer Kapazität von 8000 Plätzen, deren erstaunlicher, 100 Meter hoher Turm Teil einer imaginären Kugel mit einem Durchmesser von einem Kilometer darstellt, deren Zentrum unterhalb des Meeresspiegels im Beppu-Park liegt. Zu Isozakis aktuellen Projekten im Ausland gehört das Columbus Ohio Center of Science and Industry (COSI). Leslie Wexner, der millionenschwere Besitzer der Bekleidungskette The Limited, der in derselben Stadt Peter Eisenmans Wexner Center in Auftrag gab, betreibt und finanziert in seiner Eigenschaft als Kurator des Wexner Center das Design dieses öffentlichen Gebäudes. Durch seine lange, gekrümmte Fassade erinnert Isozakis neuer Entwurf stark an die Formen des Nara Convention Center und an das Domus-Zentrum im spanischen La Coruña, die beide in diesem Band vorgestellt werden. In einem aufschlußreichen Kommentar zu diesen drei Bauwerken erklärt Isozaki: »Es handelt sich in gewisser Weise um ›Schwester‹-Gebäude. Dennoch unterscheiden sich die urbanen Situationen in allen drei Fällen stark voneinander. Ich verwendete diese Form zum ersten Mal in Nara, als vollständige Einheit; bei den beiden anderen Projekten wurden die gebogenen Formen nicht vollendet. In La Coruña gibt es nur eine gekrümmte Seite, während die andere Seite eine Art Wandschirm darstellt. Ich vergleiche die Lösung in Columbus mit der von La Coruña, da die lange, gekrümmte Oberfläche in einer horizontal ebenen Umgebung nach Westen weist. Davor befindet sich ein Parkplatz für 1000 Fahrzeuge. Das Ganze wirkt wie ein Meer von Autos oder wie ein Hafen. Aus diesem Grunde habe ich eine ähnliche Idee verwandt. In keinem der Fälle wurde hinsichtlich der Pläne eine offenere Mauer benötigt.«[10] Ein weiteres aktuelles Projekt Isozakis ist die Saitama Arena (Saitama, 1995), für das er sich in einem Architekturwettbewerb gegen Rogers, Piano, Nouvel, Koolhaas und andere durchsetzen mußte. Zu den interessantesten Aspekten dieses Entwurfs zählt die am Computer entwickelte Form, die – zumindest für westliche Augen – an ein Piktogramm erinnert.

l'autre étant une sorte d'écran pliant. A Columbus, je compare cette solution à celle de La Corogne parce que la longue surface courbe fait face à l'ouest dans une disposition horizontale. Devant, se trouve un parking pour 1000 véhicules, comme une mer de voitures, un port. C'est la raison pour laquelle j'ai utilisé une idée similaire. Ni dans un cas, ni dans l'autre, le programme n'exigeait de mur plus ouvert.»[10] Une autre de ses commandes actuelles, la Saitama Arena (Saitama, 1995), a été remporté face à Rogers, Piano, Nouvel, Koolhaas et quelques autres. L'un des aspects les plus surprenants de sa conception est le plan généré par ordinateur qui prend une forme de pictogramme, du moins pour l'œil occidental.

Le troisième grand maître actuel de l'architecture japonaise est Kisho Kurokawa, né à Nagoya en 1934. Un des fondateurs du mouvement métaboliste dans les années 60, il a depuis mis en théorie une approche personnelle de «symbiose» entre tradition japonaise et modernité. Même s'il a remporté des commandes importantes comme le Musée d'art contemporain d'Hiroshima (1984–88), il est difficilement classable dans la même catégorie que Maki, Isozaki, et Hiroshi Hara. Son Musée d'art moderne de Wakayama (1990–94), par exemple, semble faire appel aux même recettes que ses œuvres récentes. Comme il l'indique, en référence à ce site qui appartenait jadis aux terres du château de Wakayama, «au Japon l'architecture de château a s'est développée à l'origine au XVe siècle... le dessin des toits et des avant-toits symbolise ce style... les couleurs proposées ici devraient être le noir et le blanc, qui proviennent également du style de châteaux.» Cette analyse nous ramène en terrain connu. Elle rappelle le *Teikan yoshiki* ou «style impérial de toit.» Ayant conquis leur capacité à s'appuyer sur leur propre tradition dans les années 60, les architectes japonais peuvent maintenant s'orienter vers des références plus sophistiquées. Par dessus tout, ils ont réussi, comme le montrent leurs meilleures œuvres, à créer des constructions qui affichent une maîtrise réelle des matériaux et de l'espace. Les créations de Kurokawa, comme son musée d'art moderne d'Hiroshima, peuvent sembler, par comparaison, maladroites et lourdes.

Pages 40/41: Kisho Kurokawa, Museum of Modern Art, Wakayama, Japan, 1994. A drawing shows the relationship of this large (18,000 m²) museum to Wakayama Castle.

Seite 40/41: Kisho Kurokawa, Museum of Modern Art, Wakayama, Japan, 1994. Eine Zeichnung zeigt das Verhältnis zwischen diesem großen Museum (18 000 m²) und der Burg Wakayama.

Pages 40/41: Kisho Kurokawa, Musée d'art moderne, Wakayama, Japon, 1994. Dessin montrant la relation entre ce grand musée (18 000 m²) et le château de Wakayama.

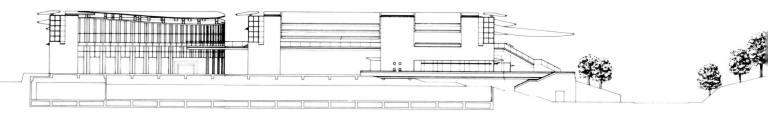

design side of this public building, acting in his capacity as a trustee of the Center. In its use of a very large curved facade, this new design strongly recalls the forms of the Nara Convention Center and Domus Center in La Coruña, Spain which are published in this volume. In a revealing comment on these three structures, Isozaki explains, "These are in a way 'sister' buildings for me. The urban situations are very different in each case though. I started to use this form in Nara, as a complete unit. In the other two cases, the curved forms are not completed. In La Coruña, there is only one side which is curved, and the other side is a kind of folding screen. In Columbus, I compare the solution to that of La Coruña because the long, curved surface is facing the west in a horizontal plane setting. In front of it, there is a parking lot for 1,000 vehicles. It's like a sea of cars, or a harbor. That is why I employed a similar idea. In neither case was a more open wall needed in terms of the programs."[10] Another of Isozaki's current projects, his Saitama Arena (Saitama, 1995), is a project that he won in a competition against Rogers, Piano, Nouvel, Koolhaas and others. One of the intriguing aspects of this design is the computer generated plan, which assumes a pictographic form, at least for Western eyes.

A third of the current masters of contemporary Japanese architects is Kisho Kurokawa, who was born in Nagoya in 1934. One of the founders of the Metabolism movement in the 1960s, he has since theorized on his own approach to a "symbiosis" between Japanese tradition and modernity. Despite winning large commissions like the Hiroshima City Museum of Contemporary Art (1984–88), it would seem that Kurokawa cannot be readily placed in the same category of inventiveness as Maki, Isozaki and Hiroshi Hara. His Museum of Modern Art in Wakayama (Wakayama, 1990–94), for example, seems to call on many of the same recipes as his other recent work. As Kurokawa says, with reference to this site located on what used to be part of the grounds of the Wakayama Castle, "Castle architecture in Japan was first developed in the fifteenth century... The design of the roof and the eaves symbolizes this style... The colors proposed here would be black and white, which is also quoted from

Der dritte der heutigen Meister der zeitgenössischen japanischen Architektur ist Kisho Kurokawa, der 1934 in Nagoya geboren wurde. Als einer der Begründer des Metabolismus in den 60er Jahren hat er sich seitdem mit Theorien seines eigenen Ansatzes einer »Symbiose« von japanischer Tradition und Moderne auseinandergesetzt. Trotz großer Bauten wie dem Hiroshima City Museum of Contemporary Art (1984–88) kann man Kurokawa nicht das gleiche innovative Vermögen zusprechen wie Maki, Isozaki oder Hiroshi Hara. Sein Museum of Modern Art in Wakayama (Wakayama, 1990–94) etwa scheint auf ebenso viele bekannte Rezepte zurückzugreifen wie seine anderen aktuellen Arbeiten.

In bezug auf das Baugelände, das auf dem Areal der ehemaligen Burg Wakayama liegt, erklärt Kurokawa: »Die Burgenarchitektur Japans entwickelte sich im 15. Jahrhundert... Das Design des Dachs und der Dachtraufen charakterisieren diesen Baustil... Die hier verwendeten Farben, Schwarz und Weiß, sind ebenfalls ein Zitat aus der traditionellen Burgenarchitektur.« Diese Analyse klingt seltsam bekannt; sie erinnert an den *Teikan yoshiki* oder »Kaiserlichen Dachstil«. Nachdem sie sich in den 60er Jahren zu ihrer eigenen Tradition zu bekennen lernten, sind die japanischen Architekten heute zu raffinierteren Anspielungen übergegangen. Darüber hinaus ist es ihnen in ihren besten Arbeiten gelungen, Bauwerke zu schaffen, die eine wahre Meisterschaft bei der Verwendung von Material und Raum verraten. Kurokawas Gebäude, wie etwa das Hiroshima Museum, wirken im Vergleich dazu klobig und schwerfällig.

Eine wesentlich interessantere Persönlichkeit ist Hiroshi Hara, der sich in letzter Zeit auf Gebäude spezialisiert zu haben scheint, die so groß sind, daß sie fast eine »Stadt in der Stadt« darstellen. Dies trifft mit Sicherheit auf die beiden hier vorgestellten Bauwerke zu, die Umeda Sky City und die Kyoto JR Station. Haras Kommentar zu diesen Projekten und seine Ansichten über den Zustand der zeitgenössischen japanischen Architektur verdienen es, ausgiebig zitiert zu werden:

Philip Jodidio: *Verwenden Sie für Ihre Projekte computergestütztes Design und sind Sie der Meinung, daß die Entwicklung des Com-*

Hiroshi Hara est un personnage fascinant qui semble s'être récemment spécialisé dans la création de bâtiments si énormes qu'ils présentent presque des caractéristiques urbaines. C'est par exemple le cas des deux immeubles reproduits ici, l'Umeda Sky City, et la gare de chemin de fer JR de Kyoto. Ses commentaires sur ces projets et ses réflexions sur l'état de l'architecture contemporaine dans son pays méritent d'être reprises ici dans leur intégralité:

Philip Jodidio: *Utilisez-vous les techniques de dessin assisté par ordinateur, et avez-vous le sentiment que l'évolution de l'informatique a modifié votre manière de concevoir?*

Hiroshi Hara: Professeur d'urbanisme à l'Université de Tokyo, je suis familiarisé avec l'utilisation de l'ordinateur depuis un certain temps. La gare de Kyoto compte 16 000 points de connexion structurelle et il a fallu trois mois à un ordinateur très puissant pour les analyser. Il est clair que pour des raisons techniques, les ordinateurs sont très utiles. Le Corbusier disait que l'architecture devait être une métaphore de la machine à l'ère de la machine. Notre tâche consiste à inventer une nouvelle métaphore pour l'ère de l'ordinateur. A mon sens, personne n'a encore trouvé de solution à ce problème. Je crois cependant qu'un aspect de la solution est de concevoir une architecture qui change ou évolue avec le temps. L'Umeda Sky City est un premier pas dans cette direction. Les images du bâtiment à différents moments de la journée montrent comment son aspect peut changer. L'architecture traditionnelle japonaise prend en compte le passage du temps, et lorsque je pense à mon architecture, j'imagine certaines vues de cerisiers en fleurs et une sorte de tuile de toit particulière. L'ordinateur lui-même semble évoluer dans une direction qui pourrait permettre de prendre en compte une notion aussi abstraite que celle du passage du temps.

Philip Jodidio: *Jugez vous votre approche typiquement japonaise, ou internationale?*

Hiroshi Hara: L'architecture traditionnelle japonaise, une fois encore, prend en compte l'idée de l'écoulement du temps. L'utilisation de la «logique floue» dans la conception par ordinateurs prouve que ceux-ci commencent à intégrer la notion d'ambi-

Hiroshi Hara, Kyoto JR Station, Shimogyo, Kyoto, Japan, 1991–97. A drawing showing the spectacular inner spaces.

Hiroshi Hara, Kyoto JR Station, Shimogyo, Kioto, Japan, 1991–97. Die Zeichnung zeigt die aufsehenerregenden Innenräume.

Hiroshi Hara, Gare JR de Kyoto, Shimogyo, Kyoto, Japon, 1991–97. Dessin représentant l'aspect spectaculaire des espaces intérieurs.

the traditional castle architecture style." This analysis has a slightly familiar ring to it. It brings to mind the *Teikan yoshiki* or "Imperial roof style." Having conquered the capacity to make reference to their own tradition in the 1960s, Japanese architects have now gone on to more sophisticated references than these. Above all, they have managed in the case of their best work to create structures which display a true mastery of the use of materials and space. Kurokawa's buildings like the Hiroshima Museum can seem by comparison to be awkward or heavy-handed.

A more fascinating figure is Hiroshi Hara, who seems to have specialized recently in the creation of buildings so large that they take on an almost urban character in their own right. This is certainly the case of the two buildings published here, his Umeda Sky City and Kyoto JR Station. His commentary on these projects, and his reflections on the state of contemporary Japanese architecture in interview form, merit being quoted here at length:

Philip Jodidio: *Do you use computer assisted design in your projects, and do you feel that the evolution of the computer and the programs has changed your way of thinking about design?*

Hiroshi Hara: As a professor of urban design at the University of Tokyo, I have been familiar with the use of computers for some time. In the Kyoto Station there are 16,000 structural connecting points, which took a very powerful computer three months to analyze. Naturally, for technical reasons, computers have been very useful. Le Corbusier said that architecture should be a metaphor for the machine in the age of the machine. Our task is to invent a new metaphor for the age of the computer. In my opinion, no one has yet found the solution to that problem. I believe, however, that one aspect of the solution is to conceive of an architecture that changes with time, or which evolves. The Umeda Sky City is a first step in this direction. Images of the building at different times of the day show how its aspect changes. Traditional Japanese architecture takes into account the passage of time, and when I think of my architecture I imagine certain views like cherry blossoms with a certain kind of roofing tile.

puters und der dazugehörigen Programme unsere Ansichten über Design verändert haben?

Hiroshi Hara: Als Professor für Stadtplanung an der Universität Tokio bin seit einigen Jahren mit dem Computer vertraut. Im Falle der Kyoto Station gab es 16 000 strukturelle Verbindungspunkte, für deren Analyse ein sehr leistungsstarker Computer drei Monate benötigte. Aus rein technischen Gesichtspunkten haben sich Computer als sehr nützlich erwiesen. Le Corbusier sagte, daß Architektur eine Metapher für die Maschine im Zeitalter der Maschine sein sollte. Unsere Aufgabe ist es, eine neue Metapher für das Zeitalter des Computers zu erfinden. Meiner Meinung nach hat bisher noch niemand eine Lösung für dieses Problem gefunden. Ich glaube jedoch, daß ein Teil der Lösung in einer Architektur besteht, die sich im Laufe der Zeit verändert oder weiterentwickelt. Umeda Sky City ist ein erster Schritt in diese Richtung: Aufnahmen des Gebäudes zu verschiedenen Tageszeiten zeigen, wie sich seine Erscheinung verändert. Die traditionelle japanische Architektur berücksichtigt den Lauf der Zeit, und wenn ich an meine Architektur denke, stelle ich mir bestimmte Bilder wie Kirschblüten in Verbindung mit einer gewissen Art von Dachziegeln vor. Einige Zeit lang habe ich mir bei jedem meiner Projekte vorzustellen versucht, wie es zu verschiedenen Tages- und Jahreszeiten aussehen würde. Die Computer selbst scheinen sich in eine Richtung zu entwickeln, die es erlaubt, einen so abstrakten Begriff wie den Lauf der Zeit berücksichtigen zu können.

Philip Jodidio: *Schätzen Sie Ihre eigene Auffassung von Architektur als typisch japanisch oder als international ein?*

Hiroshi Hara: Die traditionelle japanische Architektur bezieht die Vorstellung vom Lauf der Zeit in ihre Auffassung ein. Die Verwendung der sogenannten »Fuzzy-Logic« im Computerdesign zeigt, daß der Computer langsam beginnt, mit Mehrdeutigkeiten zu arbeiten. Die asiatische Denkweise hat seit jeher die Ambiguität des Lebens berücksichtigt. Bis vor kurzem war die westliche Logik dagegen eher positivistisch ausgerichtet. In der westlichen Logik gab es die eine Antwort, die alle anderen Antworten ungeeignet erscheinen ließ, wohingegen man in Asien nicht von einer, sondern von mehreren gleichrangigen Antworten ausgeht.

guïté. La pensée asiatique a toujours pris en compte l'ambiguïté de la vie. Jusqu'à récemment, la logique occidentale se voulait plus positiviste. Pour elle, il n'y avait qu'une réponse, les autres étant inappropriées, alors qu'en Asie, il n'y a pas une seule réponse, mais plusieurs. Des architectes comme Kenzo Tange ont imaginé une modernité qui était nécessairement liée au Japon. Je ne ressens pas le besoin d'adhérer à cette notion. Un bâtiment devrait toujours être capable de s'adapter à d'autres utilisations, et les gens devraient pouvoir se comporter différemment de ce que l'architecte a imaginé. Dans les gratte-ciel de New York, par exemple, vous ne pouvez que monter ou descendre, alors que dans l'Umeda Sky City, vous pouvez aller dans différentes directions. Dans la gare de Kyoto, vous trouverez tout un labyrinthe de directions possibles.

Philip Jodidio: *Les Futuristes, dont des architectes comme Antonio Sant'Elia, semblent avoir eu une conception similaire de l'espace, avec des passerelles dans toutes les directions...*

Hiroshi Hara: J'ai bien entendu réfléchi à des travaux comme ceux de Sant'Elia, et je suis un *fan* du film «Metropolis». Concevoir une telle architecture est une question, la construire en intégrant la problématique des tremblements de terre et de la puissance des vents en est une autre. La conception efficace de tels immeubles serait impossible sans l'aide de l'ordinateur.

Philip Jodidio: *L'Umeda Sky City aurait-il pu être construit ailleurs, où est-il spécifique à Osaka?*

Hiroshi Hara: Il aurait pu être construit partout. Je peux imaginer une ville comme New York avec des ponts entre ses gratte-ciel. Une fois encore, on y trouve une construction verticale développée, mais peu ou pas de développement horizontal au dessus du trottoir. Il n'y a toujours pas de ville qui ressemble à la Metropolis de Fritz Lang.

Philip Jodidio: *Pourquoi ne crée-t-on pas de telles liaisons entre les immeubles?*

Hiroshi Hara: Dans une société capitaliste, la réponse tient naturellement au système de propriété et de gestion. Si vous fermez les portes d'un immeuble, il est plus facile à gérer. Je pense néanmoins que cette attitude est en train d'évoluer. Il existe des

For some time, in each of my projects, I have tried to imagine what it would look like at different times of the day or in different seasons. The computer itself seems to be evolving in a direction that may permit it to take into account a notion as abstract as that of the passage of time.

Philip Jodidio: *Do you see your own approach as typically Japanese, or is it international?*

Hiroshi Hara: Traditional Japanese architecture, once again, takes into account the idea of the passage of time. The use of so-called "fuzzy logic" in computer design demonstrates that the computer is beginning to grasp the notion of ambiguity. Asian thinking has always taken the ambiguity of life into account. Until a recent date Western logic was more positivist. In Western logic, there was the answer, and the other answers were not appropriate, whereas in Asia, there is not a response, there are several. Architects like Kenzo Tange conceived of a modernity which was necessarily linked to Japan. I do not feel a need to embrace that notion. A building should always be able to serve other uses, and people should be able to behave differently than what the architect imagines. In skyscrapers in New York, for example, people can only go up and down, but in the Umeda Sky building it is possible to go in several different directions. In the Kyoto Station there will be a labyrinth of possible directions.

Philip Jodidio: *The Futurists, and architects like Antonio Sant'Elia, seem to have had a similar notion of space, with sky bridges in all directions.*

Hiroshi Hara: I certainly have thought about work like that of Sant'Elia for a long time, and I am a big fan of the movie "Metropolis." Conceiving of such an architecture is one problem; building it with problems like earthquakes and high winds is another. Efficient design of such buildings would be impossible without the computer.

Philip Jodidio: *Could the Umeda Sky building have been built anywhere, or is it specific to Osaka?*

Hiroshi Hara: The Umeda Sky building could have been built anywhere. I can imagine a city like New York with bridges between the skyscrapers. Again there is extensive vertical construc-

Architekten wie Kenzo Tange entwarfen eine Moderne, die mit Japan eng verbunden war. Ich sehe keinen Grund, diesem Ansatz folgen zu müssen. Ein Gebäude sollte immer in der Lage sein, verschiedenen Zwecken zu dienen, und die Menschen sollten immer in der Lage sein, sich anders zu verhalten, als es der Architekt geplant hat. In New Yorker Wolkenkratzern zum Beispiel können sich die Menschen nur nach oben und nach unten fortbewegen, während es im Umeda Sky Gebäude möglich ist, sich für unterschiedliche Richtungen zu entscheiden. Und in der Kyoto Station wird es ein Labyrinth möglicher Richtungen geben.

Philip Jodidio: *Die Futuristen und Architekten wie Antonio Sant'Elia schienen eine ähnliche Auffassung des Raumes zu vertreten; auch hier führen Luftbrücken in alle Richtungen.*

Hiroshi Hara: Ich habe mich natürlich lange Zeit mit Arbeiten wie denen von Sant'Elia beschäftigt, und ich bin ein großer Fan des Films »Metropolis«. Der Entwurf solcher Architektur ist eine Sache, der Bau und die damit verbundene Auseinandersetzung mit Erdbeben und Stürmen eine andere. Ein funktionsfähiges Design solcher Gebäude wäre ohne den Computer undenkbar.

Philip Jodidio: *Könnte das Umeda Sky Gebäude überall entstanden sein, oder ist es typisch für Osaka?*

Hiroshi Hara: Das Umeda Sky Gebäude hätte überall entstehen können. Ich kann mir eine Stadt wie New York vorstellen, bei der Brücken zwischen den Wolkenkratzern hin- und herführen. Dort findet man riesige vertikale Konstruktionen, aber nur wenig oder keinerlei horizontale Bewegung oberhalb des Straßenniveaus. Es gibt immer noch keine Stadt wie Fritz Langs »Metropolis«.

Philip Jodidio: *Warum werden solche Verbindungen zwischen den Gebäuden nicht angelegt?*

Hiroshi Hara: In einer kapitalistischen Gesellschaft steht die Antwort natürlich im Zusammenhang mit Management und Besitzrecht. Wenn man die Türen eines Gebäudes schließt, ist es einfacher zu verwalten; aber ich denke, daß sich diese Haltung langsam ändert. Es gibt eine ganze Reihe urbaner Bereiche, in denen unterirdische Räume entstehen, die von einer Gruppe von Gebäuden geteilt werden. Um horizontale Verbindungen zwischen Bauten herzustellen, würde es genügen, einige admini-

zones urbaines, dans lesquelles les espaces souterrains sont partagés entre un certain nombre d'immeubles. Pour construire des connexions horizontales, il suffirait de modifier certaines restrictions administratives et de modifier l'attitude de certaines personnes, mais je suis convaincu que ces changements se produiront un jour ou l'autre.[11]

L'aluminium, le béton et le nouveau maître

L'opposition entre poids et légèreté, entrevue plus haut à travers la diversité de réaction des architectes japonais face aux spécificités de leur environnement, n'est nulle part plus évidente qu'au sein d'un groupe de quatre architectes de talent, tous nés en 1940 et 1941. Trois d'entre eux explorent les capacités de l'architecture légère, et mettent l'accent sur le verre et l'aluminium. Le quatrième, Tadao Ando, est probablement l'architecte japonais vivant le plus remarquable. Sa maîtrise du béton et son vocabulaire géométrisant, volontairement restreint, témoignent d'une créativité et d'un art qui le placent dans une catégorie à part. L'aspect massif de son architecture ne l'empêche pas d'être baignée de lumière. Ando atteint parfois à une sorte de spiritualité qui représente en soi une lien profond entre le passé et le présent.

Né en 1941 à Séoul (Corée), Toyo Ito est diplômé de l'Université de Tokyo en 1965 et travaille dans l'agence de Kiyonori Kikutake jusqu'en 1969. Il crée son propre studio en 1971, qui prend le nom de Toyo Ito Architect & Associates, en 1979. Dès l'époque de sa première grande œuvre, la résidence «Hutte d'argent» (Tokyo, 1984), ou plus spectaculairement encore sa Tour des vents (Yokohama, 1986), tour d'aération de 21 m de haut en aluminium perforé et panneaux de miroir acrylique, près du terminal routier de la gare de Yokohama, il a recherché une légèreté qui tend à l'évanescence. La «Hutte d'argent» est en grande partie fermée à son environnement urbain chaotique, si ce n'est par un toit ouvert, qui la relie à la nature malgré l'omniprésence de la ville. Indubitablement influencé par Kazuo Shinohara, Ito a beaucoup travaillé dans la petite ville de Yatsushiro (Kyushu, préfecture de Kumamoto). Il y a élevé trois bâtiments: le musée

Hiroshi Hara, Umeda Sky City, Kita-ku, Osaka, Japan, 1988–93. A prototype for a series of "interconnected superskyscrapers."

Hiroshi Hara, Umeda Sky City, Kita-ku, Osaka, Japan, 1988–93. Der Prototyp für eine Reihe »intern verbundener Super-Wolkenkratzer«.

Hiroshi Hara, Umeda Sky City, Kita-ku, Osaka, Japon, 1988–93. Prototype d'une série de «super-gratte-ciel interconnectés.»

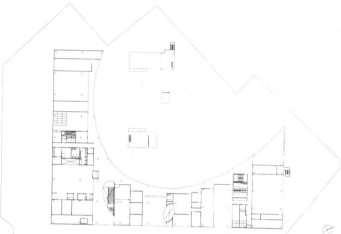

Toyo Ito, Yatsushiro Fire Station, Yatsushiro, Kumamo-to, Japan, 1992–95. A typically light design by this architect, who admits to finding similarities in his own work to that of Le Corbusier.

Toyo Ito, Feuerwache in Yatsushiro, Kumamoto, Japan, 1992–95. Ein für den Architekten, der Ähnlichkeiten zwischen seinen eigenen Arbeiten und denen Le Corbu-siers eingesteht, typisches, schwereloses Design.

Toyo Ito, caserne de pompiers de Yatsushiro, Yatsushiro, Kumamoto, Japon, 1992–95. Projet typique de la légère-té qu'aime cet architecte qui reconnaît des similarités entre son œuvre et celle de Le Corbusier.

tion but little or no horizontal movement above the sidewalk. There is still no city like Fritz Lang's "Metropolis."

Philip Jodidio: *Why aren't such connections made between buildings?*

Hiroshi Hara: In a capitalist society the answer naturally has to do with management and ownership. If you close the doors of a building, it is easier to manage, but I think that that attitude is evolving. There are a number of urban areas where underground spaces are built and shared between a number of buildings. To build horizontal connections between buildings, it would suffice to alter some administrative restrictions and to change some people's attitudes, but I am convinced that those changes will one day come about.[11]

Aluminum, concrete, and the new master

The dichotomy of lightness and weight, emphasized above to describe the differing reactions of Japanese architects to the peculiarities of their environment, is nowhere more evident than in a group of four talented architects born in 1940 and 1941. Three of them have explored the virtues of a light architecture, with an emphasis on aluminum and glass. The fourth, Tadao Ando, can perhaps claim the distinction of being the most remarkable living Japanese architect. His mastery of concrete forms in a restrained geometric vocabulary shows an inventive-ness and indeed an artistry that place him in a category apart. The solidity of his architecture does not keep it from being suf-fused with light. At his best, Ando achieves a kind of implicit spirituality, which in itself represents a deep link between the past and the present.

Born in 1941 in Seoul, Korea, Toyo Ito graduated from the Uni-versity of Tokyo in 1965, and worked in the office of Kiyonori Kikutake until 1969. He created his own office in 1971, assuming the name of Toyo Ito Architect & Associates in 1979. From the time of his first widely published work, the Silver Hut residence (Tokyo, 1984), or even more dramatically in the Tower of the Winds (Yokohama, 1986), a 21 meter high aeration stack near the bus terminal of Yokohama Station made of perforated alu-

strative Restriktionen abzuschaffen und das Verhalten einiger Personen zu verändern. Ich bin davon überzeugt, daß diese Veränderungen eines Tages Wirklichkeit werden.«[11]

Aluminium, Beton und die Neuen Meister

Die Dichotomie von Leichtigkeit und Schwere, die die unterschiedlichen Reaktionen der japanischen Architekten auf die Besonderheiten ihrer Umgebung erklärt, tritt nirgends offensichtlicher zutage als bei einer Gruppe von vier talentierten Architekten, die alle 1940 bzw. 1941 geboren wurden. Drei von ihnen erforschten die Vorzüge der Leichtbauweise und arbeiteten dabei vor allem mit Aluminium und Glas. Der vierte, Tadao Ando, kann vielleicht den Ruf des bemerkenswertesten zeitgenössischen japanischen Architekten für sich in Anspruch nehmen. Sein meisterhafter Umgang mit Betonformen im Rahmen eines beschränkten geometrischen Vokabulars zeugt von einem Erfindungsreichtum und einer Kunstfertigkeit, die ihn in eine eigene Kategorie erhebt. Trotz der massiven Strukturen seiner Architektur sind seine Bauten von Licht durchflutet. In seinen besten Momenten erreicht Ando eine implizite Spiritualität, die bereits in sich selbst eine tiefe innere Verbindung zwischen Vergangenheit und Zukunft repräsentiert.

Der 1941 in Seoul geborene Toyo Ito beendete 1965 sein Studium an der University of Tokyo und arbeitete bis 1969 im Büro von Kiyonori Kikutake. 1971 gründete er sein eigenes Büro, das seit 1979 unter dem Namen Toyo Ito Architect & Associates firmiert. Seit der Zeit seiner ersten aufsehenerregenden Arbeiten, der Silver Hut Residence (Tokio, 1984) und dem »Tower of the Winds« (Turm der Winde, Yokohama, 1986) – einem 21 m hohen Lüftungsschacht in der Nähe des Busbahnhofs der Yokohama Station, der aus perforiertem Aluminium und Acryl-Spiegelflächen besteht –, hat Ito eine zum Ätherischen neigende Leichtigkeit angestrebt. Die Silver Hut Residence ist gegenüber ihrer chaotischen urbanen Umgebung weitestgehend abgeschlossen, bis auf das offene Dach, das trotz der invasiven Präsenz der Stadt eine Verbindung zur Natur herstellt. Der ohne Zweifel von Kazuo Shinohara beeinflußte Ito baute häufig in der Kleinstadt

municipal (1989–91), un foyer de personnes âgées (1992–94) et une caserne de pompiers (1992–95). Pour le foyer de personnes âgées, il a imaginé un lien avec des mondes qui sont au delà d'une résidence de ce type. Comme il le précise: «Il n'existe pas de liens psychologiques forts entre ces résidents. S'ils vivent physiquement proches ces uns des autres... chacun dispose de son propre réseau de relations préalables et extérieures. Ces gens sont des personnes âgées dont les corps réels vivent ensemble, mais ce sont aussi des «nomades» qui, dans leur conscience, possèdent un corps fictif.» Comme pour le Musée municipal construit antérieurement et qui se dresse au sommet d'une colline artificielle tel un bateau venu d'une autre planète qui gonflerait ses voiles pour profiter des ventes intergalactiques, la résidence de personnes âgées, avec ses grandes ouvertures, évoque une sorte d'au delà. Et cependant, le vocabulaire d'Ito rappelle souvent l'un de ses célèbres prédécesseurs: «Je me retrouve toujours renvoyé à Le Corbusier. Je ne reviens jamais à lui consciemment. C'est seulement lorsque je suis presque arrivé à mon but, que ceux qui voient mes maquettes et mes dessins le remarquent, et que je réalise ce que j'ai fait.»

Comme Toyo Ito, Itsuko Hasagawa, née en 1941, dans la préfecture de Shizuoka, commence par travailler pour l'architecte Kiyonori Kikutake (1964–69). Elle est directement influencée par Kazuo Shinohara, avec lequel elle collabore plusieurs années à l'Institut de technologie de Tokyo, à partir de 1969. Elle ouvre sa propre agence, Itsuko Hasegawa Atelier, en 1978. Plus encore que Ito, elle s'efforce de donner naissance à une sorte de réalité alternative, voire à une matérialisation artificielle de la nature dans ses projets les plus importants, comme le Centre Culturel Shonandai (Fujisawa, Kanagawa, 1987–90), sorte de représentation de l'univers en réduction. Sa quête presque nostalgique d'une nature nouvelle dans laquelle pousseraient des arbres d'aluminium, pourrait bien s'expliquer par la surpopulation dramatique des zones côtières à l'est du Japon. Lorsque la nature est présente dans les cités japonaises, elle est habituellement encerclée dans une jungle artificielle de fils électriques, de panneaux publicitaires agressifs et d'horribles bâtiments. L'œuvre

minum and acrylic mirror plates, he has sought out a lightness that tends toward the ethereal. The Silver Hut is largely closed to its chaotic urban environment, except for the open roof, providing a connection to nature despite the invasive presence of the city. Ito, who was undoubtedly influenced by Kazuo Shinohara, has worked extensively in the small Kyushu city of Yatsushiro in the Prefecture of Kumamoto. He has built three structures there: the Yatsushiro Municipal Museum (1989–91); the Elderly People's Home (1992–94), and a Fire Station (1992–95). In the case of the Elderly People's Home, Ito imagines a link to worlds beyond this residence. As he says, "There are no strong psychological bonds between the residents of the Elderly People's Home. They may live in physical proximity... but each resident will no doubt already have a network of relationships to people outside the facility. These residents are elderly persons with real bodies who live together, but they are also 'nomads' who in their consciousness possess fictional bodies." Like the earlier Municipal Museum, which appears on the top of an artificial hill like a ship from another planet, its sails set to catch the galactic winds, the Elderly People's Home somehow calls out, with its large openings, to the beyond. And yet Ito's vocabulary often recalls that of a famous predecessor. As he admits, "I always find myself back at Le Corbusier. I never consciously go back to him. It is only when I am already there, and people who see my models and drawings point it out, that I realize what I have done."

Like Toyo Ito, Itsuko Hasegawa, who was born in Shizuoka Prefecture in 1941, worked with the architect Kiyonori Kikutake (1964–69) and, like him, was influenced directly by Kazuo Shinohara, with whom she worked for several years at the Tokyo Institute of Technology after 1969. She created her own office, Itsuko Hasegawa Atelier, in 1979. Even more than Ito, Itsuko Hasegawa has set out to create a kind of alternative reality or rather an artificial form of nature in her larger projects such as the Shonandai Cultural Center (Fujisawa, Kanagawa, 1987–90), which is a reduced model of the universe. Her almost nostalgic quest for a new nature where aluminum trees grow might well be related to the dramatic overcrowding of Japan's eastern coastal areas.

Yatsushiro, die auf der Insel Kyushu in der Präfektur Kumamoto liegt. Dort entstanden drei seiner Projekte: das Yatsushiro Municipal Museum (1989–91), ein Altenheim (1992–94) und eine Feuerwache (1992–95). Im Falle des Altenheims wollte Ito eine Verbindung zu Welten außerhalb dieser Wohnanlage schaffen. Er sagt dazu: »Zwischen den Bewohnern des Altenheims existieren keine starken psychologischen Bande. Sie leben zwar in unmittelbarer physischer Nachbarschaft... aber jeder Bewohner besitzt bereits ein Netz von Beziehungen zu Personen außerhalb des Heims. Diese Bewohner sind ältere Menschen mit realen Körpern, die zusammen leben; aber gleichzeitig sind sie auch ›Nomaden‹, die in ihrem Bewußtsein über einen fiktionalen Körper verfügen.« Wie Itos Municipal Museum, das auf der Spitze eines künstlich angelegten Hügels wie ein Schiff von einem anderen Planeten wirkt, welches mit gesetzten Segeln auf die galaktischen Winde wartet, scheint das Altenheim mit seinen großen Öffnungen Signale an eine andere Welt auszusenden. Dennoch erinnert Itos Formensprache häufig an die eines berühmten Vorgängers: »Ich finde mich immer bei Le Corbusier wieder. Dabei gehe ich nie bewußt zu ihm zurück. Erst wenn ich schon am Ziel bin und jemand, der meine Modelle und Zeichnungen sieht, mich darauf hinweist, entdecke ich, was ich getan habe.«

Wie Toyo Ito arbeitete auch Itsuko Hasegawa, die 1941 in der Präfektur Shizuoka zur Welt kam, für den Architekten Kiyonori Kikutake (1964–69), und ebenso wie er wurde auch sie unmittelbar von Kazuo Shinohara beeinflußt, mit dem sie nach 1969 mehrere Jahre am Tokyo Institute of Technology zusammenarbeitete. 1979 gründete sie ihr eigenes Büro, Itsuko Hasegawa Atelier. In ihren größeren Projekten wie dem Shonandai Cultural Center (Fujisawa, Kanagawa, 1987–90), das ein Modell des Universums darstellen soll, versucht Hasegawa, eine Art alternativer Realität beziehungsweise eine künstliche Natur zu schaffen. Ihre beinahe nostalgische Suche nach einer neuen Natur, in der Bäume aus Aluminium wachsen, ist in der dramatischen Überbevölkerung der Städte an der japanischen Ostküste begründet. Wenn man in japanischen Städten ein Stück Natur findet, ist es zumeist umgeben von einem künstlichen Dschungel aus Ober-

de cette architecte témoigne d'une vision d'harmonie mais éga-lement de légèreté, qui l'amène à une utilisation intensive de l'aluminium et de l'acier inoxydable. Une des premières femmes architectes à affirmer sa présence créative au Japon, elle joue sans aucun doute un rôle de modèle auprès de ses consœurs plus jeunes. Même si elle a obtenu la deuxième place au concours de l'Opéra de Cardiff, remporté par Zaha Hadid, elle ne parle presque pas l'anglais, une des raisons qui freine la notoriété de nombreux architectes japonais de talent hors de leur pays.

Ce n'est pas le cas de Shoei Yoh, né en 1940 à Kumamoto City. Yoh a étudié les beaux-arts et les arts appliqués à la Wittenberg University, Springfield, Ohio, avant de créer son agence, Shoei Yoh + Architects à Fujuoka en 1970, intervenant simultanément dans les domaines de l'architecture et du design industriel. La Maison de verre de Yoh, reproduite ici, se dresse sur une falaise de 140 m au dessus du niveau de la mer, près de Fukuoka, et jouit d'une vue à 270° sur la mer du Japon, vers le détroit de Corée. Comme le précise Shoei Yoh, il tenait à ce que la «Maison de verre ne soit pas une maison ordinaire, mais un navire flot-tant entre l'eau et les cieux.» Initialement conçue en hommage à la Farnsworth House de Mies van der Rohe (1950), cette Maison de verre a cependant pris une autre dimension: «Bien que j'aie employé des matériaux modernistes, elle revêt cependant pour moi un sens très japonais; j'ai commencé par suivre les pré-ceptes du modernisme pour finir par retrouver en eux mes racines japonaises.» En cela, comme dans sa quête d'une légèreté qui semble défier les lois de l'architecture, Yoh fait la démonstration des qualités concrètes du design japonais con-temporain. Dans cette modernité qui n'est pas fondamentale-ment opposée à la tradition, se dessine une ambition que les architectes occidentaux auraient intérêt à mieux comprendre. Il s'agit d'une recherche d'idéaux qui paraissent désormais absents de beaucoup des réalisations architecturales améri-caines ou européennes.

Considéré aujourd'hui comme l'un des grands maîtres de l'architecture en béton, Tadao Ando est né à Osaka en 1941. Ses

Pages 48/49: Itsuko Hasegawa, Shonandai Cultural Center, Fujisawa, Kanagawa, Japan, 1987–90. A reduced model of the universe or an attempt to create an "artificial nature" by a leading female architect.

Pages 48/49: Itsuko Hasegawa, Shonandai Cultural Center, Fujisawa, Kanagawa, Japan, 1987–90. Ein verkleinertes Modell des Universums oder der Versuch einer führenden Architektin, eine »künstliche Natur« zu schaffen.

Pages 48/49: Itsuko Hasegawa, centre culturel Sho-nandai, Fujisawa, Kanagawa, Japon, 1987–90. Une représentation de l'univers à échelle réduite, dans une tentative de créer une nature artificielle, signée de l'une des femmes architectes japonaises des plus éminentes.

Where nature is present in Japanese cities, it is usually circumscribed by an artificial jungle of electrical wires, garish signs and ugly buildings. In her work, there is a vision of harmony but also of lightness, as evidenced in her extensive use of aluminum or stainless steel. As one of the first woman architects to affirm a creative presence on the Japanese architectural scene, Hasegawa undoubtedly has an importance as an example to her younger female colleagues. Despite being the runner-up in the recent competition for a new opera house in Cardiff, which was won by Zaha Hadid, Itsuko Hasegawa speaks very little English. In this she is like many talented Japanese architects, who may never become well known outside of their country for this reason.

This is not the case of Shoei Yoh, born in 1940 in Kumamoto City. Yoh studied Fine and Applied Arts at Wittenberg University in Springfield, Ohio, before creating his own firm, Shoei Yoh + Architects in Fukuoka in 1970, specializing not only in architecture but also in industrial design. Yoh's Glass House, published in this volume, is set on a cliff 140 meters above sea level near Fukuoka, and has a 270° panoramic view of the Japan Sea towards the Korean Channel. As Shoei Yoh says, he was determined that "This Glass House between Sea and Sky wouldn't be an ordinary house to dwell in but a sailing boat floating between sea and sky." Initially intended as an homage to Mies van der Rohe's 1950 Farnsworth House, Yoh's Glass House somehow took on another dimension. As he says, "Though I employed modernist materials, the house possesses a very Japanese feel for me; I started out with the precepts of modernism and ended up finding my Japanese roots in them." In this, as in his quest to create a lightness beyond the real possibilities of architecture, Shoei Yoh demonstrates some of the true qualities of contemporary Japanese design. In this modernity, which is not fundamentally at odds with tradition, there is an ambition that Western architects might do well to better understand. That ambition is a search for ideals, which no longer seems to inhabit much American or European architecture.

Known today as a great master of concrete architecture, Tadao

leitungen, schreiend bunten Schildern und häßlichen Gebäuden. Hasegawas Arbeiten streben eine Vision der Harmonie, aber auch der Leichtigkeit an, wofür die ausgiebige Verwendung von Aluminium oder Edelstahl spricht. Als eine der ersten Architektinnen, die einen kreativen Einfluß auf die japanische Architekturszene ausüben, besitzt Hasegawa unzweifelhaft große Bedeutung als Beispiel für ihre jüngeren Kolleginnen. Allerdings spricht sie, trotz eines zweiten Platzes bei einem kürzlich abgehaltenen Architekturwettbewerb für ein neues Opernhaus in Cardiff, kaum Englisch. Darin ähnelt sie vielen anderen japanischen Architekten, die aus diesem Grund kaum außerhalb ihres Landes bekannt werden.

Dies gilt nicht für den 1940 in Kumamoto City geborenen Shoei Yoh. Yoh studierte Freie und Angewandte Kunst an der Wittenberg University in Springfield, Ohio, und gründete 1970 in Fukuoka seine eigene Firma, Shoei Yoh + Architects, die sich nicht nur mit Architektur, sondern auch mit Industriedesign beschäftigt. Sein Glass House steht in der Nähe von Fukuoka auf einer Klippe, die sich 140 Meter über dem Meeresspiegel erhebt. Es bietet einen 270°-Panoramablick über das Japanische Meer auf die Straße von Korea. Shoei Yoh war nach eigenen Worten fest davon überzeugt, daß »das Glass House kein gewöhnliches Haus werden würde, in dem man wohnt, sondern ein Segelboot, das zwischen Meer und Himmel treibt«. Ursprünglich als Hommage an Mies van der Rohes 1950 entstandenes Farnsworth House geplant, besitzt Yohs Glass House eine zusätzliche Dimension. Yoh sagt dazu: »Obwohl ich die Materialien der Moderne verwandte, besitzt das Haus in meinen Augen eine sehr japanische Ausstrahlung. Ich begann mit den Regeln der Moderne und fand am Ende meine japanischen Wurzeln in ihnen.« In dieser Hinsicht ebenso wie in seiner Suche nach einer Leichtigkeit, die über die realen Möglichkeiten der Architektur hinausgeht, demonstriert Shoei Yoh einige der besten Eigenschaften des zeitgenössischen japanischen Designs. In dieser Modernität, die nicht grundsätzlich im Widerstreit mit der Tradition steht, liegt ein Ehrgeiz, den westliche Architekten verstehen lernen sollten. Ein solcher Ehrgeiz – eigentlich eine Suche nach

premières années et sa formation restent enveloppées d'un certain mystère, mais il précise de lui-même qu'il est «autodidacte en architecture.» On sait qu'il a beaucoup voyagé aux Etats-Unis, en Europe et en Afrique, avant de fonder Tadao Ando Architect & Associates à Osaka en 1969. Lauréat du Prix Pritzker 1995, il ne parle pas anglais, mais il est aidé par son épouse, Yumiko, qui joue le rôle d'interprète. Ce qui semble clair dans beaucoup de ses projets c'est une quête de quelque chose qui va au delà d'une simple maîtrise de l'espace. Comme il l'explique dans son discours de réception du Prix Pritzker: «Je crois que deux dimensions bien distinctes existent en architecture. L'une est substantielle et concerne la fonction, la sécurité et l'économie, et dans la mesure où l'architecture est faite pour faciliter l'existence de l'homme, elle ne peut ignorer ces éléments de la réalité. Cependant, l'architecture peut-elle s'en contenter? Puisqu'elle est une forme d'expression humaine, quand elle s'élève au dessus des simples exigences de la construction pour ambitionner des ambitions esthétiques, la question de l'architecture en tant qu'art est posée... Je suis à la recherche d'une spatialité qui stimule l'esprit humain, éveille la sensibilité, et communique avec le plus profond de l'âme.»

La région de Mikata, dans la préfecture de Hyogo, n'est pas facile d'accès. A trois heures de voiture d'Osaka, dans une région montagneuse et boisée où se trouve une station de ski, elle est restée étonnement sauvage. Ici, l'on trouve ce type de paysage naturel et spectaculaire que les visiteurs étrangers espèrent trouver au Japon, avant d'être confrontés aux métropoles interminables de la zone côtière. En fait, parce qu'il est montagneux, l'intérieur du Japon est superbe et généralement peu fréquenté par les visiteurs étrangers. La forme ronde du Musée du bois (1993–94) de Tadao Ando qui s'élève au milieu de grands arbres, s'aperçoit de loin. Dessiné comme un anneau avec un diamètre extérieur de 46 m et comprenant espace intérieur de 22 m de diamètre, cette construction est totalement originale. Un chemin surélevé permet aux visiteurs de pénétrer jusqu'au centre, et 200 m plus loin d'accéder à un belvédère sur la face opposée. S'ils décident d'entrer, ils se trouvent confrontés à un

Shoei Yoh, Glass House, Itoshima, Fukuoka, Japan, 1984–91. A side view of this house on a hill near the city of Fukuoka, showing one of the 12 x 6 meter vertical concrete slabs used to suspend the horizontal volumes.

Shoei Yoh, Glass House, Itoshima, Fukuoka, Japan, 1984–91. Die Seitenansicht dieses Hauses auf einem Hügel in der Nähe der Stadt Fukuoka zeigt eine der 12 x 6 Meter großen, vertikalen Betonplatten, die zur Aufhängung des Baukörpers dienen.

Shoei Yoh, Maison de verre, Itoshima, Fukuoka, Japon, 1984–91. Vue latérale de cette maison située sur une colline près de la ville de Fukuoka, montrant l'une des dalles de béton verticales de 12 x 6 m, auxquelles sont arrimés les plans horizontaux.

Ando was born in Osaka in 1941. His early years and education remain shrouded in a certain mystery, but he indicates that he was "self-educated in architecture." In any case, he traveled extensively in the United States, Europe and Africa before founding Tadao Ando Architect & Associates in Osaka in 1969. Winner of the 1995 Pritzker Prize, Ando does not speak English, but he is seconded by his wife Yumiko, who acts as his interpreter. What seems clear in much of Ando's architecture is that he has sought out something more than a mastery of space in his buildings. As he said in his acceptance speech for the Pritzker Prize, "I believe that there are two separate dimensions coexisting in architecture. One is substantive, and concerns function, security and economy; inasmuch as architecture accommodates human living, it cannot ignore these elements of the real. However, can architecture be architecture with this alone? Since architecture is a form of human expression, when it steps out of the exigencies of sheer construction toward the realm of aesthetics, the question of architecture as art arises... What I have sought to achieve is a spatiality that stimulates the human spirit, awakens the sensitivity and communicates with the deeper soul."

The area of Mikata in the Prefecture of Hyogo is not an easy place to reach. Located three hours by car from Osaka in a mountainous wooded zone near a ski resort, it is surprisingly unspoiled. Here one finds the kind of spectacular natural scenery that foreigners often expect of Japan before they are confronted with the endless urban metropolises of the coastal areas. Indeed, because of the mountainous terrain, much of the interior of Japan is very attractive, and generally little visited by outsiders. Standing among the tall trees, the visitor sees the round form of Tadao Ando's Museum of Wood (1993–94) from a certain distance. Shaped like a ring with an outer diameter of 46 meters and an inner void of 22 meters, this structure is like no other. An elevated pathway permits visitors to walk right through the center and 200 meters further on to an elevated viewing platform on the opposite side if they wish. Should they choose to enter, they find an astonishing spiral exhibition space, with wooden columns reaching up as much as 18 meters.

Idealen – ist in vielen Beispielen zeitgenössischer amerikanischer und europäischer Architektur nicht mehr wahrzunehmen.

Der 1941 in Osaka geborene Tadao Ando gilt heute als einer der großen Baumeister der Betonarchitektur. Seine frühen Jahre und seine Ausbildung liegen in einem geheimnisvollen Dunkel, aber Ando behauptet von sich, daß er ein »autodidaktischer Architekt« sei. Auf jeden Fall unternahm er ausgedehnte Reisen durch die USA, Europa und Afrika, bevor er 1969 in Osaka Tadao Ando Architect & Associates gründete. Ando, der Gewinner des Pritzker Preises 1995, spricht kein Englisch, aber seine Frau Yumiko fungiert als Dolmetscherin. Aus Andos Architektur geht deutlich hervor, daß er andere Ziele anstrebt als nur eine meisterhafte Beherrschung des Raumes. So sagte er in seiner Dankesrede für den Pritzker Preis: »Ich bin der Ansicht, daß in der Architektur getrennt voneinander zwei Dimensionen existieren. Eine dieser Dimensionen ist real; sie umfaßt Funktion, Sicherheit und Wirtschaftlichkeit. Da Architektur menschliches Leben beherbergt, darf sie diese Elemente der Realität nicht ignorieren. Aber kann eine nur aus diesen Elementen bestehende Architektur wirklich Architektur sein? Architektur ist eine Form menschlichen Ausdrucks, und wenn sie sich aus der Notwendigkeit der reinen Konstruktion in das Ästhetische erhebt, stellt sich die Frage nach der Architektur als Kunstform... Ich habe versucht, Räume zu schaffen, die den menschlichen Geist inspirieren, die Sinne erwecken und mit der Seele kommunizieren.«

Das Gebiet um Mikata in der Präfektur Hyogo ist nicht einfach zu erreichen. Dieser Ort, der drei Autostunden von Osaka entfernt in einem bergigen Waldgebiet liegt, wirkt überraschend ursprünglich. Hier bietet sich dem Auge jene Art eindrucksvoller Naturlandschaft, die ausländische Besucher eigentlich von Japan erwarten, bevor sie mit den endlosen urbanen Metropolen der Küstenregion konfrontiert werden. Aufgrund der bergigen Landschaft wirkt ein großer Teil des japanischen Binnenlands zwar sehr anziehend, aber für Fremde auch sehr unzugänglich. Zwischen hohen Bäumen entdeckt der Besucher die runde Form von Tadao Andos Museum of Wood (1993–94). Geformt wie ein Ring mit einem Außendurchmesser von 46 Metern und einem

étonnant espace d'exposition en spirale à colonnes de bois qui peuvent atteindre 18 m de haut. Bien que la qualité des expositions sur l'utilisation du bois ne soit pas au niveau de celle de l'architecture, on sent que ce lieu est plus un temple dédié aux dieux de la forêt qu'un simple musée. Une indéniable présence mythique émane de cette architecture qui, dans sa conception dérive du pavillon conçu par Ando pour l'Expo '92 à Séville. Les formes sont d'une géométrie fondamentalement simple. Comme certains maîtres de la renaissance italienne, Ando prouve une fois encore que de l'union des proportions et des matériaux peut émaner un sens de la spiritualité, que ressentiront les visiteurs sensibles aux qualités profondes de son architecture. On a ici la preuve que l'architecture moderne peut parfois être autre chose qu'un objet fonctionnel, d'inspiration commerciale, et fondamentalement superficiel.

Basé à Osaka, conurbation de 2 600 000 habitants et grand centre de commerce si ce n'est de culture, Tadao Ando s'est acquis une notoriété internationale qui lui a permis de remporter non seulement le Prix Pritzker mais aussi le Prix Carlsberg (1992), encore plus prestigieux. Toutefois à part son pavillon du Japon pour Séville et un petit centre de conférences pour le fabricant de meubles Vitra (Weil am Rhein, Allemagne, 1993) presque toute son œuvre construite se trouve au Japon. Comme d'autres architectes japonais contemporains, il a très certainement été influencé par Le Corbusier. Mais il a évolué vers un vocabulaire formel assez simple qui fait généralement appel au béton. Il est d'autant plus difficile de bien appréhender son œuvre sans la voir, que les photographies ne rendent généralement pas justice à son raffinement du traitement du béton. Dans presque chacune de ses réalisations se trouve une composante de découverte et de procession, qui requiert le mouvement, et n'est donc guère traduisible en photographie. Comme dans certains temples japonais, l'entrée n'est pas toujours située là où l'on pourrait s'y attendre. Ando demande souvent au visiteur de suivre un chemin inattendu pour pénétrer dans le bâtiment, allant parfois jusqu'à fermer par un mur de béton aveugle l'entrée que l'on attendait, comme dans son Temple Hompuku-ji sur l'île d'Awaji.

Tadao Ando, Museum of Wood, Mikata-gun, Hyogo, Japan, 1993–94. In the mountain wilderness, a temple of wood related in its concept to Ando's Japanese Pavilion for Expo '92 in Seville.

Tadao Ando, Museum of Wood, Mikata-gun, Hyogo, Japan, 1993–94. Ein Tempel aus Holz in der Wildnis der Berge, dessen Konzept an Andos Japanischen Pavillon für die Expo '92 in Sevilla erinnert.

Tadao Ando, Musée du bois, Mikata-gun, Hyogo, Japon, 1993–94. Au milieu de montagnes sauvages, ce temple du bois est proche, dans son concept, du pavillon japonais édifié par Ando à l'Expo '92 de Séville.

Although the quality of the exhibitions on the use of wood is not up to the level of the architecture, one feels that this place is more a temple dedicated in and of itself to the gods of the forest than it is really a museum. There is an undeniable mystical presence in this architecture, which is derived in its conception from Ando's earlier Expo '92 Pavilion in Seville, and yet the forms themselves are fundamentally simple in their geometry. Like some masters of the Italian Renaissance, Ando has found once again that proportions and materials can be brought together in a way that will bring forth a sense of spirituality in those visitors who are sensitive to the profound quality of his architecture, without imposing such thoughts on others. There is real proof here that modern architecture can be something other than functional, commercially inspired and fundamentally superficial.

Based in Osaka, an urban sprawl with 2,600,000 residents which has a reputation as a city of commerce but little culture, Tadao Ando has reached out across the world to win not only the Pritzker Prize but also the even more prestigious 1992 Carlsberg Prize; this despite the fact that other than the Japanese Expo '92 Pavilion in Seville and a small study center for the furniture manufacturer Vitra (Weil am Rhein, Germany, 1993), almost all of his work has been located in Japan. Like other contemporary Japanese architects, he was undoubtedly influenced by Le Corbusier, but he has evolved toward a relatively simple vocabulary of forms, usually fashioned from concrete. It is all the more difficult to properly comprehend Ando's work without physically seeing it, because photographs generally do not do justice to the refinement of the concrete that he obtains. There is also an element of procession and discovery in almost every one of his buildings. Since this aspect of his work requires movement through space, it too cannot be well photographed. As in some Japanese temples, the entrance is not always located where one might count on finding it. Ando often requires the visitor to take an unexpected path to enter his buildings, bringing them sometimes, as in his Hompuku-ji Temple on the island of Awaji, onto a blank concrete wall in the place of the expected entry. But this is not a sign of aggressiveness on the

Innenraum von 22 Metern, ist dieses Bauwerk einzig in seiner Art. Ein erhöhter Weg führt die Besucher mitten durch die Konstruktion hindurch und bringt sie zu einer 200 Meter entfernt liegenden Aussichtsplattform. Wer das eigentliche Museum betritt, trifft auf einen erstaunlichen, spiralförmigen Ausstellungsraum mit bis zu 18 Meter hohen hölzernen Säulen. Obwohl die Qualität der ausgestellten Objekte zum Thema Holz nicht der umgebenden Architektur entspricht, hat der Besucher das Gefühl, sich eher in einem den Göttern des Waldes geweihten Tempel zu befinden als in einem Museum. Von diesem Bauwerk, dessen Konzeption auf Andos japanischem Pavillon für die Expo '92 in Sevilla beruht, geht eine unbestreitbar mystische Präsenz aus, und dennoch besteht es aus Formen, die in ihrer Geometrie grundlegend einfach sind. Wie einige Meister der italienischen Renaissance hat auch Ando einen Weg gefunden, Proportionen und Materialien so miteinander zu verbinden, daß die für die außergewöhnliche Qualität seiner Architektur empfänglichen Besucher ein Gefühl des Spirituellen empfinden, ohne daß anderen ein solcher Eindruck aufgedrängt würde. Dieses Bauwerk ist der Beweis dafür, daß moderne Architektur mehr als nur funktional, kommerziell und oberflächlich sein kann.

Von Osaka aus, einer sich unkontrolliert ausbreitenden Metropole mit 2,6 Millionen Einwohnern, die den Ruf einer Stadt mit viel Kommerz, aber wenig Kultur besitzt, ist es Tadao Ando gelungen, weltweit Beachtung zu finden und nicht nur den Pritzker Preis, sondern auch den noch renommierteren Carlsberg Preis von 1992 zu gewinnen – und dies trotz der Tatsache, daß er außer seinem japanischen Pavillon für die Expo '92 in Sevilla und einem kleinen Konferenzpavillon für den Möbelhersteller Vitra (Weil am Rhein, 1993) nie außerhalb Japans gebaut hat. Wie viele andere zeitgenössische Architekten wurde auch Ando von Le Corbusier beeinflußt, aber er entwickelte mit der Zeit eine relativ simple Formensprache, die er zumeist in Beton umsetzte. Es ist fast unmöglich, Andos Arbeiten wirklich würdigen zu können, ohne sie tatsächlich vor sich zu sehen. Fotografien sind nur teilweise in der Lage, den Grad der Vervollkommnung wiederzugeben, den er in seinen Betonbauten erreicht. Darüber

Mais ceci n'est pas un signe d'agressivité de sa part. Il s'agit plutôt de ce que l'on appelle une «mise en condition», une préparation à une expérience rare. A Hompuku-ji, le mur de béton incurvé guide le visiteur jusqu'à ce qu'il découvre un bassin de nénuphars ovale, qu'il pénètre littéralement par un escalier descendant qui le conduit à la grande salle: contre toute attente, le temple se trouve donc sous l'eau. Une grille serrée d'écrans de bois rouge remplace ici le gris scintillant, habituel du béton d'Ando, et la lumière pénètre dans la salle par derrière la statue de Bouddha. Plus qu'avec certains autres architectes, il est donc nécessaire «d'expérimenter» les constructions de Tadao Ando pour comprendre qu'il est réellement l'un des grands maîtres de l'architecture contemporaine, du Japon et d'ailleurs.

La génération d'après-guerre
A la différence des artistes, qui peuvent connaître la notoriété dès leur jeunesse, les architectes doivent généralement attendre la cinquantaine avant de pouvoir présenter une œuvre substantielle. La génération des architectes japonais nés après la seconde guerre mondiale commence ainsi seulement à s'affirmer. Shin Takamatsu est né dans la préfecture de Shimane en 1948. Il crée sa propre agence à Kyoto en 1980. Un certain nombre de réalisations spectaculaires, qui font appel à un vocabulaire à la fois mécaniste et anthropomorphique, attirent l'attention sur lui dès les années 80. Pour simplifier, ses bâtiments font penser à des robots ou des machines. Ce style inhabituel lui permet aussi de créer des immeubles exceptionnels comme sa tour Kirin Plaza Osaka (1985–87, Chuo-ku, Osaka). Située au croisement des rues piétonnières les plus fréquentées d'Osaka, cette construction lumineuse s'élève comme un havre de sérénité. Il est intéressant de noter que le style de Takamatsu a connu une évolution assez substantielle depuis la fin de la «l'économie de bulle». Ses œuvres récentes comme le siège social de Kirin (Chuo-ku, Tokyo, 1993–95) ou le musée de la photographie Shoji Ueda (Kishimoto-cho, Tottori, 1993–95) tendent vers un modernisme strict qui rejette les complexités mécanistes de ses réalisations précédentes. Takamatsu s'étant fait un nom comme

part of the architect. Rather it is what the French would call a "mise en condition," a preparation for an unusual experience. In Hompuku-ji, the curving concrete wall leads the visitor on until he discovers an oval water lily basin, with a stairway bisecting it leading down. Against all expectations, the temple itself is below the basin. A dense grid of red wooden screens replaces the shimmering gray of Ando's concrete here, and light enters from behind the seated statue of Buddha. More than for some other architects, it is necessary to experience the buildings of Tadao Ando to understand that he is truly one of the great masters of contemporary architecture, either in Japan for elsewhere.

The post-war generation

Unlike artists, who may become well known while they are still quite young, architects are usually fifty before they can claim to have a substantial body of built work. The generation of Japanese architects born after the end of World War II, is thus just beginning to affirm itself. One figure of this group, Shin Takamatsu, was born in Shimane Prefecture in 1948. He created his own office in Kyoto in 1980. Takamatsu became very well known in the 1980s thanks to a number of spectacular buildings that called on a mechanical vocabulary, which tended to an anthropomorphic expression. Simply put, his buildings looked like robots or machines. On occasion, Takamatsu's unusual style permitted him to create exceptional buildings, such as his 1985–87 Kirin Plaza Osaka (Chuo-ku, Osaka). Located on one of the busiest pedestrian corners in the commercial district of Osaka, this luminous tower stands out like a beacon of calm. It is very interesting to note that there has been a rather substantial shift in the style of Shin Takamatsu since the end of the "Bubble economy." His recent work, like the Kirin Headquarters (Chuo-ku, Tokyo, 1993–95) or the Shoji Ueda Museum of Photography (Kishimoto-cho, Tottori, 1993–95), tends toward a strict neo-modernism that rejects the mechanistic complexities of his earlier work. To the extent that Takamatsu made a name for himself as a "fashionable" architect, this change of course is a sure sign that neo-modernism is the trend of the moment.

hinaus besitzt fast jedes seiner Gebäude ein Element des Entdeckens. Da dieser Aspekt seiner Bauten eine Bewegung durch den Raum erfordert, läßt sich auch dieses Moment nur sehr schwer fotografisch festhalten. Ando verlangt von seinen Besuchern häufig, seine Bauten auf einem unerwarteten Weg zu betreten, der sie manchmal, wie im Falle des Hompuku-ji-Tempels auf der Insel Awaji, statt zum erwarteten Eingang vor eine kahle Betonwand führt. Aber dies ist kein Zeichen von Aggression, sondern eher eine Vorbereitung auf ein ungewöhnliches Erlebnis. Im Falle des Hompuku-ji-Tempels leitet die gekrümmte Betonwand den Besucher weiter, bis er ein ovales Seerosenbecken entdeckt, das von einer nach unten führenden Treppe in zwei Hälften geteilt wird. Der eigentliche Tempel liegt – völlig unerwartet – unter dem Bassin. Hier ersetzt ein dichtes Gitter aus roten, hölzernen Wandschirmen das schimmernde Grau des Betons, während hinter einer sitzenden Buddha-Statue Licht in den Raum dringt. Im Grunde muß man Tadao Andos Bauwerke persönlich erleben, um verstehen zu können, warum er weltweit als einer der großen Meister der zeitgenössischen Architektur gelten kann.

Die Nachkriegsgeneration

Im Gegensatz zu bildenden Künstlern, die bereits in jungen Jahren einen hohen Bekanntheitsgrad erreichen können, müssen Architekten im allgemeinen etwa 50 Jahre alt werden, bevor sie auf ein umfangreiches Œuvre verweisen können. Die nach dem Zweiten Weltkrieg geborene Generation japanischer Architekten steht daher gerade erst am Anfang größerer Bekanntheit. Ein Mitglied dieser Generation ist der 1948 in der Präfektur Shimane geborene Shin Takamatsu, der 1980 sein eigenes Büro in Kioto eröffnete. Takamatsu erlangte in den 80er Jahren durch eine Reihe aufsehenerregender Bauten Berühmtheit, deren mechanische Formensprache ihnen einen anthropomorphen Ausdruck verlieh. Mit anderen Worten: Seine Gebäude wirkten wie Roboter oder Maschinen. In einigen Fällen schuf Takamatsu mit seinem ungewöhnlichen Stil außergewöhnliche Bauten; dies gilt z.B. für seinen Kirin Plaza Osaka (Chuo-ku, Osaka, 1985–87). Dieses

architecte «à la mode», cela montre bien que ce néo-modernisme là est la tendance du moment.

Le profil personnel et professionnel de Masakazu Bokura est très différent de celui de ses confrères présentés dans cet ouvrage, et non seulement parce qu'il vit en France depuis 20 ans. Né à Tokyo en 1949, il est diplômé d'architecture et d'urbanisme de l'Université Waseda en 1976, et architecte D.P.L.G. de l'Ecole des Beaux-Arts (U.P. 6) de Paris, en 1979. Il est très inhabituel pour un architecte japonais de s'établir de façon permanente hors de son pays, mais Bokura est resté en contact avec Tokyo, travaillant à l'occasion avec Arata Isozaki, et actuellement sur un grand projet d'immeubles de logements à Kobe. Sa plus importante réalisation à ce jour est le Pôle agro-alimentaire de Saint-Lô, en Normandie, exercice fascinant d'innovation architecturale avec un budget très limité. Très observateur, très informé sur les tendances de l'art et de l'architecture d'aujourd'hui, Bokura a réussi à utiliser des matériaux apparemment banals d'une manière à la fois séduisante et pratique. Il admet que l'un des bâtiments de Saint-Lô rappelle la forme du bombardier B-29 qui fit tant de ravages au Japon pendant la seconde guerre mondiale. La puissance de références culturelles de ce type, les allusions à la tradition japonaise et la pensée architecturale contemporaine nourrissent son œuvre. Encore peu connu aujourd'hui, il est peut-être l'un des premiers architectes à apporter à l'Europe le sentiment de l'importance de l'architecture de son pays.

Kazuyo Sejima, née dans la préfecture d'Ibaraki en 1956, a travaillé dans l'agence de Toyo Ito de 1981 à 1987. Elle a fondé Kazuyo Sejima et Associés à Tokyo en 1987. Son dortoir pour femmes Saishunkan Seiyaku à Kumamoto (1990–1991) figurait sur la couverture du catalogue de l'exposition «Light Architecture» en 1995, organisée par Terry Riley au Museum of Modern Art de New York. Il n'en fallait pas plus pour attirer l'attention internationale sur une œuvre encore relativement limitée, qui comprend par ailleurs trois curieux clubs de *pachinko*. Installée à Tokyo dans un petit bureau encombré, elle fournit des réponses assez surprenantes aux questions sur le rôle de la femme dans l'architecture, et sa situation au Japon. En un sens, ses réactions

Shin Takamatsu, Kirin Plaza Osaka, Chuo-ku, Osaka, Japan, 1985–87. A beacon of calm in the midst of one of the most agitated pedestrian areas of central Osaka.

Shin Takamatsu, Kirin Plaza Osaka, Chuo-ku, Osaka, Japan, 1985–87. Ein Leuchtfeuer der Ruhe inmitten einer der belebtesten Fußgängerzonen Osakas.

Shin Takamatsu, Kirin Plaza Osaka, Chuo-ku, Osaka, Japon, 1985–87. Un havre de calme au cœur de l'une des zones piétonnières les plus animées du centre d'Osaka.

Masakazu Bokura, Saint-Lô Agricultural Study Center, Saint-Lô, France, 1993–94. A futuristic design built with a low budget for an industry that does not often show concern with its architectural image.

Masakazu Bokura, Saint-Lô Studienzentrum für Agrarwirtschaft, Saint-Lô, Frankreich, 1993–94. Ein mit einem niedrigen Budget verwirklichtes, futuristisches Design für eine Wirtschaftsbranche, die nur selten Interesse für ihr architektonisches Image zeigt.

Masakazu Bokura, Pôle agro-alimentaire de Saint-Lô, Saint-Lô, France, 1993–94. Projet futuriste édifié dans le cadre d'un budget limité, pour une industrie qui ne se préoccupe habituellement pas de son image architecturale.

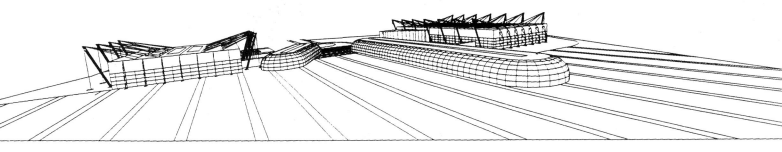

The personal and professional profile of Masakazu Bokura is very different from that of the other architects presented in this book, if only because he has been living in France for the past twenty years. Born in Tokyo in 1949, he received a degree in Architecture and Urbanism from Waseda University in 1976, and then a second degree in Paris (D.P.L.G.) from the Ecole des Beaux-Arts (U.P.6) in 1979. It is indeed unusual for Japanese architects to establish themselves permanently outside of their country, but Bokura has kept in close touch with Tokyo, working with Arata Isozaki on occasion, and currently on a large housing project in Kobe. Masakazu Bokura's largest built work to date, the Agricultural Study Center in Saint-Lô in Normandy, is a fascinating exercise in architectural innovation with a very restricted budget. Observant and very much aware of trends in contemporary art and architecture, Bokura has succeeded in using apparently banal materials in an attractive and practical way. He admits that one of the buildings in Saint-Lô brings to mind the shape of the B-29 aircraft that devastated Japan during the War. The power of cultural references of this type, as well as that of allusion to Japanese tradition and current architectural thinking, informs the work of Masakazu Bokura. Little known today, he may be one of the first architects to bring a sense of the importance of contemporary Japanese architecture to Europe.

Kazuyo Sejima, who was born in Ibaraki Prefecture in 1956, worked in the office of Toyo Ito from 1981 to 1987. She established Kazuyo Sejima and Associates in Tokyo in 1987. Her Saishunkan Seiyaku Women's Dormitory in Kumamoto, Kumamoto (1990–91)

Gebäude liegt an einer der belebtesten Fußgängerzonen Osakas und wirkt dort wie ein Leuchtturm der Ruhe. Es ist interessant, daß sich der Stil Shin Takamatsus seit dem Ende der »Seifenblasenökonomie« tiefgreifend verändert hat. Seine aktuellen Arbeiten, wie das Kirin Headquarters (Chuo-ku, Tokio, 1993–95) oder das Shoji Ueda Museum of Photography (Kishimoto-cho, Tottori, 1993–95) tendieren in Richtung einer strengen Neomoderne, die die mechanistische Komplexität seiner früheren Werke ablehnt. Da Takamatsu den Ruf eines »Mode«-Architekten hat, ist dieser Kurswechsel ein sicheres Zeichen dafür, daß die Neomoderne zur Zeit stark im Trend liegt.

Das persönliche und berufliche Profil Masakazu Bokuras unterscheidet sich deutlich von dem der anderen, hier vorgestellten Architekten – und sei es auch nur, weil er die letzten 20 Jahre in Frankreich verbracht hat.

Der 1949 in Tokio geborene Bokura schloß 1976 sein Studium der Architektur und Stadtplanung an der Waseda University ab, dem er 1979 einen zweiten akademischen Grad (D.P.L.G.) an der Ecole des Beaux-Arts (U.P.6) in Paris folgen ließ. Es ist äußerst ungewöhnlich, daß sich japanische Architekten dauerhaft außerhalb ihres Landes niederlassen. Aber Bokura blieb eng mit Tokio verbunden, wo er gelegentlich mit Arata Isozaki zusammenarbeitete; momentan stellt er ein großes Wohnbauprojekt in Kobe fertig.

Masakazu Bokuras größte, bisher realisierte Arbeit ist das Studienzentrum für Agrarwirtschaft in Saint-Lô in der Normandie – eine faszinierende Übung in architektonischer Innovation im Rahmen eines eng begrenzten Budgets. Immer offen für die neuesten Entwicklungen in der zeitgenössischen Kunst und Architektur, gelang es Bokura, augenscheinlich banale Materialien auf attraktive und praktische Weise zu verwenden. Er räumt ein, daß eines seiner Gebäude in Saint-Lô an die Form der B-29-Bomber erinnert, die Japan während des Zweiten Weltkriegs verwüsteten. Die Kraft derartiger kultureller Bezüge durchdringt die Arbeiten Masakazu Bokuras ebenso wie seine indirekte Bezugnahme auf japanische Traditionen und zeitgenössisches architektonisches Denken. Der heute kaum bekannte Bokura könnte einer der

offrent une conclusion pertinente à ce survol de l'état actuel de l'architecture au Japon.

Philip Jodidio: *Vous participez au projet de reconstruction de logements Gifu Kitagata avec d'autres femmes architectes. Les femmes conçoivent-elles le logement d'une manière différente des hommes?*

Kazuyo Sejima: Pas du tout. On trouve des hommes qui peuvent parfaitement concevoir des logements, et des femmes qui ne savent pas comment s'y prendre. Peut-être une fois le projet achevé, peut-on ressentir certaines qualités dues à une intervention féminine.

Philip Jodidio: *Vos interlocuteurs réagissent-ils différemment aujourd'hui à l'idée d'une femme architecte qu'ils auraient pu le faire il y a quelques années?*

Kazuyo Sejima: Lorsque j'étais étudiante en architecture, nous étions peu nombreuses, ce qui n'est plus le cas aujourd'hui. Après l'université, j'ai travaillé pendant dix ans avec Toyo Ito. Lorsque j'ai commencé à travailler à mon propre compte, les attitudes avaient déjà changé. Aujourd'hui, je pense que ce n'est plus un handicap d'être femme architecte, et je ne rencontre pas d'hostilité particulière. Je ne travaille que sur deux ou trois projets par an. Si je voulais réussir, en tant que «femme d'affaires», j'aurais sans doute quelques difficultés. Mais à mon rythme actuel de travail, je ne rencontre pas de problème. Dans quelques années, lorsque les femmes commenceront à s'attaquer aux grandes commandes publiques, il y aura peut-être plus de résistance. Actuellement, Itsuko Hasegawa est la seule femme architecte au Japon qui reçoivent des commandes importantes.

Philip Jodidio: *Votre attitude a-t-elle évolué avec la récession économique? Utilisez-vous, par exemple, des matériaux différents?*

Kazuyo Sejima: Je me suis mise à mon compte juste avant l'effondrement de la «bulle» immobilière. Je n'ai jamais travaillé pour moi au cours de la période d'euphorie qui a précédé. Aussi, je ne pense pas que les problèmes économiques aient changé quoi que ce soit à ma manière de travailler.

Philip Jodidio: *La conception assistée par ordinateur influence-t-elle votre travail?*

was on the cover of the 1995 "Light Architecture" exhibition, organized by Terry Riley at the Museum of Modern Art in New York. This fact in itself is sufficient to bring international attention to her still relatively limited œuvre, which also includes three unusual *pachinko* parlors. Based in a tiny, crowded office in Tokyo, she gives rather surprising answers to questions about the role of women in architecture, and about the situation in Japan. In a sense, her reactions provide a fitting conclusion to this overview of the current state of Japanese architecture.

Philip Jodidio: *You are participating in the Gifu Kitagata Apartment Reconstruction Project with other female architects. Do women see housing in a different way than men?*

Kazuyo Sejima: Not at all. There are men who can build housing very well and women who have absolutely no idea what to do. Perhaps once everything is built some people will feel that certain qualities have been obtained because the housing was built by women.

Philip Jodidio: *Do the people you deal with react differently now to the idea of a woman architect than they may have in Japan a few years ago?*

Kazuyo Sejima: When I studied architecture, there were very few women, whereas now there are many more women studying architecture. I worked for ten years after my studies with Toyo Ito. When I started working on my own, attitudes had already changed. Today I believe that it is not a handicap to be a female architect, and there is no particular hostility that I encounter. I work on only two or three projects a year. If I wanted to succeed as a "businesswoman" I might have some problems, but at the rhythm at which I am presently working, there is no problem. In a few years, when women begin building larger public commissions, there may be more resistance. For the time being, Itsuko Hasegawa is the only woman architect in Japan building large commissions.

Philip Jodidio: *Has your attitude evolved as a result of Japan's economic recession? Do you use different materials for example?*

Kazuyo Sejima: I began to work on my own just before the real estate "bubble" burst. I never worked on my own in the period of

ersten Architekten sein, der etwas von der Bedeutung der zeitgenössischen japanischen Architektur nach Europa vermittelt.

Kazuyo Sejima wurde 1956 in der Präfektur Ibaraki geboren und arbeitete von 1981–87 im Büro von Toyo Ito. 1987 gründete sie Kazuyo Sejima and Associates in Tokio. Ihr Saishunkan Seiyaku-Wohnheim in Kumamoto (1990–91) zierte das Plakat der Ausstellung »Light Architecture«, die Terry Riley 1995 im New Yorker Museum of Modern Art organisierte. Diese Tatsache allein genügt, ihr immer noch begrenztes Œuvre – das auch drei ungewöhnliche Pachinko-Spielhallen umfaßt – ins Licht internationaler Beachtung zu rücken. In ihrem winzigen, überfüllten Büro in Tokio gibt sie überraschende Antworten auf die Frage nach der Rolle der Frau in der japanischen Architektur. In gewisser Hinsicht bilden ihre Reaktionen einen passenden Abschluß dieses Überblicks über die aktuelle japanische Architektur.

Philip Jodidio: *Sie nehmen zusammen mit anderen Architektinnen am Gifu Kitagata Apartment Reconstruction Project teil. Sehen Frauen den Wohnungsbau anders als Männer?*

Kazuyo Sejima: Überhaupt nicht. Es gibt Männer, die großartige Wohnbauten errichten und Frauen, die absolut keine Ahnung haben, was sie tun sollen. Vielleicht trifft es zu, daß man nach der Fertigstellung feststellen kann, daß die Häuser bestimmte Eigenschaften aufweisen, weil sie von Frauen gebaut wurden.

Philip Jodidio: *Reagieren die Menschen, mit denen Sie zu tun haben, heute anders auf die Vorstellung einer Frau als Architekt, als es noch vor einigen Jahren in Japan der Fall war?*

Kazuyo Sejima: Als ich Architektur studierte, gab es nur wenige Frauen, während heute immer mehr Frauen diesen Studiengang wählen. Nach meinem Studium arbeitete ich zehn Jahre für Toyo Ito. Als ich mit meinem eigenen Büro begann, hatten sich die Verhältnisse bereits geändert. Heute bin ich der Meinung, daß es kein Handicap darstellt, ein weiblicher Architekt zu sein; ich erlebe auch keine feindselige Haltung mir gegenüber. Ich arbeite nur an zwei bis drei Projekten pro Jahr. Wenn ich Erfolg als »Geschäftsfrau« anstreben würde, bekäme ich vielleicht einige Probleme, aber bei meinem momentanen Arbeitsrhythmus stellt sich die Frage nicht. Wenn in einigen Jahren Frauen die ersten

Kazuyo Sejima: Je ne suis pas encore équipée, mais je suis impressionnée par la liberté que cela peut donner aux architectes, et je vais certainement m'y mettre. Certaines formes qui n'auraient pu exister dans le passé peuvent aujourd'hui être créées par des ordinateurs.

Philip Jodidio: *Toyo Ito, avec lequel vous avez travaillé, parle souvent de la nécessité d'une traduction de la nouvelle société «électronique» en forme architecturale. Est-ce également l'une de vos préoccupations? Ito influence-t-il encore votre travail?*

Kazuyo Sejima: Il est certainement exact qu'il devient très difficile d'ignorer l'influence des ordinateurs. Néanmoins, je ne pense pas que l'architecture de Toyo Ito soit réellement une réflexion sur une nouvelle société de l'électronique émergente. C'est maintenant que nous pouvons commencer à concevoir des bâtiments qui répondront dans le futur à cet esprit.

Philip Jodidio: *Dans une direction opposée, êtes-vous influencée par la tradition japonaise, par exemple celle des paravents shoji?*

Kazuyo Sejima: Je ne suis pas spécifiquement attentive à l'architecture traditionnelle. C'est probablement dans mon sang, quelque part, mais je crois que les Occidentaux analysent davantage que nous l'architecture japonaise en ces termes.[12]

Kazuyo Sejima, Saishunkan Seiyaku Dormitory, Kumamoto, Kumamoto, Japan, 1990–91. Large, light communal living spaces for this company-owned dormitory for women.

Kazuyo Sejima, Saishunkan Seiyaku-Wohnheim, Kumamoto, Kumamoto, Japan, 1990–91. Dieses Wohnheim für weibliche Angestellte der Saishunkan Company besitzt große, lichte Gemeinschaftsräume.

Kazuyo Sejima, Foyer Saishunkan Seiyaku, Kumamoto, Kumamoto, Japon, 1990–91. Vastes et lumineux espaces de vie commune dans ce foyer pour femmes, construit pour une entreprise.

A view from the Gepparo Tea Pavilion, Katsura Palace, Kyoto, Japan, early 17th century. No clear boundary between the interior and the exterior, and a simple, geometric design, a tradition that approaches modernity.

Blick aus dem Gepparo Teepavillon im Katsura-Palast, Kioto, Japan, frühes 17. Jahrhundert. Zwischen Innen und Außen besteht keine klare Grenze, und das traditionelle, schlichte, geometrische Design des Pavillons erinnert an die Moderne.

Vue du pavillon de thé Gepparo, Palais de Katsura, Kyoto, Japon, début XVIIe siècle. Aucune frontière précise entre l'intérieur et l'extérieur, dans ce plan simple et géométrique, proche de la modernité.

euphoria that preceded. So I feel that the economic problems that the country may encounter change nothing in my way of working.

Philip Jodidio: *Has computer assisted design had any influence on your work?*

Kazuyo Sejima: I am not yet equipped with computers, but I am impressed with the liberty they can now give architects, and I will try to begin using them. Certain forms can now be created with computers that could not have existed in the past.

Philip Jodidio: *Toyo Ito, with whom you worked, has often spoken of the necessity of translating the new electronic society into an architectural form. Is that also one of your preoccupations? Does Ito still influence your work?*

Kazuyo Sejima: It is certainly true that it is becoming very difficult to ignore the influence of computers. I do not feel, however, that the architecture of Toyo Ito is really a reflection of the new emerging society of electronics. It is now that we can begin to conceive buildings that will in the future be in this spirit.

Philip Jodidio: *In the opposite direction, are you influenced by Japanese tradition, for example that of shoji screens?*

Kazuyo Sejima: I do not specifically look at traditional architecture. It is probably in my blood somewhere, but I believe that it is Westerners who analyze Japanese architecture in these terms more than we do.[12]

größeren Bauaufträge realisieren werden, kann es zu größerem Widerstand kommen. Aber im Augenblick ist Itsuko Hasegawa die einzige Architektin, die in Japan größere Aufträge realisiert.

Philip Jodidio: *Inwieweit hat die wirtschaftliche Rezession in Japan Einfluß auf Ihre Arbeit gehabt? Verwenden Sie heute z.B. andere Baumaterialien?*

Kazuyo Sejima: Ich hatte mich gerade erst selbständig gemacht, als die Immobilien-»Seifenblase« platzte. Während der vorhergehenden Boomjahre habe ich also keinerlei eigene Aufträge bearbeitet. Daher glaube ich, daß die wirtschaftlichen Probleme des Landes nichts an meiner Arbeitsweise geändert haben.

Philip Jodidio: *Hat computergestütztes Design Ihre Arbeiten beeinflußt?*

Kazuyo Sejima: Mein Büro ist noch nicht mit Computern ausgestattet, aber ich bin beeindruckt von der Freiheit, die sie den heutigen Architekten ermöglichen, und ich werde versuchen, mit ihnen zu arbeiten. Mit Hilfe des Computers lassen sich bestimmte Formen erzeugen, die in der Vergangenheit nicht realisierbar waren.

Philip Jodidio: *Toyo Ito, mit dem Sie zusammenarbeiteten, sprach oft von der Notwendigkeit, die neue elektronische Gesellschaft in eine architektonische Form umzusetzen. Beschäftigen Sie sich auch mit diesem Ziel, und ist Ito immer noch ein Einfluß für Sie?*

Kazuyo Sejima: Es ist sicherlich richtig, daß sich der Einfluß des Computers heute nur sehr schwer ignorieren läßt. Dennoch bin ich nicht der Ansicht, daß die Architektur Toyo Itos tatsächlich eine Reflexion der neuen elektronischen Gesellschaft darstellt. Erst jetzt können wir damit beginnen, Bauten zu entwerfen, die diesen Geist in der Zukunft beinhalten werden.

Philip Jodidio: *Einmal andersherum gefragt: Sind Sie von der japanischen Tradition, beispielsweise von den shoji-Wandschirmen beeinflußt worden?*

Kazuyo Sejima: Ich beschäftige mich nicht bewußt mit traditioneller Architektur. Vielleicht liegt sie mir einfach im Blut. Ich glaube jedoch, daß man sich im Westen mehr mit der diesbezüglichen Analyse japanischer Architektur befaßt als in Japan selbst.[12]

Notes | Anmerkungen

1   *Illusion and Remembrance, Installations by Kimio Tsuchiya,*
    Hara Museum of Contemporary Art, Tokyo, 1996.

2   Interview with Arata Isozaki, Tokyo, April 1, 1996.

3   Barber, Lionel: "A Deeper Transformation",
    The Financial Times, April 10, 1996.

4   Doi, Yoshitake: "The Calamities of 1995 Came on the Streetcar
    named Desire", *The Japan Architect,* n°20, Winter 1995.

5   Coaldrake, William: *Order and Anarchy: Tokyo from 1868 to
    the present,* in: Tokyo, Form and Spirit:
    Walker Art Center. Harry N. Abrams, New York, 1986.

6   Wright, Frank Lloyd: *An Autobiography,*
    Duell, Sloan and Pearce, New York, 1943.

7   Isozaki, Arata: *Katsura: a Model for Post-Modern Architecture,*
    in: Katsura Villa – Space and Form. Iwanami Shoten
    Publishers, Tokyo, 1983.

8   Interview with Kenzo Tange, Tokyo, December 1992.

9   Interview with Fumihiko Maki, Tokyo, April 8, 1996.

10 Interview with Arata Isozaki, Tokyo, April 1, 1996.

11 Interview with Hiroshi Hara, Tokyo, April 1, 1996.

12 Interview with Kazuyo Sejima, Tokyo, April 8, 1996.

1 Ando: Naoshima Museum and Hotel, Naoshima, Kagawa
2 Ando: Museum of Wood, Mikata-gun, Hyogo
3 Hara: Umeda Sky City, Kita-ku, Osaka
4 Hara: Kyoto JR Station, Shimogyo, Kyoto
5 Hasegawa: Museum of Fruit, Yamanashi-shi, Yamanashi
6 Isozaki: Nagi MoCA, Nagi-cho, Okayama
7 Isozaki: Concert Hall, Kyoto
8 Isozaki: Nara Convention Hall, Nara
9 Ito: Shimosuwa Lake Suwa Museum, Shimosuwa-machi, Nagano
10 Maki: Kirishima Concert Hall, Aira, Kagoshima
11 Sejima: Saishunkan Seiyaku Dormitory, Kumamoto, Kumamoto
12 Sejima: Pachinko Parlor III, Hitachi, Ibaraki
13 Takamatsu: Kunibiki Messe, Matsue, Shimane
14 Yoh: Glass House, Itoshima, Fukuoka

CHINA

RUSSIA

SEA OF
OKHOTSK

HOKKAIDO

• Sapporo

• Hakodate

HONSHU

SEA OF JAPAN

KOREA

Matsue

13

2

6

4 7 Kyoto

Kobe

8 Nara

3 Osaka

Nagoya

9

5

Tokyo

Yokohama

12

Hiroshima

1

AWAJI

Takamatsu

INLAND SEA

14 Fukuoka

KYUSHU

SHIKOKU

gasaki

11 Kumamoto

10

PACIFIC

OCEAN

124 miles

200 km

Tadao Ando

Known today as a great master of concrete architecture, Tadao Ando was born in Osaka in 1941. His early years and education remain shrouded in a certain mystery, but he indicates that he was "self-educated in architecture." In any case, he travelled extensively in the United States, Europe and Africa before founding Tadao Ando Architect & Associates in Osaka in 1969. Winner of the 1995 Pritzker Prize, he has been a visiting professor at Harvard, Columbia and Yale. Numerous exhibitions of his work in Europe and the United States have made him very popular with architectural students around the world. Some of his most significant buildings, always impregnated with his sense of geometric rigor, are the Rokko Housing (1983–93) in Kobe, his Church on the Water, located in Hokkaido (1988), the Japan Pavilion for Expo '92, Seville (1992), and his recent Suntory Museum in Osaka (1994). Neither photographs nor exhibitions give a clear idea of the most compelling aspect of Ando's architecture, its spirituality, expressed for example in the unusual indirect approach paths favored by the architect, and quite simply in his sense of space.

Der 1941 in Osaka geborene Tadao Ando gilt heute als einer der großen Baumeister der Betonarchitektur. Über seine ersten Lebensjahre und seine schulische bzw. universitäre Ausbildung hüllt sich Ando in Schweigen; er gibt jedoch an, »Autodidakt auf dem Gebiet der Architektur« zu sein. Fest steht, daß er die Vereinigten Staaten, Europa und Afrika vielfach bereiste, bevor er 1969 sein Büro Tadao Ando Architect & Associates in Osaka gründete. Der Gewinner des Pritzker Preises 1995 dozierte als Gastprofessor in Harvard, Columbia und Yale. Zahlreiche Ausstellungen seiner Werke in Europa und den Vereinigten Staaten brachten ihm einen hohen Bekanntheitsgrad bei Architekturstudenten in der ganzen Welt ein. Zu seinen bedeutendsten Bauwerken – die stets von seinem Gefühl für geometrische Strenge durchdrungen sind – gehören: die Rokko-Wohnsiedlung (1983–93) in Kobe, seine Church on the Water in Hokkaido (1988), der japanische Pavillon für die Expo '92 in Sevilla (1992) und sein Suntory Museum in Osaka (1994). Aber weder Fotografien noch Ausstellungen vermitteln einen klaren Eindruck des herausragendsten Aspekts in Andos Architektur – einer Spiritualität, die sich z.B. in den vom Architekten bevorzugten, ungewöhnlichen indirekten Zugangswegen und vor allem in seinem Raumgefühl äußert.

Né à Osaka en 1941, Tadao Ando est reconnu aujourd'hui comme l'un des grands maîtres de l'architecture japonaise. Sa formation et ses débuts restent entourés d'un certain mystère, mais il précise qu'il est «autodidacte en architecture». Il a beaucoup voyagé aux Etats-Unis, en Europe et en Afrique, avant de fonder Tadao Ando Architect & Associates à Osaka (1969). Lauréat du Prix Pritzker 1995, il est professeur invité à Harvard, Columbia et Yale. De nombreuses expositions consacrées à son œuvre en Europe et aux Etats-Unis l'ont rendu très célèbre auprès des étudiants du monde entier. Parmi ses réalisations les plus significatives, toujours imprégnées de son sens rigoureux de la géométrie: l'immeuble de logements Rokko (1983–93) à Kobe, l'Eglise sur l'eau, à Hokkaido (1988), le pavillon japonais d'Expo '92 à Séville (1992), ou son récent Musée Suntory pour Osaka (1994). Ni les photographies ni les expositions ne peuvent donner une idée précise de l'aspect le plus convaincant de son architecture, une spiritualité, exprimée entre autres dans de curieux cheminements d'approche, et un sens particulier de l'espace.

Museum of Wood, Mikata-gun, Hyogo, Japan, 1993–94.

Museum of Wood, Mikata-gun, Hyogo, Japan, 1993–94.

Musée du bois, Mikata-gun, Hyogo, Japon, 1993–94.

Naoshima Museum and Hotel

Naoshima, Kagawa, Japan, Phase I, 1990–1992;
Phase II, 1994–1995

This complex is located on an elevated cape at the southern end of the relatively unspoiled island of Naoshima, in the Inland Sea of Japan. The island is reached by ferry from neighboring ports such as Takamatsu and Uno. The complex itself can be entered either by road, or from an arrival pier and stepped plaza. In Phase I, Tadao Ando designed a large exhibition space for art and a small hotel, with a total floor area of 3,643 m². In this instance, Ando combined the use of stone rubble walls and concrete. Because it is part of a national park site, environmental requirements dictated that more than half of the volume be under ground. The main exhibition hall, sunken below grade, is two levels high, 50 meters long and 8 meters wide, and is used to exhibit contemporary art, with works by artists such as Frank Stella. Phase II, used mainly as hotel space, measures 551 m² of floor area. Since regulations would have required this building to have a pitched roof, Ando placed the structure underground. It is a one-level building with an oval plan, and an oval courtyard covered with water. By digging into the site, Tadao Ando has created something akin to an earthwork. As he says, "There is a plan to have me design one building a year all over this area. Every time you go, there will be something under construction. This will be kept up for ten, twenty years. This project in its conception is very much like contemporary art."

Dieser Komplex auf einem Kap der relativ naturbelassenen Insel Naoshima ist nur mit dem Schiff von benachbarten Fährhäfen wie Takamatsu und Uno zu erreichen. Zum Museum gelangt man über eine Straße oder über einen Landungspier und einen terrassenförmig abgestuften Platz. In Phase I entwarf Ando eine große Ausstellungshalle für Kunst und ein kleines Hotel mit einer Gesamtfläche von 3643 m². Er verwandte Natursteinmauern in Kombination mit Beton. Da sich das Gebäude in einem Nationalpark befindet, schrieben die örtlichen Umweltschutzbestimmungen vor, daß mehr als die Hälfte der Konstruktion unter Planum liegen müsse. Die unterirdische Ausstellungshalle besteht aus zwei 50 Meter langen und 8 Meter breiten Geschossen und dient zur Präsentation zeitgenössischer Kunst. Phase II des Bauwerks, hauptsächlich als Hotel genutzt, weist eine Gesamtfläche von 551 m² auf. Da die örtlichen Baubestimmungen ein Satteldach vorsahen, senkte Ando diesen Teil – ein eingeschossiges Gebäude von ovalem Grundriß sowie ein ovaler, wasserbedeckter Innenhof – ebenfalls unter Planum. Durch die Erdarbeiten schuf Ando eine Art »Erdkunstwerk«. Er erklärte: »Es bestehen Pläne, daß ich in dieser Gegend jedes Jahr ein neues Bauwerk errichten soll. Jedesmal, wenn man hierher kommt, befindet sich gerade ein anderes Gebäude im Bau. Und das soll zehn, zwanzig Jahre so weitergehen. Dieses Projekt entspricht in seiner Konzeption durchaus einem zeitgenössischen Kunstwerk.«

Cet ensemble est situé sur un cap élevé, à la pointe sud de l'île relativement protégée de Naoshima, dans la mer intérieure du Japon. On y accède par ferry à partir des ports voisins de Takamatsu et Uno. Les constructions sont accessibles par la route ou par une jetée et une place en escaliers. La Phase I, consiste en un vaste espace pour expositions artistiques et un petit hôtel. La surface totale est de 3643 m². Ando a marié ici des murs en moellons de pierre et le béton. Le site faisant partie d'un parc national, la réglementation exigeait que plus de la moitié du volume construit soit souterrain. Le principal hall d'exposition, enfoui sous terre (50 m x 8 m), comporte deux niveaux. Il sert à présenter des œuvres d'art contemporain comme, par exemple, celles de Frank Stella. Le bâtiment de la Phase II – qui concerne essentiellement l'hôtel – mesure 551 m² de surface utile. La réglementation locale exigeant un toit à pentes, Ando a décidé d'installer le volume en sous-sol. Sur un seul niveau, le bâtiment présente un plan ovale avec une cour ovale recouverte d'eau. Cette œuvre souterraine s'apparente presque au «land art». Comme il le fait remarquer: «D'après le programme, je dois construire sur ce site un bâtiment par an. A chaque fois que vous venez ici, quelque chose est donc en cours de construction. Ceci se poursuivra pendant dix ou vingt ans. La conception de ce projet le rapproche beaucoup de l'art contemporain.»

View toward Honshu from the small island of Naoshima.

Blick von der kleinen Insel Naoshima auf Honshu.

Vue vers Honshu, prise de la petite île de Naoshima.

Page 70: *A view from below the landing point looking up toward the Phase I building.* **Page 71:** *An outdoor terrace and the large round, interior exhibition space, used for temporary shows.*

Seite 70: *Blick vom Landungspier auf die Gebäude der Phase I.* **Seite 71:** *Eine Terrasse sowie die große, runde Ausstellungshalle für Wechselausstellungen.*

Page 70: *Vue du point d'accostage, face au bâtiment de la phase I.* **Page 71:** *Terrasse extérieure et le vaste espace d'exposition intérieur circulaire, réservé aux expositions temporaires.*

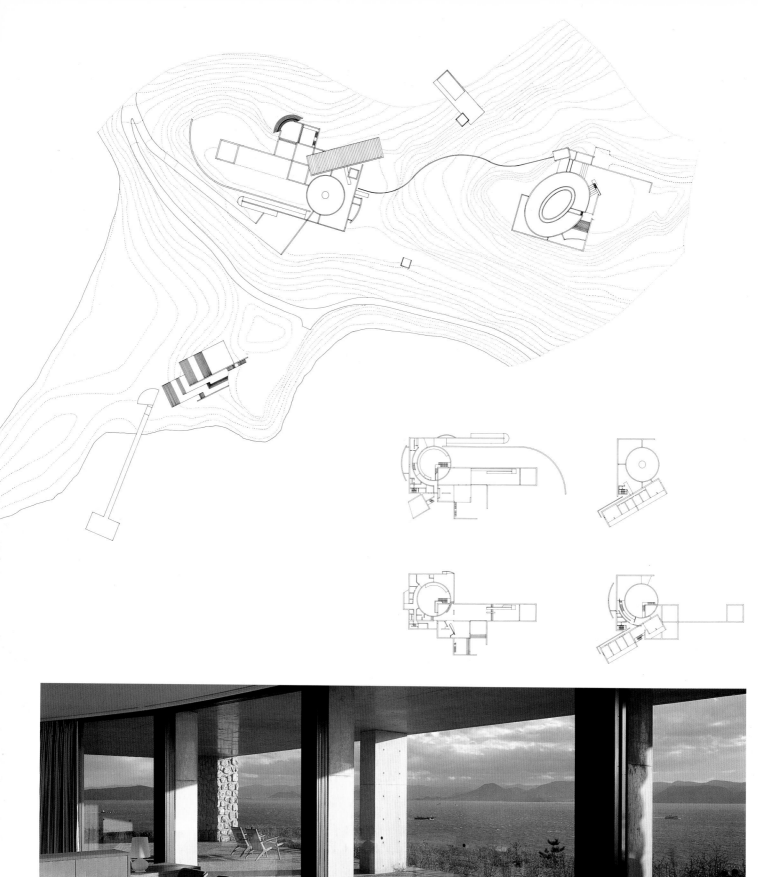

Pages 72/73: Plans show the relationship of Phase I structures (landing and volume with circular exhibition space) to Phase II (the oval form). The central feature of Phase II is the oval opening of the structure overlooking the Inland Sea.

Seite 72/73: Die Baupläne zeigen das Verhältnis zwischen den Gebäuden der Phase I (Landungspier und der Baukörper mit dem runden Ausstellungsraum) und der Phase II (die ovale Form). Das zentrale Merkmal von Phase II ist die ovale Öffnung des Bauwerks mit Blick auf die Japanische Inlandsee.

Page 72/73: Les plans montrent la relation entre les constructions de la phase I (accostage et espace circulaire d'exposition) et celles de la phase II (forme ovale). L'élément le plus caractéristique de la Phase II est l'ouverture ovale du bâtiment dominant la mer intérieure du Japon.

Tadao Ando: Naoshima Museum and Hotel, 1990–95 **73**

Museum of Wood

Mikata-gun, Hyogo, Japan, 1993–1994

This remarkable museum was built to commemorate the forty-fifth wood festival in Hyogo Prefecture, which occurs on Arbor Day, a ceremony founded by the Emperor in the 1950s following the wartime destruction of the forests. Located three hours by car from Osaka near a ski resort, the remote, wooded site covers an area of 168,310 m². Built of wood with a steel frame and reinforced concrete, the museum features a ring-shaped exhibit hall with a 46 meter outer diameter and a 22 meter void within. The access bridge cuts directly through the structure, bridging over a central fountain, and leading visitors 200 meters further on to an observation deck and guest house. Inside the museum, a sloping floor guides visitors down along a spiral path, which takes them twice into the central void. Locally milled Hyogo cedar was used for the posts and beams. The enormous laminated wood columns, rising to a height of 16 meters, are arranged in a manner that recalls the forest. Unfortunately, the quality of the exhibits, with models of wooden houses and light-box images, is not up to the extraordinary quality of the architecture. Although not specifically reminiscent of any particular temple, this structure does give at the very least an impression of communion with nature. Visitors are required to remove their shoes and put on slippers, as in most Japanese temples.

Dieses bemerkenswerte Museum in der Präfektur Hyogo wurde zum Gedenken des 45. Holzfestes errichtet, das am »Tag des Baumes« stattfindet und vom japanischen Kaiser in den 50er Jahren nach der kriegsbedingten Zerstörung der Wälder eingeführt wurde. Das abgelegene, bewaldete Gelände liegt etwa drei Autostunden von Osaka entfernt in der Nähe eines Skigebietes und umfaßt eine Fläche von 168 310 m². Das in Stahlskelettbauweise aus Holz und Stahlbeton erbaute Museum besitzt eine ringförmige Ausstellungshalle mit einem Außendurchmesser von 46 Metern und einem Innenraum von 22 Metern. Die Eingangsrampe, die über einen zentralen Springbrunnen führt, schneidet mitten durch die Konstruktion hindurch und bringt die Besucher zu einer 200 Meter entfernt liegenden Aussichtsplattform mit Gästehaus. Im Inneren des Museums führt ein leicht abfallender Boden den Besucher in einer langen Spirale bis zum Erdgeschoß, wobei der Innenraum zweimal durchquert wird. Sämtliche Stützpfeiler und Balken bestehen aus einheimischer Hyogo-Zeder; die gewaltigen, bis zu 16 Meter hohen Säulen aus Schichtholz wurden so arrangiert, daß ihre Anordnung an einen Wald erinnert. Leider entspricht die Qualität der Ausstellungsobjekte – Modelle von Holzhäusern und Bilder in Leuchtpultrahmen – nicht der außerordentlichen Qualität der Architektur. Obwohl dieses Gebäude nicht an einen bestimmten Tempel erinnert, erweckt es den Eindruck einer innigen Verbundenheit mit der Natur. Und wie in den meisten japanischen Tempeln werden die Besucher gebeten, ihre Schuhe auszuziehen und das Museum nur mit Hausschuhen zu betreten.

Ce musée remarquable a été construit à l'occasion de la 45ème fête du bois dans la préfecture de Hyogo. Cette manifestation se déroule le Jour de l'Arbre, cérémonie instituée par l'empereur dans les années 50, à la suite de la destruction de forêts pendant la guerre. Situé à trois heures de voiture d'Osaka, près d'une station de ski, ce site isolé et boisé couvre environ 168 310 m². Elevé en bois sur une structure d'acier et de béton armé, le musée possède un hall d'exposition en forme d'anneau de 46 de diamètre qui laisse un vide intérieur de 22 m de diamètre. La passerelle d'accès traverse directement la structure, au dessus d'une fontaine centrale, et conduit les visiteurs, 200 m plus loin, à un belvédère et une maison d'hôtes. A l'intérieur, un sol en pente les guide le long d'un cheminement en spirale, qui les fait pénétrer à deux reprises dans le vide central. Les poutres et piliers sont en cèdre Hyogo, travaillé sur place. Les énormes colonnes de bois laminé qui s'élèvent à 16 m de haut, font partie de l'exposition. Leur disposition rappelle la forêt. Malheureusement, la qualité des pièces exposées, avec des maquettes de maisons de bois et des images projetées, n'est pas au niveau de l'extraordinaire qualité de l'architecture. Bien qu'elle ne rappelle aucun temple en particulier, cette construction exprime un sentiment de communion avec la nature. Les visiteurs sont priés d'ôter leurs chaussures et de chausser des mules comme dans la plupart des temples japonais.

Page 75: An aerial view shows the unspoiled surroundings of the Museum. The long, elevated walkway to the rear of the museum leads to an observation platform and guest house.

Seite 75: Eine Luftaufnahme zeigt die unberührte Natur rund um das Museum. Der lange, ansteigende Weg auf der Rückseite des Museums führt zu einer Aussichtsplattform mit Gästehaus.

Page 75: Vue aérienne de l'environnement vierge autour du musée. Le long cheminement surélevé à l'arrière mène à un belvédère et une maison d'hôtes.

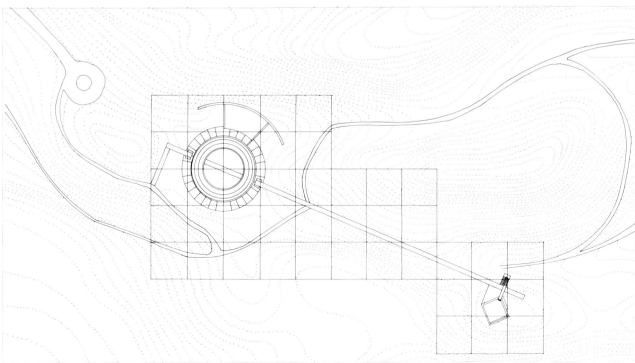

Tadao Ando: Museum of Wood, 1993–94 **75**

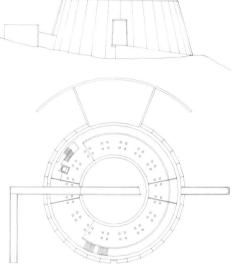

Pages 76/77: *Visitors, even those who have not actually entered the museum, can walk through its center, with a circular opening above, and a fountain below.*

Seite 76/77: *Auch die Besucher, die nicht das Museum selbst betreten, können das Gebäude auf einer Rampe durchqueren, unter der ein Springbrunnen angelegt ist. Nach oben weist das Zentrum eine kreisförmige Öffnung auf.*

Pages 76/77: *Les visiteurs, même ceux qui n'ont pas encore pénétré dans le musée peuvent en traverser le centre, dominé par une grande ouverture circulaire zénithale et donnant sur une fontaine en dessous.*

Meditation Space, UNESCO
Paris, France, 1994–1995

This small structure, with a floor area of only 33 m², is located on a 350 m² site squeezed between Marcel Breuer's UNESCO Headquarters (1953–58) and the adjacent Conference Hall designed by Pier Luigi Nervi. Significantly, it is also next to the Japanese garden created by Isamu Noguchi (1956–58) with 88 tons of stone brought from Shikoku. Finally, on a wall near the entrance ramp of the Contemplation Space hangs the "Angel of Nagasaki," a small sculpture that was part of the Urakami Church in that city, when the bomb exploded on August 9, 1945. Ando uses granite irradiated by the atomic bomb here for the basin and for the interior paving. Inside the 6.5 meter high concrete cylinder, which has two openings, but no doors, light enters through a narrow strip skylight running around the perimeter. Once again, Tadao Ando has created a space that gives a strong sense of spirituality, this time in a very difficult site. He even manages to fit a metal spiral staircase leading up toward the Conference Hall into this composition as though it had always belonged there. The gently running water below the approach ramps gives a feeling of calm, which is confirmed by the powerful simplicity of the structure itself. Within, two armchairs by Ando are the only decor.

Dieses kleine Gebäude mit einer Grundfläche von nur 33 m² befindet sich auf einem 350 m² großen Gelände zwischen Marcel Breuers UNESCO-Hauptgebäude (1953–58) und dem angrenzenden Konferenzsaal von Pier Luigi Nervi. Bezeichnenderweise liegt das Gebäude außerdem in direkter Nachbarschaft zu Isamu Noguchis Japanischem Garten (1956–58), für den 88 Tonnen Gestein aus Shikoku importiert wurden. Darüber hinaus befindet sich an einer Mauer in der Nähe des Eingangsbereichs der »Engel von Nagasaki«, eine kleine Skulptur, die zu Nagasakis Urakami-Kirche gehörte, als am 9. August 1945 die Bombe fiel. Ando verwandte radioaktiv verstrahlten Granit für das Becken und den Fußbodenbelag im Inneren des Gebäudes. Bei diesem 6,5 Meter hohen Betonzylinder – der zwei Öffnungen, aber keine Türen besitzt – fällt nur durch ein schmales schlitzförmiges Oberlicht Licht ins Innere. Wieder einmal schuf Tadao Ando einen Raum von starker spiritueller Ausstrahlung, und in diesem Fall auf einem besonders schwierigen Gelände. Es gelang ihm sogar, wie selbstverständlich eine metallene Wendeltreppe zum Konferenzsaal in diesen Raum zu integrieren. Das sanft plätschernde Wasser unterhalb der Eingangsrampe verströmt ein Gefühl der Ruhe, das von der kraftvollen Schlichtheit der Konstruktion – deren einziges Innendekor aus zwei von Ando entworfenen Sesseln besteht – zusätzlich betont wird.

Cette petite construction de 33 m² seulement de surface au sol se trouve sur un terrain de 350 m² enserré entre le siège de l'UNESCO construit par Marcel Breuer (1953–58) et la salle de conférence de Pier Luigi Nervi. Elle se trouve également proche du jardin japonais créé par Isamu Noguchi (1956–58) et de ses 88 tonnes de pierre importées de Shikoku. Sur un mur, près de la rampe d'entrée, est accroché «l'ange de Nagasaki», petite sculpture qui se trouvait dans l'église Urakami de cette ville, lorsque la bombe atomique explosa le 9 août 1945. Pour le bassin et le pavement intérieur Ando s'est servi de granit irradié par la bombe. La lumière pénètre à l'intérieur de ce cylindre de béton armé de 6,5 m de haut à deux ouvertures, mais sans porte, par une mince verrière qui court sur son périmètre. Une fois encore, Ando a su créer un espace qui offre un puissant sentiment de spiritualité, et ce dans un site très difficile. Il a même réussi à insérer un escalier métallique en spirale qui mène vers la salle de conférences, comme s'il s'était toujours trouvé là. L'eau qui coule doucement, sous la rampe d'approche, donne un sentiment de calme, confirmé par la puissante simplicité de la construction. Deux fauteuils d'Ando, sont les seuls éléments de décor.

Pages 78/79: *The cylindrical volume of the Meditation Space is surrounding by a gently sloping water basin. It is located on a restricted plot between the buildings of Breuer and Nervi.*

Seite 78/79: *Der zylindrische Baukörper des Meditation Space, der sich auf einem eng begrenzten Gelände zwischen zwei Bauten von Breuer und Nervi befindet, ist von einem leicht abschüssigen Wasserbecken umgeben.*

Pages 78/79: *Le volume cylindrique de l'Espace de méditation est entouré d'un petit bassin d'eau, doucement incliné. Il est situé sur un petit espace libre entre les bâtiments de Breuer et de Nervi.*

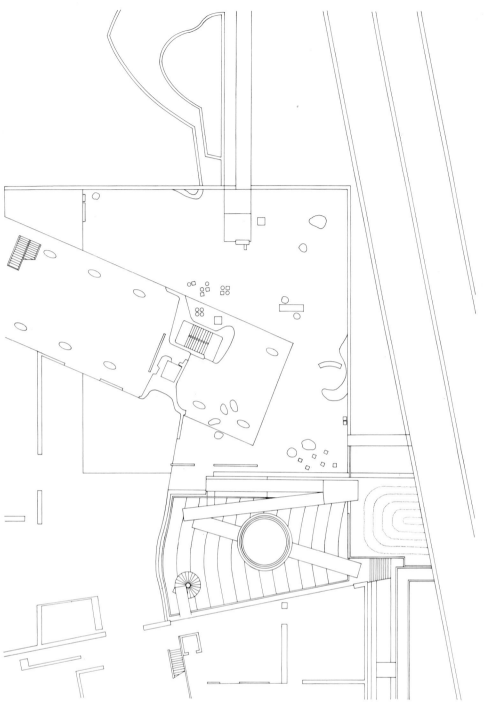

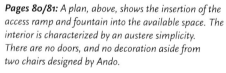

Pages 80/81: *A plan, above, shows the insertion of the access ramp and fountain into the available space. The interior is characterized by an austere simplicity. There are no doors, and no decoration aside from two chairs designed by Ando.*

Seite 80/81: *Ein Grundriß (oben) zeigt, wie die Eingangsrampe und der Brunnen in den vorhandenen Raum eingefügt wurden. Die von einer strengen Schlichtheit beherrschte Innenausstattung der Konstruktion besitzt keine Türen und keinerlei Dekor – abgesehen von zwei von Ando entworfenen Sesseln.*

Pages 80/81: *Le plan (en haut) montre l'insertion de la rampe d'accès et de la fontaine, dans l'espace disponible. L'intérieur se caractérise par une austère simplicité. Aucune porte, aucune décoration, en dehors de deux sièges dessinés par Ando.*

Masakazu Bokura

Masakazu Bokura is an unusual figure in that he has lived for twenty years outside of his native Japan. Born in 1949, he received a degree in Architecture and Urbanism from Waseda University in 1976. He received his qualification as an architect in France (D.P.L.G.) from the Ecole des Beaux-Arts in Paris (U.P.6) in 1979. He has taught at the Parsons School of Design (Paris, 1985–88) and more recently at the Ecole Spéciale d'Architecture (ESA) in Paris. Having worked with Arata Isozaki, as well as with I.M. Pei on the Grand Louvre project, he has begun to affirm a style that is highly contemporary in its use of materials and in its capacity to respect restrictive budgets. Well traveled and very much aware of contemporary art and architecture, Masakazu Bokura blends the influences that have formed him in a unique way. Although a number of Japanese architects like Arata Isozaki travel widely and build frequently outside of Japan, Masakazu Bokura has succeeded in bringing a touch of his own culture to Europe.

Masakazu Bokura bildet insofern eine Ausnahme in der japanischen Architekturwelt, als daß er seit 20 Jahren im Ausland lebt. Er wurde 1949 geboren, machte 1976 seinen Abschluß in Architektur und Stadtplanung an der Waseda University und erhielt 1979 sein Diplom als Architekt in Frankreich (D.P.L.G.) an der Ecole des Beaux-Arts in Paris (U.P.6). Anschließend unterrichtete er an der Parsons School of Design (Paris, 1985–88) und später an der Ecole Spéciale d'Architecture (ESA) in Paris. Nach seiner Zusammenarbeit mit Arata Isozaki, und seiner Arbeit mit I.M. Pei für das Grand Louvre-Projekt, entwickelte er einen eigenen Stil, der in der Verwendung der Materialien und der Fähigkeit mit einem begrenzten Budget zu arbeiten, als ausgesprochen modern bezeichnet werden kann. Dank seiner ausgedehnten Reisen und seiner Beschäftigung mit zeitgenössischer Kunst und Architektur läßt Masakazu Bokura die Einflüsse, die ihn geprägt haben, auf einzigartige Weise in seine Werke einfließen. Obwohl auch zahlreiche andere japanische Architekten wie Arata Isozaki viel reisen und ebenfalls häufig außerhalb Japans tätig sind, ist es vor allem Masakazu Bokura gelungen, einen Hauch seiner eigenen Kultur nach Europa zu bringen.

Masakazu Bokura est un représentant hors normes des architectes japonais, dans la mesure où il a vécu vingt ans loin de son pays. Né en 1949, il est diplômé en architecture et urbanisme de l'Université Waseda en 1976, et devient architecte D.P.L.G. après des études à l'Ecole des Beaux-Arts de Paris (U.P.6), en 1979. Il enseigne à la Parsons School of Design (Paris, 1985–88), et plus récemment à l'Ecole Spéciale d'Architecture (ESA) toujours à Paris. Après avoir travaillé avec Arata Isozaki, et avec I.M. Pei sur le projet du Grand Louvre, il affirme un style très contemporain, dans son recours aux matériaux modernes, et sa capacité à respecter des budgets restreints. Grand voyageur, et très au fait de l'actualité de l'art et de l'architecture, M. Bokura marie de façon originale diverses influences. Si un certain nombre d'architectes nippons, comme Arata Isozaki, voyagent et construisent souvent hors du Japon, Masakazu Bokura réussit à acclimater en Europe une partie de sa propre culture.

Saint-Lô Agricultural Study Center, Saint-Lô, France, 1993–94.

Saint-Lô Studienzentrum für Agrarwirtschaft, Saint-Lô, Frankreich, 1993–94.

Pôle agro-alimentaire de Saint-Lô, Saint-Lô, France, 1993–94.

Saint-Lô Agricultural Study Center

Saint-Lô, France, 1993–1994

This 5,500 m² group of buildings was built for a cost of only 21 million francs using materials such as galvanized metal and aluminum. Located 5 kilometers from the small city of Saint-Lô, it features an administrative building aligned on the city's church, and a low-maintenance garden designed by the landscape architect Laure Quoniam. This in itself is innovative in that industrial buildings are usually built without the least consideration for their urban environment, and little consideration for the quality of architecture. The architect contrasts his approach here with that of the Russian Constructivists, "The architects of the Russian avant-garde," he says, "imagined modern industry that did not exist so that it might one day exist. My approach is exactly the opposite. The French agribusiness is an important and often high-technology industry, but its image is usually not up to its technical performances. My goal was to create an image for this industry that corresponds to its truly modern nature." Aside from its metallic purity, little marks this complex as being Japanese, with the possible exception of the long, low classroom building, which Masakazu Bokura compares to the form of American B-29 bombers.

Die Baukosten für diesen 5500 m² großen Gebäudekomplex aus Zinkblech und Aluminium betrugen lediglich 21 Millionen Francs. Das 5 Kilometer von der kleinen Stadt Saint-Lô entfernte Studienzentrum umfaßt ein auf die Kirche des Ortes ausgerichtetes Verwaltungsgebäude und einen pflegeleichten Garten, den der Gartenarchitekt Laure Quoniam entwarf. Dieser Aspekt ist insofern ein Novum, als Industriebauten im allgemeinen ohne besondere Rücksicht auf ihre städtische Umgebung oder gar auf die Qualität der Architektur errichtet werden. Der Architekt kontrastiert seinen Ansatz mit dem der russischen Konstruktivisten: »Die Architekten der russischen Avantgarde hatten eine moderne Industrie vor Augen, die noch nicht bestand, aber eines Tages existieren sollte. Ich vertrete den genau entgegengesetzten Ansatz. Die französische Agrarwirtschaft ist eine bedeutende und hochtechnologisierte Industrie, deren Image meist jedoch nicht ihren technischen Möglichkeiten entspricht. Mein Ziel ist es, für diesen Wirtschaftszweig ein Image zu schaffen, das seinem wahrhaft modernen Charakter entspricht.« Abgesehen von seiner metallischen Reinheit deutet bei diesem Gebäudekomplex nur wenig auf die japanische Herkunft des Architekten hin – mit einer möglichen Ausnahme: Das lange, niedrige Gebäude mit den Schulungsräumen verglich Masakazu Bokura mit der Form eines amerikanischen B-29-Bombers.

Ce groupe de bâtiments de 5500 m² a été construit pour de 21 millions de francs seulement, avec des matériaux comme le métal galvanisé et l'aluminium. Situé à 5 kilomètres de la petite ville de Saint-Lô, il se compose d'un bâtiment administratif aligné sur l'église de la ville, et d'un jardin naturel dessiné par l'architecte paysager Laure Quoniam. En soi il est une innovation tant les bâtiments industriels sont souvent construits sans la moindre considération pour l'environnement urbain ou la qualité architecturale. L'architecte fait remarquer la différence entre son approche et celle des constructivistes russes: «Les architectes de l'avant-garde russe,» dit-il, «imaginaient une industrie moderne qui n'existait pas, afin qu'elle puisse exister un jour. Mon approche est exactement le contraire. L'agriculture française est une industrie importante, souvent de haute technologie, mais son image n'est généralement pas au niveau de ses performances. Mon but a été de donner à cette industrie une image qui corresponde à sa vraie nature.» Mise à part sa pureté et son éclat métallique, peu d'éléments évoquent une intervention japonaise, si ce n'est la longue salle de cours que Masakazu Bokura compare à un bombardier B-29.

Pages 84/85: Located in a typical industrial park, the Study Center is nonetheless partially aligned with the church of Saint-Lô. The four sections correspond to the functions required by the program: laboratories, offices, classrooms and space for rental.

Seite 84/85: Das in einem typischen Industriepark gelegene Studienzentrum ist teilweise auf die Kirche von Saint-Lô ausgerichtet. Die vier Bereiche entsprechen den Funktionen des Zentrums: Laboratorien, Büroräume, Schulungsräume und Mieträume.

Pages 84/85: Situé dans un parc d'activités industrielles banal, le centre de recherche n'en est pas moins partiellement aligné sur l'église de Saint-Lô. Ses quatres parties correspondent aux fonctions requises par le programme: laboratoires, bureaux, salles de cours et espace à louer.

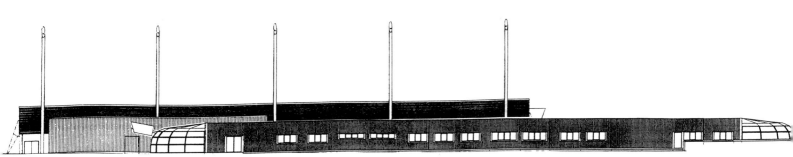

Masakazu Bokura: Saint-Lô Agricultural Study Center, 1993–94 **85**

Light materials like perforated aluminum and simple ones like concrete paving for interior floors permitted the architect to respect the rigorous budget for this project.

Leichte und schlichte Materialien wie perforiertes Aluminium bzw. Betonplatten für die Böden im Inneren ermöglichten es dem Architekten, das eng gesteckte Budget dieses Projektes nicht zu überschreiten.

Des matériaux légers, comme l'aluminium perforé, ou très simples, comme le pavement de béton des sols intérieurs, ont permis à l'architecte de respecter le budget très serré de ce projet.

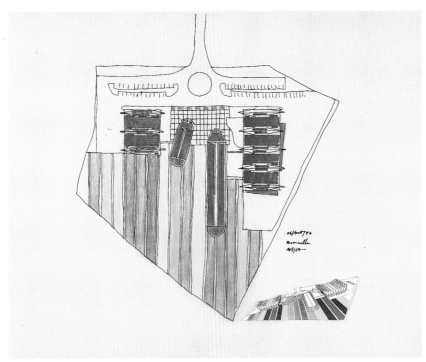

The drawing (above) shows the alignment of the garden designed by Laure Quoniam with the main fuselage-like volume. The apparently low ceiling levels here are in fact quite adequate. **Pages 88–89:** A night view shows the transparency of the building.

Die Zeichnung (oben) zeigt die Ausrichtung des von Laure Quoniam entworfenen Gartens auf den großen, röhrenförmigen Baukörper. Die scheinbar zu niedrige Deckenhöhe reicht tatsächlich völlig aus. **Seite 88–89:** Eine Nachtansicht, die die Transparenz des Gebäudes dokumentiert.

Le croquis (en haut) montre l'alignement du jardin, dessiné par Laure Quoniam, et du volume en forme de fuselage. Les plafonds, apparemment bas, ne posent en réalité aucun problème. **Pages 88–89:** Vue de nuit montrant la transparence du bâtiment.

Hiroshi Hara

Born in 1936 in Kawasaki, Japan, Hiroshi Hara was educated at the University of Tokyo. Because he has taught at the University of Tokyo both in the faculty of architecture and at the Institute of Industrial Science (since 1982), Hara has had a considerable influence on younger Japanese architects. His influence is also undoubtedly due to the spectacular nature of many of his buildings, such as the widely published Yamato International Building (Ota-ku, Tokyo, 1985–86) or, more recently, the Umeda Sky City building in Osaka. A slight man with a commanding voice, Hara has frequently explained his elaborate architectural forms with equally elaborate theories, but he remains a master of space and architectural detail. Beyond his individual structures, he has dreamed of creating entire cities of interconnected skyscrapers, even imagining contemporary architecture as a stepping stone to construction in outer space. Currently being completed, his enormous Kyoto JR Station will be a defining image of this ancient capital of Japan, now a large, modern city. Like an urban landscape in itself, this station, together with the Umeda Sky Building, places Hiroshi Hara in a category apart from his colleagues.

Hiroshi Hara wurde 1936 in Kawasaki (Japan) geboren und erhielt seine Ausbildung zum Architekten an der University of Tokyo. Da er sowohl an der Fakultät für Architektur als auch am Institut für Wirtschaftswissenschaften (seit 1982) lehrte, hat Hara beträchtlichen Einfluß auf die jungen japanischen Architekten. Aber sein Einfluß begründet sich auch auf der aufsehenerregenden Natur vieler seiner Bauwerke, u.a. des vielbesprochenen Yamato International City Gebäudes (Ota-ku, Tokio, 1985–86) und des vor kurzem fertiggestellten Umeda Sky City Gebäudes in Osaka. Obwohl dieser zierliche Architekt mit der gebieterischen Stimme seine kunstvollen architektonischen Formen bereits mehrfach in ebenso kunstvollen Theorien darlegte, bleibt er stets ein Meister des Raums und des architektonischen Details. Neben seinen eigenen Konstruktionen träumte er von der Gestaltung ganzer Städte aus miteinander verbundenen Wolkenkratzern und betrachtete die moderne Architektur sogar als Sprungbrett für die Errichtung von Bauwerken im All. Seine vor kurzem fertiggestellte, gewaltige Kyoto JR Station wird sich zu einem prägenden Merkmal von Japans ehemaliger Hauptstadt entwickeln. Dieser an eine urbane Landschaft erinnernde Bahnhof und das Umeda Sky City sind der Grund dafür, daß Hiroshi Hara in eine Klasse für sich eingestuft werden muß.

Né en 1936 à Kawasaki (Japon), Hiroshi Hara fait ses études à l'Université de Tokyo. Enseignant à l'Université de Tokyo (faculté d'architecture), et à l'Institut de la science industrielle (depuis 1982) il exerce une influence considérable sur les jeunes générations d'architectes. Ce rayonnement est également due à la nature spectaculaire de plusieurs de ses réalisations, comme le Yamato International Building (Ota-ku, Tokyo, 1985–86), très commenté, ou plus récemment l'Umeda Sky City à Osaka. Petit homme à la voix pleine d'autorité, Hara a souvent expliqué ses formes architecturales élaborées et ses théories recherchées. Il reste un maître de l'espace et du détail. En dehors de ses projets ponctuels, il rêve de créer des cités entières composées de tours interconnectées, imaginant même une architecture contemporaine qui servirait de point de départ de constructions dans l'espace. En cours d'achèvement, son énorme gare JR de Kyoto donnera une nouvelle image de cette ancienne capitale, aujourd'hui grande ville moderne. En soi élément de paysage urbain, cette gare et l'Umeda Sky City, placent Hiroshi Hara un peu à part de ses confrères.

Umeda Sky City, Kita-ku, Osaka, Japan, 1988–93.
Umeda Sky City, Kita-ku, Osaka, Japan, 1988–93.
Umeda Sky City, Kita-ku, Osaka, Japon, 1988–93.

Umeda Sky City
Kita-ku, Osaka, Japan, 1988–1993

Though still the tallest building in West Japan, the Umeda Sky City building is surrounded by a growing number of other tall buildings in this area that has been compared to Tokyo's Shinjuku district. It remains an unusually strong presence on the skyline of a city still dominated by low-rise structures. The forty-story, 173 meter high double tower, with its two sections 54 meters apart, features a "Floating Garden" 150 meters above the ground. This 54 x 54 meter area is served by two transparent elevators. A 6 meter wide steel bridge at the twenty-second level also links the buildings. The total floor area of the complex is 147,398 m². Although Arata Isozaki proposed a "City in the Air" in 1960, this is one of the first structures to attempt to create what Hiroshi Hara calls an "interconnected superskyscraper." He says, "We must develop and practice living in a variety of high-density modes." This remark is particularly valid in such a densely crowded city as Osaka. As numerous critics have pointed out, the Umeda Sky building makes reference to the hanging gardens of Babylon, or perhaps to the flying island of Laputa imagined by Jonathan Swift in *Gulliver's Travels*. Going beyond the earthbound design of any building, Hara has imagined the Umeda Sky City as being a kind of gateway for what he calls the Leo (Low Earth Orbit) Ring, a round space station of the future, which he has depicted as floating above the ring-shaped opening between the Umeda towers.

Obwohl es sich bei dem Umeda Sky City nach wie vor um Westjapans höchstes Gebäude handelt, füllt sich diese Gegend in zunehmendem Maße mit hohen Bauwerken. Dennoch bleibt dieser Wolkenkratzer ein ungewöhnlicher Anblick in einem Stadtbild, das von eingeschossigen Bauten beherrscht wird. Der 40-geschossige, 173 Meter hohe Doppelturm, dessen beide Teile 54 Meter auseinanderliegen, besitzt einen »Schwebenden Garten« in 150 Metern Höhe. Dieser 54 x 54 Meter große Bereich ist über zwei transparente Aufzüge erreichbar, während eine sechs Meter breite Stahlbrücke im 22. Stockwerk beide Gebäudeteile zusätzlich miteinander verbindet. Die Gesamtfläche des Komplexes beträgt 147398 m². Obwohl Arata Isozaki bereits 1960 eine »Stadt in der Luft« vorschlug, zählt dieses Gebäude zu den ersten Bauwerken, die als »intern verbundener Super-Wolkenkratzer« (so der Architekt) konzipiert wurden. Hiroshi Hara erklärt: »Wir müssen verschiedene Techniken entwickeln, um in dichtbesiedelten Gebieten leben zu können.« Dies gilt besonders für eine so dicht besiedelte Stadt wie Osaka. Einige Architekturtheoretiker vertreten die Ansicht, daß das Umeda Sky City Bezüge zu den hängenden Gärten Babylons oder zur fliegenden Insel Laputa aufweise, deren Bild Jonathan Swift in »Gullivers Reisen« entwarf. Losgelöst vom erdverbundenen Design eines Gebäudes sieht Hara sein Umeda Sky City als eine Art Tor zum »LEO (Low Earth Orbit)-Ring« – so bezeichnet er eine runde Weltraumstation, die in seiner Phantasie über der ringförmigen Öffnung der beiden Umedatürme schwebt.

Bien qu'il demeure l'immeuble le plus haut du Japon, l'Umeda Sky City est de plus en plus entouré d'autres tours dans ce quartier d'Osaka comparable au Shinjuku, à Tokyo. Néanmoins, il impose toujours sa forte présence dans le panorama d'une ville où prédominent les constructions de faible hauteur. Cet immeuble, composé de deux tours de 40 niveaux de 173 m de haut à 54 m l'une de l'autre, s'orne d'un «jardin flottant» à 150 m au dessus du niveau du sol. De forme carrée, cet espace de 54 m x 54 m est desservi par deux ascenseurs transparents. Une passerelle d'acier de 6 m de large relie les deux bâtiments à la hauteur du 22ème niveau. La surface totale de l'ensemble est de 147398 m². Si Arata Isozaki avait déjà proposé une «cité dans les airs» en 1960, cette réalisation est l'une des premières tentatives de création de ce que Hara appelle un «super-gratte-ciel interconnecté». Il déclare: «Nous devons nous habituer à exister dans toute une variété de styles de vie de haute intensité.» Cette remarque est particulièrement pertinente dans une ville aussi peuplée qu'Osaka. Comme de nombreux critiques l'ont remarqué, l'Umeda Sky City est une référence aux jardins suspendus de Babylone, ou peut-être à l'île volante de Laputa, imaginée par Jonathan Swift dans «Les Voyage de Gulliver». Allant au delà des constructions qui prennent racine sur le sol, Hara a imaginé son Umeda Sky City comme une sorte de porte d'entrée vers ce qu'il appelle le LEO Ring (Low Earth Orbit, orbite terrestre basse), station spatiale circulaire du futur. Il la décrit comme flottant au dessus de l'ouverture en forme d'anneau, entre les tours Umeda.

Pages 92/93: Although it stands out less now than when it was completed because this area of Osaka has more and more high-rise buildings, the Umeda Sky City nonetheless makes its mark on the skyline. Sky bridges facilitate movement between the two parts of the tower.

Seite 92/93: Obwohl das Umeda Sky City Gebäude heute weniger aus der Skyline Osakas herausragt als früher – da sich dieser Bezirk zunehmend mit hohen Bauwerken füllt – bildet es nach wie vor einen wichtigen Bezugspunkt im Stadtbild. Brücken ermöglichen es, von einem Turm in den anderen zu gelangen.

Pages 92/93: Même s'il se détache moins aujourd'hui sur le panorama de la ville que lors de sa construction – ce quartier d'Osaka s'est enrichi depuis de plusieurs immeubles de grande hauteur – l'Umeda Sky City n'en affirme pas moins son originalité. Des passerelles permettent la circulation entre les deux tours.

Pages 94/95: Imagined by its architect like a city floating in the clouds, the Umeda Sky City does tend, because of its mirrored glass cladding, to change its exterior appearance according to the time of day.

Seite 94/95: Das von seinem Architekten als in den Wolken schwebende Stadt gedachte Umeda Sky City Gebäude scheint sein Erscheinungsbild – dank der Spiegelglasverkleidung – zu jeder Tageszeit zu verändern.

Pages 94/95: Imaginé par l'architecte comme une ville flottant dans les nuages, l'apparence de l'Umeda Sky City change au cours de la journée, grâce à sa peau de verre réfléchissant.

Hiroshi Hara: Umeda Sky City, 1988–93 **95**

Page 96 top: *Visitors can reach the highest level of the building, around the central opening.*

Seite 96 oben: *Das oberste Geschoß des Gebäudes rund um die zentrale Öffnung steht Besuchern offen.*

Page 96 en haut: *Les visiteurs peuvent se promener au sommet du bâtiment, autour de l'ouverture centrale.*

Pages 96/97: *A correspondence between interior and exterior design and an extreme attention to details and the quality of construction mark the Umeda Sky City as a very Japanese structure despite its modernist aspects.*

Seite 96/97: *Eine Beziehung zwischen dem Design des Gebäudes und seiner Innenausstattung sowie die große Liebe zum Detail und zur Bauausführung kennzeichnen das Umeda Sky City als sehr japanisch – ungeachtet seiner modernen Aspekte.*

Pages 96/97: *L'accord entre la conception de l'intérieur et de l'extérieur, l'extrême attention aux détails, et la qualité de la construction, font de l'Umeda Sky City une réalisation typiquement japonaise, malgré ses aspects modernistes.*

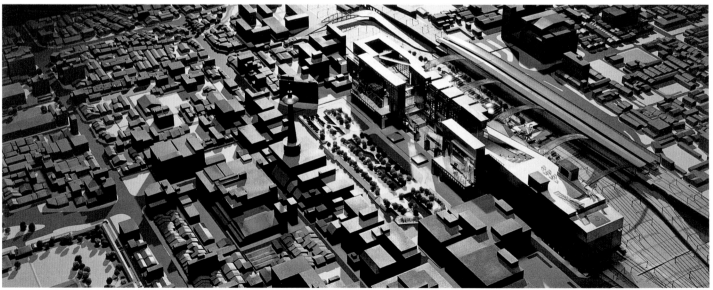

98 Hiroshi Hara: Kyoto JR Station, 1991–97

Kyoto JR Station
Shimogyo, Kyoto, Japan, 1991–1997

The massive silhouette of the new Kyoto JR Station, conceived of as part of the celebrations of the 1200th anniversary of the city, was partially dictated by the unusually narrow form of the 3.8 hectare site. Consisting of three basements, sixteen stories and a one-story penthouse, this complex is no less than 470 meters long, for a total floor area of 235,257 m². More than anything else, it resembles an inhabited wall, or the skyline of an entire city, if not a horizontal skyscraper fully as complex as Hara's Umeda Sky City. As Hiroshi Hara points out, "The station itself occupies only one tenth of the total area, the rest being occupied by hotels, stores and offices. It is designed so that the persons visiting the train station will not necessarily be aware of the other activities, or of the overall size of the building." As in the case of the Umeda project, linking bridges connect different parts of the structure. Hara explains that "In the Kyoto JR Station, the site itself and the nature of the project assume the existence of multiple levels of communication. The subway passes below and there is the train above. This type of complexity," he concludes, "naturally has an effect on the building, since elevators cannot be placed just anywhere, for example." Hiroshi Hara was chosen in a 1991 competition for this project, over Tadao Ando, Kisho Kurokawa, James Stirling, Bernard Tschumi and others.

Die massive Silhouette des neuen Bahnhofs, der als Teil der Jubiläumsfeiern zum 1200-jährigen Bestehen der Stadt Kioto entworfen wurde, ist geprägt von der ungewöhnlich schmalen Form des 3,8 Hektar großen Geländes. Dieser aus 3 Tiefgeschossen, 16 Stockwerken und einem eingeschossigen Penthouse bestehende Gebäudekomplex weist eine Länge von 470 Metern und eine Gesamtfläche von 235 257 m² auf. Seine Form erinnert in erster Linie an eine bewohnte Mauer oder die Skyline einer ganzen Stadt – wenn nicht sogar an einen horizontalen Wolkenkratzer von einer Komplexität wie etwa Haras Umeda Sky City. Hiroshi Hara erklärte dazu: »Der Bahnhof selbst nimmt nur ein Zehntel der Gesamtfläche ein, den Rest bilden Hotels, Geschäfte und Büroräume. Der Komplex ist so konzipiert, daß sich der Bahnreisende nicht notwendigerweise der anderen Bereiche oder der Größe des gesamten Gebäudes bewußt wird.« Genau wie bei seinem Umeda-Projekt verbinden auch hier mehrere Brücken die einzelnen Bereiche des Gebäudes. Hara fährt fort: »Bei der Kyoto JR Station legen das Gelände und die Art des Projektes die Existenz verschiedener Kommunikationsebenen nahe. Die U-Bahn befindet sich im Untergeschoß und die Bahnlinie darüber. Diese Komplexität wirkt sich natürlich auf das Gebäude aus, da beispielsweise nicht überall Aufzüge eingerichtet werden können.« Den Auftrag zu diesem Projekt erhielt Hiroshi Hara 1991 nach einer Ausschreibung, an der sich u.a. auch Tadao Ando, Kisho Kurokawa, James Stirling und Bernard Tschumi beteiligten.

La silhouette massive de la nouvelle gare de chemin de fer JR de Kyoto, édifiée dans le cadre des célébrations du 1200ème anniversaire de la fondation de la cité, est en partie dictée par l'étroitesse inhabituelle de son site de 3,8 hectares. Composé de trois niveaux en sous-sol, de 16 étages et d'une *penthouse*, cet ensemble ne mesure pas moins de 470 m de long, pour une surface totale de plus de 235 000 m². Aussi complexe que l'Umeda City Sky, il fait surtout penser à une muraille, au panorama d'une ville, voire à un gratte-ciel horizontal. Comme le note Kiroshi Hara: «La gare elle-même n'utilise qu'un dixième de la surface totale, le reste est occupé par des hôtels, des magasins, et des bureaux. L'ensemble est conçu de telle façon que les personnes qui se rendent à la gare, peuvent ne pas être conscientes des autres activités, ni de la taille réelle du bâtiment.» Comme pour le projet Umeda, des passerelles relient les différentes parties de l'ensemble. Hara explique que: «Le site lui-même et la nature du projet supposent l'existence de multiples niveaux de communication. Le métro passe en dessous, le train au dessus. Ce type de complexité a bien entendu exercé son effet sur la conception, puisque, par exemple, les ascenseurs ne peuvent être placés n'importe où.» Hiroshi Hara a remporté le concours pour cette gare en 1991, face à Tadao Ando, Kisho Kurokawa, James Stirling, Bernard Tschumi, et d'autres.

Kyoto JR Station, Shimogyo, Kyoto, Japan, 1991–97. Two model views showing the articulation of the 470 meter long structure.

Kyoto JR Station, Shimogyo, Kioto, Japan, 1991–97. Zwei Ansichten des Modells zeigen die Gliederung des 470 Meter langen Komplexes.

Gare JR de Kyoto, Shimogyo, Kyoto, Japon, 1991–97. Deux vues de la maquette, montrant l'articulation de cette construction de 470 m de long.

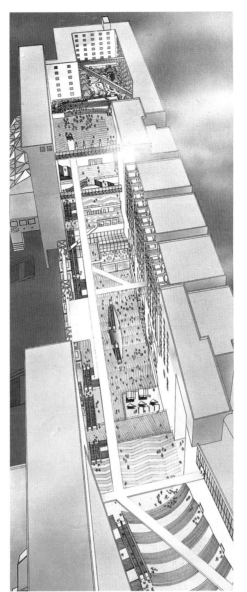

Pages 100/101: *A canyon-like central interior volume and other large spaces give some idea of the complexity of the Kyoto JR Station. As is already the case in many Japanese railway stations, there will be multiple levels of communication and movement throughout the structure.*

Seite 100/101: *Ein schluchtartiger Innenraum und andere große Räume vermitteln eine Vorstellung von der Komplexität der Kyoto JR Station. Wie bei vielen anderen japanischen Bahnhöfen werden auch hier zahlreiche Kommunikations- und Bewegungsebenen durch das Gebäude führen.*

Pages 100/101: *Un volume intérieur central aux profondeurs de canyon et d'autres grands espaces donnent une première idée de la complexité de cette gare de Kyoto. Comme dans de nombreuses gares japonaises, on y trouve de multiples niveaux de communication et d'animation.*

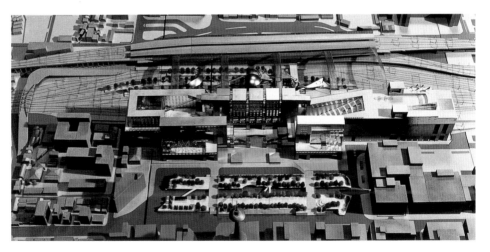

Itsuko Hasegawa

Like Toyo Ito, Itsuko Hasegawa worked with the architect Kiyonori Kikutake (1964–69), and like him, she was influenced directly by Kazuo Shinohara, with whom she worked for several years at the Tokyo Institute of Technology after 1969. She created her own office, Itsuko Hasegawa Atelier, in 1979. She has been a lecturer at Waseda University, at the Tokyo Institute of Technology, and in 1992 at the Harvard Graduate School of Design. Even more than Ito, Itsuko Hasegawa has set out to create a kind of alternative reality or rather an artificial form of nature in her larger projects such as the Shonandai Cultural Center (Fujisawa, Kanagawa, 1987–90), which is a reduced model of the universe. More recent work includes the Oshima-machi Picture Book Museum (Imizu, Toyama, 1992–94) and the Sumida Culture Factory (Sumida, Tokyo, 1991–94). Born in 1941, Itsuko Hasegawa was one of the first women to establish a high reputation as an architect in Japan. Her example has inspired many others.

Wie Toyo Ito war auch Itsuko Hasegawa für den Architekten Kiyonori Kikutake (1964–69) tätig, und wie Ito wurde auch sie von Kazuo Shinohara beeinflußt, mit dem sie nach 1969 mehrere Jahre am Tokyo Institute of Technology zusammenarbeitete. 1979 gründete sie Itsuko Hasegawa Atelier; außerdem war sie als Dozentin an der Waseda University, am Tokyo Institute of Technology und an der Harvard Graduate School of Design (1992) tätig. Mit ihren größeren Projekten – wie etwa dem Shonandai Cultural Center (Fujisawa, Kanagawa 1987–90), das ein verkleinertes Modell des Universums darstellt – strebt sie in noch stärkerem Maße als Ito eine alternative Realität oder eine künstliche Form der Natur an. Zu ihren unlängst fertiggestellten Bauwerken gehören u.a. das Oshima-machi Picture Book Museum (Imizu, Toyama, 1992–94) und die Sumida Culture Factory (Sumida, Tokio, 1991–94). Die 1941 geborene Itsuko Hasegawa zählt zu den ersten Frauen, die sich in Japan als Architektin einen Namen machten, und ihr Beispiel dient vielen anderen als Vorbild.

Comme Toyo Ito, Itsuko Hasegawa travaille pour l'architecte Kiyonori Kitukate (1964–69), et comme lui, elle est directement influencée par Kazuo Shinohara, avec lequel elle collabore plusieurs années à l'Institut de technologie de Tokyo, à partir de 1969. Elle crée sa propre agence, Itsuko Hasegawa Atelier en 1979. Elle est lectrice à l'Université Waseda, à l'Institut de technologie de Tokyo, et, en 1992, à l'Harvard Graduate School of Design. Plus encore qu'Ito, Itsuko Hasegawa s'efforce de créer une sorte de réalité alternative, voire de nature artificielle, dans ses grands projets comme le centre culturel Shonandai (Fujisawa, Kanagawa, 1987–90), qui représente l'univers en réduction. Plus récemment, elle a réalisé le Musée Oshima-machi du livre d'images (Imuzu, Toyama, 1992–94) et l'Atelier culturel Sumida (Sumida, Tokyo, 1991–94). Née en 1941, Itsuko Hasegawa est l'une des premières femmes japonaises à s'être fait un nom dans la profession. Son exemple inspire de nombreuses étudiantes.

Museum of Fruit, Yamanashi-shi, Yamanashi, 1993–95, interior view.

Innenansicht des Museum of Fruit, Yamanashi-shi, Yamanashi, 1993–95.

Musée du fruit, Yamanashi-shi, Yamanashi, 1993–95, vue intérieure.

Museum of Fruit

Yamanashi-shi, Yamanashi, Japan, 1993–1995

Yamanashi-shi is a small rather unattractive rural town with extensive agricultural activity. This museum is located on a hill above the town, which is covered with vineyards and fruit trees. Greenhouses, which recall the forms of the museum, are scattered across the hillside. On a generous park site of 195,000 m², with a distant view of Mount Fuji, this group of buildings includes a total floor area of 6,459 m². The architect describes her own concept in rather poetic terms: "When we started thinking about a museum devoted to fruit," she says, "we were faced with the spiritual aspects such as sensuality, intelligence, and human desires, as well as global ecological issues surrounding our physical environment. The museum takes the form of a group of shelters and underground spaces set into sloped ground, each of which accommodates specific programs. It is also a metaphor of a group of seeds, an expression of the fertility and vitality of fruit. The shelters are constructed in different sizes and materials, either planted firmly in the ground or attempting to reject the earth, as if they had just landed from the air or are trying to fly away. The vitality of the fruit and the museum, as an alien visitor landing and taking-off in the sloped orchard, fuse into one science fiction ecological totality."

Yamanashi-shi ist eine kleine, eher unattraktive, ländliche Stadt mit intensiver Agrarwirtschaft. Das Museum befindet sich auf einem mit Wein- und Obstgärten bedeckten Hügel oberhalb der Stadt, dessen zahlreiche Treibhäuser an die Form des Museums erinnern. Der in einem weitläufigen, 195 000 m² großen Park gelegene Museumskomplex mit Blick auf den Fudschijama besitzt eine Gesamtfläche von 6459 m². Die Architektin beschreibt ihr Werk in eher poetischen Begriffen: »Als wir mit der Planung eines Museums der Früchte begannen, wurden wir sowohl mit spirituellen Aspekten wie Sinnlichkeit, Intelligenz und menschlichen Bedürfnissen als auch mit globalen ökologischen Themen konfrontiert, die unsere natürliche Umwelt betreffen. Das Museum besitzt die Form einer Reihe von Schutzräumen und unterirdischen Räumlichkeiten, die in den Hang gebaut wurden und jeweils unterschiedliche Aufgaben erfüllen. Dabei handelt es sich auch um die Metapher in die Erde gepflanzter Samenkerne – Ausdruck der Fruchtbarkeit und Lebenskraft der Früchte. Die Schutzräume wurden aus unterschiedlichen Materialien und in verschiedenen Größen konzipiert und entweder direkt in die Erde »gepflanzt« oder so konstruiert, daß sie der Erde zu widerstehen scheinen – als seien sie gerade erst aus der Luft gelandet oder im Begriff davonzufliegen. Die Lebenskraft der Früchte und das Museum – das an ein UFO erinnert, welches in dem schräg ansteigenden Obstgarten landet und wieder abhebt – verschmelzen zu einer ökologischen Science-fiction-Einheit

Yamanashi-shi est une petite ville rurale d'assez peu d'intérêt si ce n'est sa spécificité agricole. Le musée est situé sur une colline couverte de vignes et de vergers, qui domine la ville. Au centre d'un vaste parc de 195 000 m², avec le Mont Fuji dans le lointain, ce groupe de bâtiments représente une surface totale de 6459 m². L'architecte en décrit le concept en termes presque poétiques: «Lorsque nous avons commencé à réfléchir à un musée consacré au fruit, nous avons été confrontés aux aspects spirituels de problèmes comme la sensualité, l'intelligence, le désir, et les enjeux écologiques de notre environnement physique. Le musée a la forme d'un groupe d'abris et d'espaces souterrains implanté sur un terrain en pente, chacun consacré à un programme d'exposition spécifique. C'est aussi la métaphore de quelques graines, l'expression de la fertilité et de la vitalité du fruit. Les abris sont de différentes tailles et matériaux, solidement plantés dans le sol, ou tentant de quitter la terre, comme s'ils venaient d'atterrir ou essayaient de s'envoler. Ici, la vitalité du fruit et le musée, visiteur venu d'ailleurs, atterrissant ou s'envolant de ce verger pentu, fusionnent en une unité écologique de science-fiction.»

Pages 106/107: Plans and a night view give a sense of the organic forms of the Museum of Fruit. It is set on a hillside that is actively cultivated with fruit trees and vineyards.

Seite 106/107: Die Baupläne und eine Nachtansicht vermitteln eine Vorstellung von der organischen Form des Museum of Fruit, das an einem von Obst- und Weingärten überzogenen Hang liegt.

Pages 106/107: Plans et vue nocturne soulignant le caractère organique des formes du Musée du fruit. Il est construit sur une colline, plantée d'arbres fruitiers et de vignes.

On a clear day, Mount Fuji is visible from the site
of the Museum of Fruit. The main greenhouse,
though visually spectacular, is planted, through
no fault of the architect, in an uninspired way.

An klaren Tagen kann man vom Gelände des Museum
of Fruit den Fudschijama sehen. Leider zeichnet sich
das optisch aufsehenerregende Hauptgewächshaus
durch eine phantasielose Bepflanzung aus, wofür die
Architektin jedoch nicht verantwortlich ist.

Par temps clair, le Mont Fuji est visible du Musée du
fruit. La serre principale, bien que très spectaculaire,
est plantée d'une manière très conventionnelle dont
l'architecte n'est pas responsable.

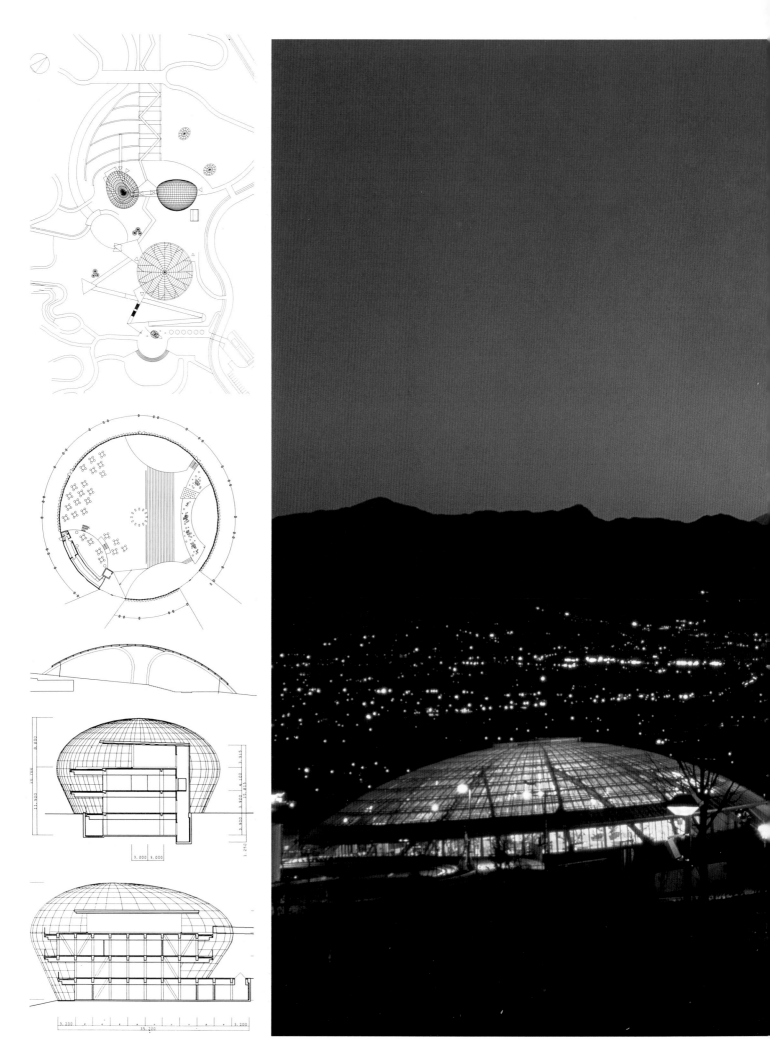

Arata Isozaki

Arata Isozaki is one of the unquestioned masters of late twentieth century architecture. Especially in his native Japan, he plays a considerable role through his own buildings, but also in encouraging younger architects, as in the case of the 1992 Kumamoto Artpolis project, or the current Gifu Kitagata Apartment Reconstruction Project for which he has selected only young female designers. Isozaki has also built a number of seminal buildings outside of Japan, including the Los Angeles Museum of Contemporary Art (MoCA, 1981–86), or the Center for Japanese Art and Technology in Cracow, Poland (1991–94). Current projects include the 60,000 m² Higashi Shizuoka Plaza Cultural Complex in Shizuoka and Ohio's Center of Science and Industry (COSI), located in Columbus, Ohio. Never one to persist in a single uncompromising style, Isozaki has gone further than almost any of his colleagues in creating the forms of a contemporary Japanese architecture that has its place anywhere in the world. He is a master of materials, creating unusual juxtapositions of stones, metal and wood, and he is also a willing participant in international colloquiums and competitions.

Arata Isozaki zählt unbestritten zu den herausragenden Meistern der Architektur des ausgehenden 20. Jahrhunderts. Insbesondere in seiner Heimat Japan spielt er eine bedeutende Rolle – nicht nur wegen seiner eigenen Bauwerke, sondern auch wegen seines Engagements für junge Architekten, wie etwa bei dem Kumamoto Artpolis-Projekt (1992) oder seinem derzeitigen Bauvorhaben, der Sanierung der Gifu Kitagata Appartements. Für dieses Projekt engagierte er ausschließlich junge Architektinnen. Aber auch außerhalb Japans errichtete Isozaki eine Reihe zukunftsweisender Gebäude, u.a. das Los Angeles Museum of Contemporary Art (MoCA, 1981–86) und das Zentrum für japanische Kunst und Technologie im polnischen Krakau (1991–94). Zu seinen gegenwärtigen Projekten zählen der 60000 m² große Higashi Shizuoka Plaza Cultural Complex in Shizuoka und das Columbus Ohio Center of Science and Industry (COSI) in Columbus, Ohio. Isozaki war nie jemand, der nur an einem einzigen, eindeutigen Stil festhielt, und er trug in erheblich stärkerem Maße als die meisten seiner Kollegen zur Entwicklung einer modernen japanischen Architektur bei, die überall auf der Welt ihren Platz findet. Er versteht sich auf den meisterhaften Umgang mit Materialien und schuf ungewöhnliche Kombinationen aus Stein, Metall und Holz. Darüber hinaus beteiligt er sich gerne und ausgiebig an internationalen Kolloquien und Wettbewerben.

Arata Isozaki est, sans conteste, l'un des maîtres de l'architecture de la fin de ce siècle. En particulier dans son propre pays, il joue un rôle considérable à travers ses réalisations, mais également ses encouragements aux jeunes architectes. C'est le cas du projet Kumamoto Artpolis de 1992, ou celui de rénovation de logements Gifu Kitagata pour lequel il a sélectionné de jeunes architectes femmes. Isozaki a également construit un certain nombre de bâtiments importants hors du Japon, dont le Los Angeles Museum of Contemporary Art (MoCA, 1981–86), ou le Centre japonais d'art et de technologie de Cracovie, Pologne (1991–94). Parmi ses récents projets figurent le complexe culturel Higashi Shizuoka Plaza de 60000 m² à Shizuoka, et l'Ohio's Center of Science and Industry (COSI), à Columbus, Ohio. Peu enclin à persister dans le même style, Isozaki est allé plus loin que beaucoup de ses confères dans la création de formes contemporaines japonaises qui ont trouvé leur place partout dans le monde. Il maîtrise magnifiquement les matériaux, créant des rapprochements inhabituels de pierre, de métal et de bois, et participe volontiers aux colloques et concours internationaux.

Nagi MoCA, Nagi-cho, Okayama, Japan, 1992–94.

Nagi MoCA, Nagi-cho, Okayama, Japan, 1992–94.

Musée d'art contemporain Nagi, Nagi-cho, Okoyama, Japon, 1992–94.

Nagi MoCA

Nagi-cho, Okayama, Japan, 1992–1994

According to Satoshi Takatori, the director of this small (1,887 m²) museum located in a rural area, the 7,000 inhabitants of the town do not always understand the meaning of this structure, which absorbed more than one-third of the city budget for its construction. 40,000 people nonetheless visited it the first year, and 20,000 the second, many of them obviously attracted from outside the area by the reputations of the architect and the artists. Arata Isozaki designed the tripartite structure intentionally for three artists, giving each a cosmological significance: Shusaku Arakawa (Sun); Kazuo Okazaki (Moon); and Aiko Miyawaki (Earth). Arakawa's highly unusual mirror image of Ryoan-ji garden is situated in the tube-like form, its angle making it very difficult for visitors to know how to stand up straight, while Okazaki's minimal crescent-shaped moon room is occupied only by two simple Okayama granite benches and three gold colored "organic" forms, which the artist calls *hisashi* or eaves. One interesting feature of this peaceful room is the multiple echo of visitors' voices. Aiko Miyawaki's arcing steel *Utsurohi* sculptures occupy an area close to the entrance and fill their space with a delicate, poetic atmosphere. The museum is oriented on the nearby "sacred" mountain Nagi-san, although a recently built housing complex partially blocks the view. The museum also includes a public library for the town, and an elegant café looking out onto the courtyard with Aiko Miyawaki's work.

Nach Aussage Satoshi Takatoris, des Direktors dieses kleinen (1887 m²), in einer ländlichen Gegend gelegenen Museums, wissen die 7000 Einwohner der Stadt die Bedeutung des Gebäudes nicht immer richtig einzuschätzen, dessen Bau immerhin ein Drittel des städtischen Etats in Anspruch nahm. Nichtsdestotrotz zählte das Museum im ersten Jahr 40 000 und im zweiten Jahr 20 000 Besucher, die durch die Reputation des Architekten und der ausstellenden Künstler auch aus anderen Regionen angelockt wurden. Arata Isozaki entwarf die dreiteilige Konstruktion ursprünglich für drei Künstler und gab ihnen jeweils eine kosmologische Bedeutung: Shusaku Arakawa (Sonne), Kazuo Okazaki (Mond) und Aiko Miyawaki (Erde). Arakawas höchst ungewöhnliches Abbild des Ryoan-ji-Gartens befindet sich in der Röhrenform, deren Neigungswinkel es den Besuchern sehr erschwert, aufrecht zu stehen, während Okazakis minimaler halbmondförmiger Raum von zwei schlichten Okayama-Granitbänken und drei goldfarbenen »organischen« Formen belegt ist, die der Künstler als *hisashi* oder Traufe bezeichnet. Einen interessanten Aspekt dieses ruhigen Raumes bildet das vielfache Echo der Stimmen der Besucher. Und Aiko Miyawakis bogenförmige Stahlskulpturen *Utsurohi* erzeugen in der Nähe des Eingangs eine zarte, fast poetische Atmosphäre. Das Museum wurde auf den nahegelegenen »heiligen« Berg Nagi-san ausgerichtet – obwohl ein vor kurzem fertiggestellter Wohnungskomplex die Sicht auf den Berg teilweise versperrt. Neben der städtischen Bücherei gehört zum Museum ein elegantes Café mit Blick auf Aiko Miyawakis Arbeiten im Innenhof.

Selon Satoshi Takatori, directeur de ce petit musée (1887 m²) situé en zone rurale, les 7000 habitants de Nagi n'ont pas toujours compris cette construction qui a absorbé plus du tiers du budget de la ville. Elle a néanmoins reçu 40 000 visiteurs la première année, et 20 000 la seconde, beaucoup d'entre eux étant des étrangers à la région attirés par la notoriété de l'architecte et des artistes. Arata Isozaki a volontairement conçu sa structure en trois parties, destinées à trois artistes, et donné à chacune d'elles un sens cosmologique: Shusaku Arakawa (le soleil), Kazuo Okazaki (la lune), et Aiko Miyawaki (la terre). La très étonnante image en miroir du jardin du Ryoan-ji d'Arakawa est disposée dans un espace en forme de tube, selon un angle qui déstabilise les visiteurs, tandis que la salle en croissant de lune minimaliste d'Okazaki n'est occupée que par deux simples banquettes de granit d'Okayama et trois formes «organiques» dorées que l'artiste appelle *hisashi* ou chêneaux. Cette salle paisible s'emplit de l'écho des voix des visiteurs. Les sculptures en arcs d'acier *Utsurohi* d'Aiko Miyawaki se dressent dans un espace proche de l'entrée qu'elles emplissent d'une manière poétique et délicate. Le musée est orienté vers la montagne «sacrée» toute proche de Nagi-san, bien qu'un immeuble de logement récemment construit en bouche en partie la vue. Le bâtiment comprend également une bibliothèque municipale de prêt et un élégant café qui donne sur l'œuvre d'Aiko Miyawaki.

Page 110: An overall view across a flooded rice paddy.

Seite 110: Eine Gesamtansicht des Bauwerks, mit einem überfluteten Reisfeld im Vordergrund.

Page 110: Vue du musée avec, en premier plan, une rizière inondée.

Page 111: The "Moon" room with the bench and sculptural forms designed by Kazuo Okazaki.

Seite 111: Der »Mond«-Raum mit einer Bank und skulpturalen Formen von Kazuo Okazaki.

Page 111: La salle «lune», avec le banc et les formes sculpturales de Kazuo Okazaki.

Top left: The suspended reproductions of Ryoan-ji garden by Shusaku Arakawa are intended to leave the visitor in disequilibrium. **Bottom left:** The view toward Mount Nagi is unfortunately blocked by a recently built prefectural housing structure.

Links oben: Die aufgehängten Reproduktionen des Ryoan-ji-Gartens von Shusaku Arakawa lassen den Besucher bewußt im Ungleichgewicht. **Links unten:** Der Blick zum Berg Nagi wird leider von einem erst kürzlich errichteten Gebäude der Präfektur verstellt.

A gauche en haut: Les reproductions du jardin du Ryoan-ji de Shusaku Arakawa mettent le visiteur en déséquilibre. **A gauche en bas:** Vue vers le Mont Nagi malheureusement obturée par un immeuble de logements, récemment construit par l'administration.

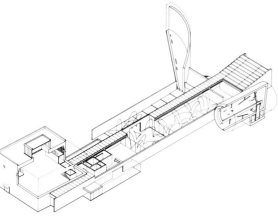

The most succesful of the installations at Nagi MoCA is that of Aiko Miyawaki. Her delicate sculpture, representing the "earth," makes the transition between the interior and the exterior of the area near the entrance.

Die erfolgreichste Installation des MoCA stammt von Aiko Miyawaki. Ihre zarte Skulptur, die die »Erde« darstellen soll, bildet den Übergang zwischen dem inneren und dem äußeren Bereich nahe des Eingangs.

L'installation la plus réussie de ce musée est celle d'Aiko Miyawaki. Sa sculpture délicate, représentant la «Terre» fait transition entre l'intérieur et l'extérieur de la zone près de l'entrée.

Concert Hall
Kyoto, Japan, 1992–1995

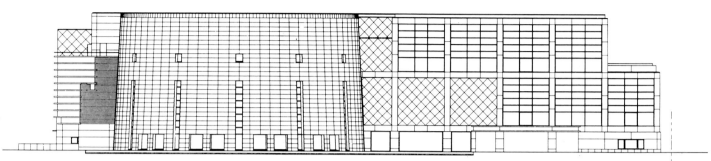

This is a 22,442 m² concrete structure with five floors above ground and two basement levels. The main concert hall seats 1,839, while the smaller Ensemble Hall Murata seats 514 for piano or chamber music recitals. Underground parking for 145 vehicles and a restaurant seating 100 are also part of the structure. Isozaki won this commission, another of the planned commemorations of the 1200th anniversary of Kyoto, in a 1991 limited competition against Fumihiko Maki, Shin Takamatsu, Kazuhiro Ishii, and Sakakura Associates. Its surprising entrance hall features a *trompe-l'œil* floor pattern and twelve pillars representing the twelve zodiac symbols of ancient Eastern astrology. This is a strong building, marked on the street side by the undulating bands of its facade. The main entrance is unexpectedly located on the side, leading to a processional spiraling slope, which the architect invites the visitor to take before finally discovering the main hall. The overall impression is one of a stony solidity and undoubted virtuosity. Using Italian *pietra serena* stone extensively, and tweaking the standard shoebox form of the hall slightly by including an off-axis pipe organ, Isozaki creates a masterpiece here, which calls on Western tradition as well as Japanese tradition as seen in the *shoji*-like screens hovering above the waiting areas, in the curved stone bridge leading to the café from the exterior, or in the rough-hewn stone block benches outside, which recall the work of Isozaki's friend Noguchi.

Diese 22 442 m² große Betonkonstruktion mit fünf oberirdischen Geschossen und zwei Untergeschossen umfaßt eine große Konzerthalle mit 1839 Plätzen, eine kleinere Ensemblehalle Murata für Klavier- und Kammermusik mit 514 Plätzen, ein unterirdisches Parkhaus mit 145 Stellplätzen sowie ein Restaurant mit Sitzgelegenheiten für 100 Gäste. Isozaki gewann den Auftrag für dieses Projekt – ebenfalls Teil der 1200-Jahrfeier Kiotos – in einem 1991 veranstalteten, geschlossenen Wettbewerb, an dem sich auch Fumihiko Maki, Shin Takamatsu, Kazuhiro Ishii und Sakakura Associates beteiligt hatten. Die überraschende Eingangshalle des Gebäudes präsentiert einen *trompe l'œil*-Fußboden sowie zwölf Pfeiler, die die zwölf Tierkreiszeichen der antiken östlichen Astrologie symbolisieren. Das ausdrucksstarke Bauwerk ist auf der Straßenseite durch seine wellenförmigen Fassadenbänder geprägt, wobei der Haupteingang überraschenderweise an einer Seite des Gebäudes liegt und die Besucher zu einer spiralförmig ansteigenden Rampe führt bevor sie schließlich die große Halle betreten. Die Konzerthalle verströmt den Eindruck massiver Kompaktheit und unbestrittener Virtuosität. Durch seine ausgiebige Verwendung von italienischem *pietra serena*-Gestein und indem er die Standardform der schuhkartonähnlichen Halle durch die Integration einer seitlich zur Achse versetzten Orgel durchbrach, gelang Isozaki ein Meisterwerk, das sich nicht nur auf die westliche Tradition, sondern auch auf sein japanisches Erbe beruft – wie sich in den *shoji*-ähnlichen Wandschirmen oberhalb der Wartehalle, der geschwungenen Steinbrücke zum Café oder in den roh behauenen Natursteinbänken zeigt, die an die Arbeiten von Isozakis Freund Noguchi erinnern.

Ce bâtiment de cinq niveaux dont deux en sous-sol mesure 22 442 m². La salle principale peut accueillir 1839 auditeurs, et la plus petite, l' «Ensemble Hall Murata», 514, pour des récitals de piano ou de musique de chambre. Un parking souterrain pour 145 véhicules et un restaurant de 100 places sont également prévus. C'est en 1991 qu'Isozaki a remporté cette commande, dans le cadre des célébrations du 1200ème anniversaire de la fondation de Kyoto face à Fumihiko Maki, Shin Takamatsu, Kazuhiro Ishii, et Sakakura Associates. Son étonnant hall d'entrée met en scène un sol en trompe-l'œil de marbre et douze piliers symbolisant les douze signes du zodiaque orientaux. Cette puissante réalisation, est marquée, côté rue, par de longs bandeaux ondulés qui animent sa façade. Curieusement, l'entrée principale est déportée sur le côté, ce qui crée une sorte de cheminement que le visteur est invité à parcourir avant la salle principale. L'impression dominante est de puissance minérale et de remarquable virtuosité. A grand renfort de *pietra serena* italienne, et en pinçant la forme classique «en boite de chaussure» de la salle (qui comprend un orgue désaxé), Isozaki a créé ici un chef d'œuvre. Il rappelle aussi bien les traditions occidentales que nippones, en particulier à travers les écrans de style *shoji* suspendus au dessus des principaux espaces d'attente, le pont de pierre incurvé qui de l'extérieur mène au café, et les bancs en blocs de pierre brute qui rappellent les œuvres de son ami Noguchi.

A drawing, above, shows the entrance side of the Concert Hall, perpendicular to the street facade shown opposite.

Die Zeichnung oben zeigt die Eingangsseite der Concert Hall, die rechtwinklig zur Straßenansicht (Seite 115) angeordnet wurde.

En haut, croquis de l'entrée de la salle de concert, perpendiculaire à la façade sur rue, visible page de droite.

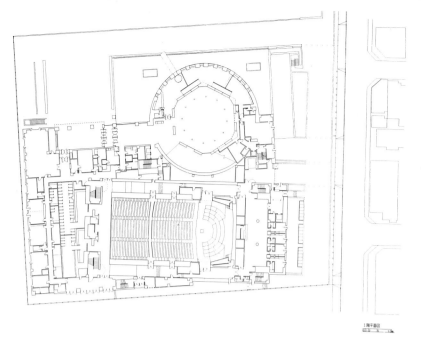

The spectacular trompe-l'œil floor design of the entrance foyer (round area in the plan on the left) leads visitors to an entrance ramp, which spirals up toward the main concert hall. **Above:** A full view of the street-side facade. The passage to the entrance is located on the right.

Der aufsehenerregende trompe l'œil-Fußboden des Eingangsbereichs (runder Bereich auf dem Grundriß links) leitet die Besucher zu einer Eingangsrampe, die spiralförmig zur großen Konzerthalle führt. **Oben:** Ansicht der Straßenseite. Der Durchgang zum Haupteingang liegt auf der rechten Seite.

Le spectaculaire motif en trompe-l'œil du foyer d'entrée (zone circulaire sur le plan, à gauche), conduit le visiteur vers une rampe d'accès qui monte en spirale vers la salle de concert principale. **Ci-dessus:** Vue générale de la façade sur rue. Le passage vers l'entrée se situe à droite.

Nara Convention Hall

Nara, Japan, 1992–1998 (project)

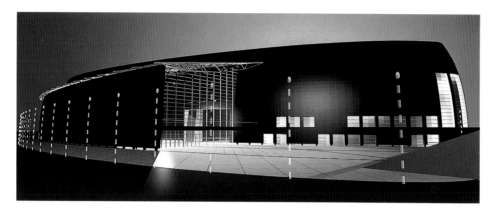

Arata Isozaki was one of five architects selected from several hundred applicants for this prestigious project in the ancient capital of Japan. Also participating in the second stage were Hans Hollein, Christian de Portzamparc, Mario Botta and Tadao Ando. The chairman of the jury was Kisho Kurokawa, and other members were Richard Meier, James Stirling, Vittorio Lampugnani, Kazuo Shinohara and Hiroshi Hara. The intention was obviously to give an international flavor to the competition, and a similar legitimacy to the final choice. The 23,462 m² structure by Isozaki will be an enormous ellipse, 138 meters long, 42 meters wide and 25 meters high, with its long axis defined by Nara's ancient city plan. The flared plaza and entrance lobby takes advantage of the angle of the train line as opposed to the main axis of the hall, providing a dynamic entrance to the stable, and rather mysterious, oval form of the main building. Plans call for the erection of a precast concrete interior wall, with a steel space truss with attached tiles forming the exterior wall. Located near the Nara JR Station, this monolithic form is intended to recall the large roofs or pagodas of Nara's temples, Todai-ji, Kofuku-ji and Toshodai-ji. The building will contain two halls, the largest of which will seat 1,700 persons, and feature a flexible seating arrangement. The smaller hall has a seating capacity of 450.

Arata Isozaki gehört zu den fünf Architekten, die aus einer Gruppe von mehreren 100 Bewerbern für dieses prestigeträchtige Projekt in der alten Hauptstadt Japans ausgewählt wurden. Neben Isozaki gelangten auch Hans Hollein, Christian de Portzamparc, Mario Botta und Tadao Ando in die zweite Ausscheidungsrunde; die Jury bestand neben Kisho Kurokawa als Vorsitzendem aus Richard Meier, James Stirling, Vittorio Lampugnani, Kazuo Shinohara und Hiroshi Hara. Dadurch sollte die Ausschreibung internationales Flair und die endgültige Entscheidung eine ähnliche Legitimität erhalten. Bei der von Isozaki entworfenen, 23 462 m² großen Konstruktion wird es sich um eine gewaltige Ellipsenform von 138 Metern Länge, 42 Metern Breite und 25 Metern Höhe handeln, deren Längsachse sich an Naras altem Stadtplan orientiert. Der erweiterte Platz und die Eingangshalle profitieren von der zur Hauptachse der Halle schräg verlaufenden Bahnlinie, wodurch die stabile und geheimnisvolle ovale Form des Hauptgebäudes einen dynamischen Eingang erhält. Die Baupläne sehen die Errichtung einer Fertigbeton-Innenwand mit einem räumlichen Stahltragwerk vor, an dem Kacheln befestigt sind, die die Außenwand bilden. Die monolithische Form der in der Nähe der Nara JR Station gelegenen Convention Hall soll an die großen Dächer bzw. Pagoden von Naras Tempeln – Todai-ji, Kofuku-ji und Toshodai-ji – erinnern. Das Gebäude soll zwei Hallen umfassen: Eine große Halle mit 1700 Plätzen und einem flexiblen Bestuhlungsplan sowie eine kleine Halle mit einer Kapazität von 450 Personen.

Avec Hans Hollein, Christian de Portzamparc, Mario Botta et Tadao Ando, Arata Isozaki fait partie des cinq architectes sélectionnés, parmi des centaines de candidats, pour ce prestigieux projet destiné à l'ancienne capitale du Japon. Le jury présidé par Kisho Kurokawa comptait également parmi ses membres Richard Meier, James Stirling, Vittorio Lampugnani, Kazuo Shinohara, et Hiroshi Hara. L'intention était à la fois de donner un caractère international à ce concours et de légitimer le choix final. L'énorme ellipse de 138 m de long, 42 de large et 25 de haut, dont l'axe est défini par l'ancien plan de la ville, représente une surface de 23 462 m². La place évasée et le hall d'entrée s'alignent en fonction de l'angle déterminé par une voie de chemin de fer opposée à l'axe principal du hall, offrant une entrée dynamique à l'ovale massif et assez mystérieux du bâtiment principal. Les plans prévoient l'érection d'un mur intérieur en béton préfabriqué avec une charpente d'acier plaquée de carrelages et formant le mur extérieur. Dressée près de la gare de chemin de fer JR de Nara, cette forme monolithique est censée évoquer les grands toits et les pagodes des temples de Nara, Todai-ji, Kofuku-ji et Toshodai-ji. Le bâtiment contiendra deux grandes salles dont la plus grande pourra accueillir 1700 personnes, avec un système de sièges modulable. La plus petite salle est conçue pour 450 personnes.

Pages 118/119: Computer-generated images give an idea of the unsual and rather massive aspect of the Nara Convention Hall, which does bring to mind the impressive size of temples in Nara, and in particular Todai-ji.

Seite 118/119: Vom Computer erzeugte Bilder vermitteln einen Eindruck der ungewöhnlichen, recht massiven Außenansicht der Nara Convention Hall, die an die beeindruckende Größe der Tempel von Nara, und vor allem an den Todai-ji-Tempel denken läßt.

Pages 118/119: Ces images de synthèse donnent une idée de l'aspect inhabituel et assez massif du Hall de congrès de Nara, qui rappelle la taille impressionnante des temples de la ville, en particulier du Todai-ji.

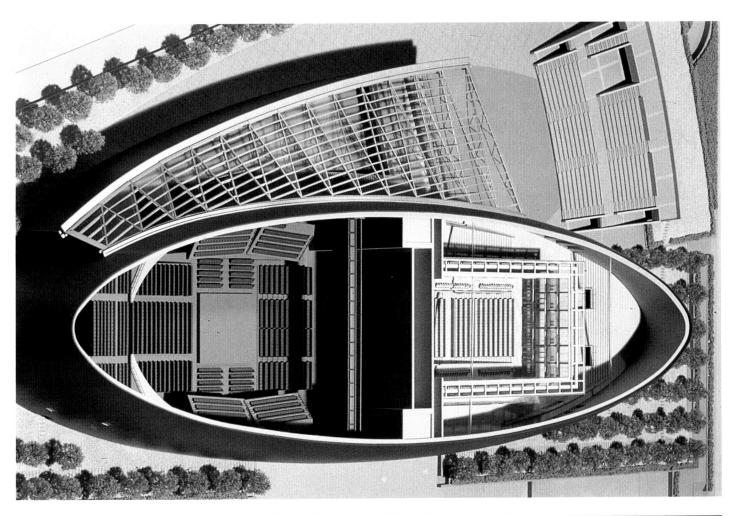

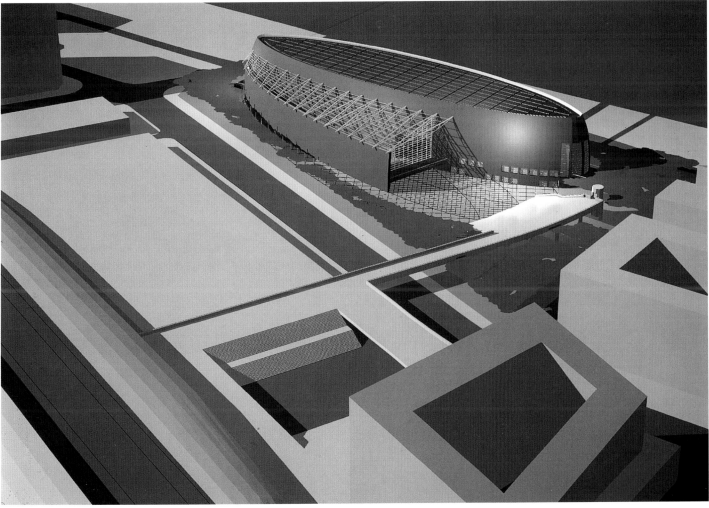

Domus: La Casa Del Hombre

La Coruña, Spain, 1993–1995

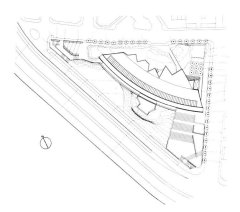

Despite his extensive use of Galician stone in this 4,019 m² project, Arata Isozaki insists on his intention to make the whole building look light or even weightless. It has a very large (94 x 17 meters) curved wall "set like a mask" or a sail facing the sea. It is made of precast concrete panels clad with 3 centimeter thick slate boards. The form of this complex curve was naturally calculated with the assistance of a computer. On the opposite side, there is a wall built on exposed bedrock, following the jagged line of the site itself. It is made of site-cast concrete covered by thick pale gray Mondariz granite, with an average height of 11 meters. The architect compares this facade to the form of a Japanese folding screen. Devoted to exhibitions about mankind, whether in its physical or psychological aspects, this unusual museum is set on a coast that is otherwise occupied by undistinguished architecture. The interior is designed around an overlapping group of exhibition spaces, defined by the large curve of the seaside wall. Arata Isozaki describes the Casa Del Hombre as "an evocative singularity," and compares its large curved wall not only to a mask, but also to "skin on a body." In this way, the function of the museum itself finds an expression in the architecture in an abstract form.

Located in the northwestern corner of Spain in the province of Galicia, facing out onto the Atlantic, La Coruña's seafront is characterized by undistinguished modern architecture, which makes Arata Isozaki's building stand out all the more in the image to the left.

Die Seeseite der in der spanischen Provinz Galizien gelegenen Stadt La Coruña wird von recht durchschnittlicher moderner Architektur beherrscht – wodurch Arata Isozakis Bauwerk um so deutlicher hervorsticht (links).

Au nord-ouest de l'Espagne, dans la province de Galice, face à l'Atlantique, le front de mer de La Corogne se caractérise par une architecture moderne sans intérêt, qui fait encore mieux ressortir le bâtiment édifié par Arata Isozaki (à gauche).

Trotz der massiven Verwendung von galizischem Stein für dieses 4019 m² große Projekt beharrte Arata Isozaki auf seiner Absicht, eine leichte und schwerelos wirkende Konstruktion erbauen zu wollen. Auf der Meerseite befindet sich eine sehr große (94 x 17 Meter), geschwungene Wand, die an eine »Maske« oder ein Segel erinnert und aus Betonfertigelementen und einer 3 Zentimeter dicken Schieferplattenverkleidung besteht. Die Form dieser komplexen Kurvung wurde mit Hilfe eines Computers berechnet. Auf der anderen Seite besitzt das Gebäude eine durchschnittlich 11 Meter hohe Mauer aus Gußbeton, die mit hellgrauem Mondariz-Granit verkleidet ist und auf nacktem Fels der Linienführung des zerklüfteten Geländes folgt. Der Architekt vergleicht diese Fassade mit der Form eines japanischen Wandschirms. Das ungewöhnliche Museum, das ausschließlich Ausstellungen zum Thema Mensch – sowohl physische als auch psychische Aspekte – gewidmet ist, befindet sich auf einem Küstenstreifen, den ansonsten eine eher durchschnittliche Architektur kennzeichnet. Die Innenausstattung wurde um eine Reihe ineinander übergehender Ausstellungsräume herum konzipiert, die von der Form der Mauer auf der Meerseite beherrscht sind. Arata Isozaki beschreibt die Casa Del Hombre als »eine sinnträchtige Einzigartigkeit« und vergleicht ihre große geschwungene Mauer nicht nur mit einer Maske, sondern mit der »Haut eines Körpers«. Auf diese Weise findet die Funktion des Museums ihren Ausdruck in der abstrakten Form seiner Architektur.

Bien qu'il ait beaucoup utilisé la pierre de Galice pour ce projet de 4019 m², Arata Isozaki insiste sur sa volonté de donner à cette construction un aspect léger, voire d'apesanteur. Elle présente un très important mur incurvé (94 x 17 m) «posé comme un masque» ou une voile face à l'océan, constitué de panneaux de béton préfabriqué plaqués d'ardoises de 3 cm d'épaisseur. La forme de cette courbe complexe a été naturellement calculée par ordinateur. Du côté opposé, se trouve un mur de béton coulé sur place d'une hauteur moyenne de 11 m, recouvert de granit gris pâle de Mondariz et appuyé sur un rocher naturel. L'architecte compare cette façade à un paravent japonais. Consacré à des expositions sur l'homme, que ce soit sous ses aspects physiques ou psychologiques, ce musée inhabituel se trouve sur une côte dont l'architecture n'offre rien de très remarquable par ailleurs. L'intérieur s'articule autour d'un groupe d'espaces d'exposition entrelacés, définis par la large courbe du mur côté mer. Pour Arata Isozaki, cette Casa Del Hombre avec ses grands murs incurvés est comme un masque, ou une «peau tendue sur un corps». Ainsi, la fonction du musée lui-même trouve-t-elle son expression dans une architecture de forme abstraite.

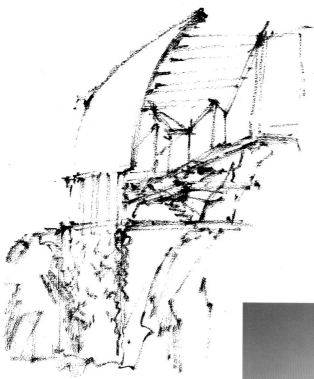

Pages 122/123: A drawing by Arata Isozaki, above, and the photographs to the right, show his concept of the seafront facade as a "mask," while the image below on this page shows the other side of the building, which he likens to a Japanese folding screen.

Seite 122/123: Diese Zeichnung Arata Isozakis und die Bilder rechts vermitteln sein Konzept von der zum Meer gewandten Fassade als »Maske«. Das Foto unten zeigt die andere Seite des Gebäudes, die Isozaki mit einem japanischen Wandschirm vergleicht.

Pages 122/123: Le dessin d'Arata Isozaki, ci-dessus, et les photographies, à droite, illustrent le concept de façade maritime en «masque». En dessous, l'autre façade du bâtiment, comparable à un paravent japonais.

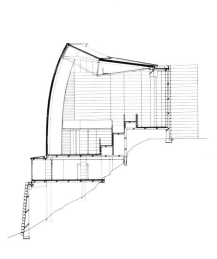

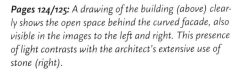

Pages 124/125: *A drawing of the building (above) clearly shows the open space behind the curved facade, also visible in the images to the left and right. This presence of light contrasts with the architect's extensive use of stone (right).*

Seite 124/125: *Auf dem Querschnitt des Gebäudes (oben) sowie auf den Bildern links und rechts erkennt man deutlich den offenen Raum hinter der gekrümmten Fassade. Dieser ständige Lichteinfall kontrastiert mit der massiven Verwendung von galizischem Stein (rechts).*

Pages 124/125: *Le dessin ci-dessus montre clairement l'espace ouvert derrière la façade en courbe également visible dans les photographies de droite et de gauche. Cette présence de lumière contraste avec l'usage intensif de la pierre (à droite).*

Arata Isozaki: Domus: La Casa Del Hombre, 1993–95 **125**

Toyo Ito

Toyo Ito is a leading representative of what some have called the post-Shinohara or post-Isozaki generation. Stylistically, he is undoubtedly linked more to the first figure than to the second. His work has always been characterized by an almost ethereal lightness, as evidenced in his Silver Hut residence (Tokyo, 1984), or even more dramatically in the Tower of the Winds (Yokohama, 1986), a 21 meter high aeration stack near the bus terminal of Yokohama Station, made of perforated aluminum and acrylic mirror plates. In works such as his Pao 2 Dwelling for Tokyo Nomad Woman, erected in Brussels in 1989, or his "Dreams" sequence for the 1991–92 "Visions of Japan" show at London's Victoria & Albert Museum, Ito has emphasized the necessity of finding a new type of design for an age of impermanence and electronics. Finely crafted and interesting spaces are a hallmark of this architect's work. Recent work includes his Elderly People's Home located in Yatsushiro (1992–94), and the fire station in the same southern city (1992–95).

Toyo Ito ist der führende Vertreter einer von manchen als »Post-Shinohara« oder »Post-Isozaki« bezeichneten Architektengeneration. Stilistisch steht er Shinohara jedoch bedeutend näher als Isozaki. Seine Bauten sind stets von einer fast ätherischen Leichtigkeit geprägt, wie seine Silver Hut Residence (Tokio, 1984) oder sein aufsehenerregender Tower of the Winds (Yokohama, 1986) dokumentieren. Bei letzterem Gebäude handelt es sich um einen 21 Meter hohen Lüftungsschacht aus perforierten Aluminium- und Acrylspiegelglasplatten in der Nähe des Busbahnhofs der Yokohama Station. In seinen Bauwerken wie dem Pao 2 Dwelling for Tokyo Nomad Woman (1989 in Brüssel errichtet) oder seiner »Dreams«-Sequenz für die Ausstellung »Visions of Japan« im Victoria & Albert Museum in London (1991–92) betonte Ito die Notwendigkeit, für ein Zeitalter der Vergänglichkeit und der Elektronik eine neue Art von Design zu entwickeln. Typisches Kennzeichen der Werke dieses Architekten sind seine hervorragend gestalteten, interessanten Räume. Zu den vor kurzem fertiggestellten Bauten zählen ein Altenheim in Yatsuhiro (1992–94) und die Feuerwehrwache in derselben Stadt (1992–95).

Toyo Ito est l'un des principaux représentants de ce que l'on a pu appeler la génération post-Shinohara, ou post-Isozaki. Stylistiquement, il est certainement davantage lié au premier qu'au second. Son œuvre s'est toujours caractérisée par une légèreté éthérée, comme dans sa résidence la «Hutte d'argent» (Tokyo, 1984), ou plus spectaculairement encore dans la Tour des vents (Yokohama, 1986), structure d'aération de 21 m de haut, en aluminium perforé, et panneaux de miroirs acryliques, près du terminal routier de la gare de Yokohama. Dans des réalisations comme son immeuble d'habitation Pao 2 pour Tokyo Nomad Woman (Bruxelles, 1989), ou sa séquence «Dreams» pour l'exposition «Visions du Japon» au Victoria & Albert Museum de Londres, Ito a mis l'accent sur la nécessité d'élaborer un nouveau type de conception pour l'âge de l'éphémère et de l'électronique. Des espaces intéressants et soigneusement traités sont l'une des marques de son œuvre. Parmi ses réalisations récentes: un foyer pour personnes âgées à Yatsushiro (1992–94), et la caserne des pompiers de la même ville (1992–95).

Shimosuwa Lake Suwa Museum, Shimosuwa-machi, Nagano, Japan, 1990–93.

Shimosuwa Lake Suwa Museum, Shimosuwa-machi, Nagano, Japan, 1990–93.

Le musée Shimosuwa du lac Suwa, Shimosuwa-machi, Nagano, Japon, 1990–93.

Shimosuwa Lake Suwa Museum
Shimosuwa-machi, Nagano, Japan, 1990–1993

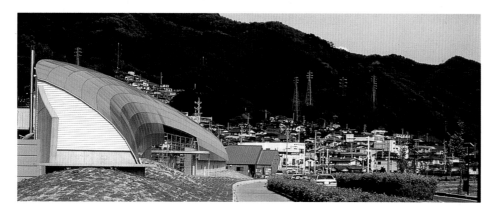

This museum was intended as a commemoration of the centennial of the incorporation of Shimosuwa, a small town in the center of Nagano Prefecture, located on the banks of a rather scenic lake. The museum houses two permanent collections, one related to the life of a local poet, Akahiko Shimaki (1876–1926), and the other more specifically based on the history and natural environment of Lake Suwa. The site is 200 meters long, but very narrow, and situated between a four-lane prefectural highway, and band including railroad tracks and another road. A curious figurative sculpture, with which the architect had nothing to do, greets visitors near the entrance to the museum, recalling that Lake Suwa was one of the first locations where ice skating was practiced in Japan. As is appropriate to both the site and the function of the building, Toyo Ito imagined his structure in the shape of an overturned boat, complete with an emerging concrete rudder at the rear. Despite the relatively literal nature of this reference, Ito has made the overall form sufficiently abstract for it to be quite spectacular. A sophisticated computer system derived from CAD was created to cut the aluminum panels that form the skin of the structure. The smoothness of this skin is one of the reasons that the pure esthetic effect sought by the architect succeeds brilliantly. A small cubic volume on the inner side houses special exhibition rooms, but the only clearly visible section is the aluminum curve of the main building.

Das Museum wurde anläßlich der Hundertjahrfeier der Eingemeindung Shimosuwas errichtet, einer kleinen, an einem malerischen See gelegenen Stadt inmitten der Präfektur Nagano. Das Museum beherbergt zwei ständige Sammlungen, von denen eine dem regional bekannten Dichter Akahiko Shimaki (1876–1926), und die andere der Geschichte und der natürlichen Umgebung des Suwa-Sees gewidmet ist. Das Gelände ist 200 Meter lang, sehr schmal und liegt zwischen einer vierspurigen Autobahn und dem Ufer, an dem eine Bahnlinie und eine weitere Straße entlangführten. Eine kuriose Skulptur am Eingang des Museums, für die der Architekt nicht verantwortlich zeichnet, erinnert daran, daß der Suwa-See zu den ersten Gewässern zählte, auf denen man in Japan Schlittschuh laufen konnte. Passend zum Gelände und zur Funktion entwarf Ito seine Konstruktion in Form eines umgedrehten Bootes, inklusive eines herausragenden Heckruders aus Beton. Trotz der recht offenkundigen Anspielung gelang es Ito, dem Museum eine ausreichend abstrakte Gesamtform zu verleihen, die das Bauwerk zu etwas Besonderem macht. Für die Anfertigung der Aluminiumplatten, die die Außenhaut der Konstruktion bilden, wurde ein spezielles, CAD-ähnliches Computersystem entwickelt. Gerade die glatte Oberfläche dieser Außenhaut ist einer der Gründe dafür, daß der vom Architekten angestrebte ästhetische Effekt seine Wirkung nicht verfehlt. Ein kleiner kubischer Baukörper auf der Innenseite bietet zusätzliche Ausstellungsräume, aber die Aluminiumkurvatur des Hauptgebäudes bildet den einzigen deutlich sichtbaren Teil der Konstruktion.

Ce musée a été construit pour commémorer l'érection en municipalité de Shimosuwa, petite ville du centre de la préfecture de Nagano, au bord d'un lac assez spectaculaire. Il abrite deux collections permanentes, l'une consacrée à la vie d'un poète local, Akahiko Shimaki (1876–1926), et l'autre à l'histoire et à l'environnement naturel du lac Suwa. Le terrain très étroit mesure 200 m de long, mais il est coincé entre une rocade à quatre voies, des voies de chemin de fer et une autre route. A l'entrée du musée, une curieuse sculpture figurative, non choisie par l'architecte, accueille les visiteurs. Elle rappelle que le Lac Suwa a été l'un des premiers endroits où l'on a pratiqué le patin à glace au Japon. Toyo Ito a imaginé une solution adaptée au site et à la fonction du bâtiment: une structure en forme de bateau renversé, y compris son gouvernail en béton. Si cette référence est un peu littérale, l'architecte l'a rendue suffisamment abstraite pour lui conférer un aspect spectaculaire. Un programme informatique sophistiqué a facilité la découpe des panneaux d'aluminium qui forment la peau de la structure. La douceur de ce revêtement explique en partie la perfection esthétique de l'effet. Un petit volume cubique a été conçu, côté intérieur, pour des expositions temporaires, mais la seule section clairement visible est la courbe d'aluminium du bâtiment principal.

Page 129 top: Although it does face Lake Suwa, the museum is separated from the water's edge by a four lane highway. Page 129 bottom: The entrance area demonstrates Ito's typical mastery of materials, dedicated to creating a sense of architectural lightness.

Seite 129 oben: Obwohl es dem Suwa-See zugewandt liegt, ist das Museum durch eine vierspurige Schnellstraße vom Ufer getrennt. Seite 129 unten: Der Eingangsbereich dokumentiert Itos meisterhaften Umgang mit den Baumaterialien, der dem Betrachter ein Gefühl architektonischer Leichtigkeit vermittelt.

Page 129 en haut: Edifié face au lac Suwa, le musée est séparé de ses rives par une route à quatre voies. Page 129 en bas: La zone d'entrée montre une maîtrise des matériaux typique d'Ito, qui sait créer ce sens de légèreté architecturale.

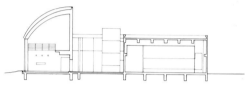

Pages 130/131: *Although the image of an overturned boat comes first to mind, the curvature of the museum, as seen in the plan below, also resembles a fish, in particular because of the silvery aluminum cladding. The egg-like form seen in the plan below corresponds to the entrance canopy (left).*

Seite 130/131: *Obwohl sich sofort der Eindruck eines umgedrehten Bootes aufdrängt, erinnert die Kurvatur des Museums (siehe Grundriß unten), insbesondere aufgrund der silbrigen Aluminiumverkleidung auch an einen Fisch. Die Eiform im Grundriß entspricht dem Vordach über dem Eingang (links).*

Pages 130/131: *Si la première image qui vienne à l'esprit est celle d'un bateau retourné, la courbe du musée et sa couverture en aluminium argenté, comme le montre le plan ci-dessous, fait également penser à un poisson. La forme en œuf sur le plan, correspond au dais de l'entrée (photo de gauche).*

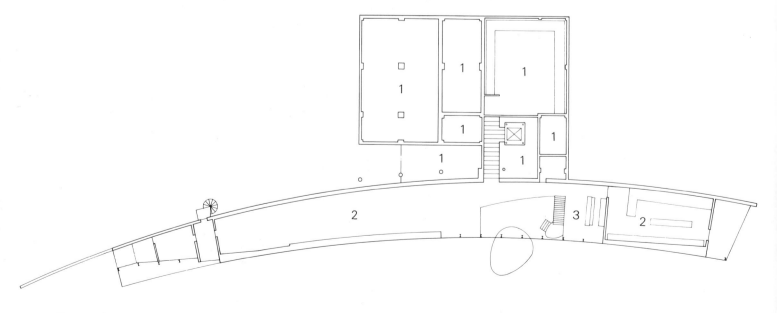

Fumihiko Maki

One of the most cosmopolitan of contemporary Japanese architects, Fumihiko Maki was born in 1928 in Tokyo. Having been educated at the University of Tokyo, the Cranbrook Academy of Art and the Harvard Graduate School of Design (M.Arch. 1954), he worked for Skidmore, Owings and Merrill in New York and Sert Jackson and Associates in Cambridge, Massachusetts before creating Maki and Associates in Tokyo in 1965. Winner of the 1993 Pritzker Prize, Fumihiko Maki is best known for buildings like his 1989 Tepia in the Minato-ku area of Tokyo or his 1984 Fujisawa Municipal Gymnasium in Kanagawa Prefecture. Often incorporating indirect references to traditional Japanese architecture in his work, Maki's recent projects vary between the elegant simplicity of his 1995 Church of Christ (Shibuya-ku, Tokyo) and the more spectacular forms of the Kirishima International Concert Hall (Makizono, Kagoshima, 1994). Current work includes the large Phase II extension of his own Nippon Convention Center Makuhari Messe (Chiba, Chiba), due to be completed in 1997.

Fumihiko Maki, einer der kosmopolitischsten Vertreter zeitgenössischer japanischer Architektur, wurde 1928 in Tokio geboren. Er studierte an der University of Tokyo sowie an der Cranbrook Academy of Art und der Harvard Graduate School of Design (Master of Architecture 1954). Danach war er für Skidmore, Owings & Merill in New York sowie für Sert Jackson & Associates in Cambridge, Massachusetts tätig, bevor er 1965 sein eigenes Büro Maki & Associates in Tokio gründete. Als Gewinner des Pritzker Preises 1993 erlangte Maki den größten Bekanntheitsgrad durch Gebäude wie das Tepia im Minato-ku-Viertel von Tokio (1989) oder das Fujisawa Municipal Gymnasium in der Präfektur Kanagawa. Während Fumihiko Makis frühere Bauten häufig indirekte Bezüge zur traditionellen japanischen Architektur aufweisen, schwanken seine jüngeren Projekte zwischen der eleganten Schlichtheit seiner 1995 fertiggestellten Church of Christ, (Shibuya-ku, Tokio) und der aufsehenerregenden Formensprache der Krishima International Concert Hall, Makizono, Kagoshima (1994). Zu seinen gegenwärtigen Projekten zählen u.a. Phase II des Erweiterungsbaus seines eigenen Nippon Convention Center Makuhari Messe (Chiba, Chiba), die 1997 fertiggestellt werden soll.

L'un des architectes japonais contemporains les plus cosmopolites, Fumihiko Maki, est né en 1928, à Tokyo. Après avoir fait ses études à l'Université de Tokyo, à la Cranbrook Academy of Art et à l'Harvard Graduate School of Design (Master en Architecture en 1954), il travaille pour Skidmore Owings and Merill à New York, et Sert Jackson & Associates à Cambridge Massachusetts, avant de fonder Maki and Associates à Tokyo en 1965. Lauréat du Prix Pritzker 1993, il est surtout connu pour des immeubles comme son Tepia pour Minato-ku, un quartier de Tokyo (1989), ou son gymnase municipal de Fujisawa (préfecture de Kanagawa). Incorporant souvent dans son œuvre des références à l'architecture traditionnelle nippone, ses projets récents oscillent entre l'élégante simplicité de son Eglise du Christ (Shibuya-ku, Tokyo, 1995) et les formes plus spectaculaires de la salle de concert internationale Kirishima (Makizono, Kagoshima, 1994). Il travaille actuellement à la vaste extension de Phase II du Centre de Congrès Nippon de Makuhari (Chiba, Chiba) qui devrait être achevé en 1997.

Center for the Arts, Yerba Buena Gardens,
San Francisco, California, United States, 1991–93.

Center for the Arts, Yerba Buena Gardens, San
Francisco, Kalifornien, 1991–93.

Yerba Buena Center, San Francisco, Californie,
Etats-Unis, 1991–93.

Center for the Arts, Yerba Buena Gardens

San Francisco, California, United States, 1991–1993

Fumihiko Maki's first building designed in the United States in more than thirty years, this Kunsthalle type structure is part of the 40 hectare Yerba Buena development zone, which was intended to give San Francisco a new cultural area near the downtown office towers. It is situated next to Mario Botta's new San Francisco Museum of Modern Art and to the Theater for the Arts designed by James Stewart Polshek. One very unusual feature of the 5,338 m² building is that it is not built on solid ground but rather on the top of the nearby Moscone Convention Center's underground extension. As the architect says, "Because of the limitations the underground Moscone Center imposed on the site, the Center for the Arts is forced literally to float within its dense urban context. The apparent weightlessness of this light, diaphanous metallic building also expresses the temporality and changeability inherent in the Center's contemporary art programs, consciously avoiding any suggestion of the monumentality we associate with conventional museums." It is obvious that the Yerba Buena Center is a far more successful and lighter building in every respect than the SFMoMA building. Indeed, it is unfortunate that in spite of their proximity, the elements of the Yerba Buena development zone were not designed with any particular urban concept or harmony.

Das Yerba Buena Center, eine kunsthallenähnliche Konstruktion und Fumihiko Makis erstes in den Vereinigten Staaten entworfenes Gebäude, ist Teil des 40 Hektar großen Yerba Buena-Sanierungsgebietes, das der Stadt San Francisco in der Nähe seines Geschäftsviertels ein neues kulturelles Zentrum schenken sollte. Makis Gebäude liegt neben Mario Bottas neuem San Francisco Museum of Modern Art und einem von dem New Yorker Architekten James Stewart Polshek erbauten Theater. Eine der ungewöhnlichsten Eigenschaften dieses 5338 m² großen Bauwerks ist die Tatsache, daß es nicht auf festem Boden errichtet wurde, sondern auf dem unterirdischen Erweiterungsbau des nahegelegenen Moscone Convention Center. Maki erklärte dazu: »Aufgrund der Beschränkungen, die das unterirdische Moscone Center dem Gelände auferlegt, ist das Yerba Buena Center buchstäblich gezwungen, innerhalb seiner dichtbebauten urbanen Umgebung zu schweben. Die scheinbare Schwerelosigkeit dieses leichten, transparentmetallischen Gebäudes bringt auch die Vergänglichkeit und Veränderlichkeit der vom Zentrum gezeigten zeitgenössischen Kunst zum Ausdruck. Dabei wurde bewußt auf jede Andeutung von Monumentalität verzichtet, wie wir sie mit herkömmlichen Museen verbinden.« Das Yerba Buena Center kann in jeder Hinsicht als erheblich gelungener und transparenter als das benachbarte SFMoMA bezeichnet werden. Und es ist sehr bedauerlich, daß die einzelnen Projekte des Yerba Buena-Sanierungsgebietes trotz ihrer unmittelbaren Nachbarschaft nicht Teil eines speziell für diesen Bezirk entwickelten Städtebauprogramms bilden.

Première réalisation de Fumihiko Maki aux Etats-Unis en plus de trente ans d'activité, ce centre d'exposition artistiques fait partie de la zone de rénovation de Yerba Buena, nouveau quartier culturel de San Francisco, non loin des tours de bureaux du centre ville. Il est situé juste à côté du nouveau Museum of Modern Art de San Francisco de Mario Botta, et d'un théâtre conçu par James Stewart Polshek. L'une des caractéristiques les plus curieuses de ce bâtiment de 5338 m² est de reposer non pas sur le sol, mais au dessus d'une extension souterraine du Centre de congrès Moscone tout proche. Comme le précise l'architecte: «Du fait des contraintes imposées par la partie souterraine du Moscone Center, le Center for the Arts était littéralement obligé de «flotter» dans ce contexte urbain très dense. Pour ce bâtiment métallique léger et diaphane l'absence apparente de masse exprime également les concepts de temps et de polyvalence inhérents à sa vocation d'expositions contemporaines. Cela évite consciemment toute suggestion de cette monumentalité que l'on associe d'habitude aux musées.» Il est clair que le Yerba Buena Center est plus réussi et plus léger, à tous égards, que le nouveau Musée d'Art moderne de San Francisco. D'ailleurs, il est dommage que, malgré leur proximité, les divers éléments de ce quartier de Yerba Buena n'aient pas été conçus plus harmonieusement, ou selon un projet urbanistique plus cohérent.

Located near Mario Botta's recent San Francisco Museum of Modern Art building, visible on the plan and aerial photo below, Fumihiko Maki's Yerba Buena Center is characterized by light, flexible spaces. **Top right:** The entrance foyer. **Bottom right:** The forum exhibition area.

Fumihiko Makis Yerba Buena Center, das unmittelbar neben Mario Bottas neuem Museum of Modern Art liegt (siehe Plan und Luftaufnahme unten), wird gekennzeichnet durch seine hellen, flexiblen Räume. **Rechts oben:** Die Eingangshalle. **Rechts unten:** Die Ausstellungshalle.

Situé non loin du récent Museum of Modern Art de San Francisco construit par Mario Botta, visible sur le plan et la photo aérienne (ci-dessous), le Yerba Buena Center de Fumihiko Maki se caractérise par des espaces souples et aériens. **A droite en haut:** Le foyer d'entrée. **A droite en bas:** Le forum d'exposition.

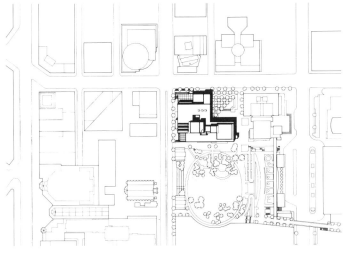

Fumihiko Maki: Center for the Arts, Yerba Buena Gardens, 1991–93 **135**

Fumihiko Maki's original drawings for the building stressed its resemblance to a ship, floating on the underground spaces of the Moscone Convention Center. In this image, Botta's museum appears to the right.

Fumihiko Makis Originalzeichnungen für sein Bauwerk betonen dessen Ähnlichkeit mit einem Schiff, das auf den unterirdischen Räumen des Moscone Convention Center treibt. Auf diesem Bild ist auf der rechten Seite Mario Bottas Museum zu erkennen.

Le projet original de Fumihiko Maki accentue la ressemblance avec un bateau, qui flotterait au dessus des espaces souterrains du Moscone Convention Center. A droite, le musée de Mario Botta.

Kirishima Concert Hall
Aira, Kagoshima, Japan, 1993–1994

Set on a 4.8 hectare site in a range of volcanic mountains on the island of Kyushu, the Kirishima Concert Hall is a 4,904 m² facility that is intended as the basis for a future cultural park in Kirishima, which each year hosts an internationally recognized music festival. An outdoor amphitheater with seating for 4,000 spectators is one feature of this complex, which is centered on the main concert hall, seating 770. Devoted to classical music, the hall, with its warm texture due to the use of Canadian maple, is best suited to chamber music, and is configured in a "transformed shoebox" shape. Also included are practice and rehearsal rooms. As the architect says, the roof of the Kirishima Concert Hall does form a distinctive silhouette, "but dispenses as much as possible with the massive quality typical of concert halls." The shape of this roof does bring to mind an abstract version of the neighboring mountains, but it also recalls the dynamic forms of the roofs of Maki's Fujisawa and Tokyo gymnasiums. Through a close link to nature in this instance, and perhaps more specifically to other shapes like the helmets of samurai warriors in the case of the sports facilities, Fumihiko Maki creates a truly modern building, which nonetheless has a timeless quality to it.

Die 4904 m² große Kirishima Concert Hall liegt auf einem 4,8 Hektar großen Gelände inmitten einer vulkanischen Gebirgskette auf der Insel Kyushu. Sie wurde als Grundstein eines zukünftigen Kulturparks der Stadt Kirishima geplant, die jedes Jahr ein international bekanntes Musikfestival veranstaltet. Eine Freilichtbühne mit 4000 Sitzplätzen ist nur ein Teil dieses Gebäudekomplexes, dessen Zentrum die Hauptkonzerthalle mit 770 Sitzplätzen bildet. Die der klassischen Musik gewidmete Konzerthalle mit ihrer warmen Ausstrahlung – die sie der Verwendung von kanadischem Ahornholz verdankt – eignet sich am besten für Kammermusik und zeichnet sich durch ihre »abgewandelte Schuhkartonform« aus. Darüber hinaus verfügt das Bauwerk über diverse Probe- und Übungsräume. Maki erklärte, daß das Dach der Kirishima Concert Hall eine charakteristische Silhouette besitzt, das Gebäude aber »weitestgehend auf das typisch massive Erscheinungsbild der meisten Konzerthallen verzichtet.« Die Gestalt des Dachs erinnert an eine abstrakte Version der benachbarten Berge, aber sie verweist auch auf die dynamischen Dachformen von Makis Sportstadien in Fujisawa und Tokio. Durch die enge Verknüpfung mit der Natur und insbesondere durch die Verwendung eigenwilliger Formen – wie etwa die Helme von Samuraikämpfern bei den Sporteinrichtungen – schuf Fumihiko Maki ein durch und durch modernes Gebäude von zeitloser Schönheit.

Implanté sur 4,8 hectares, au cœur d'une chaîne de montagnes volcaniques sur l'île de Kyushu, la salle de concert de Kirishima (4904 m²) se veut la base du futur parc culturel de Kirishima, ville qui chaque année accueille un festival musical de renommée internationale. Un amphithéâtre extérieur, prévu pour 4000 spectateurs, est l'une des installations les plus caractéristiques de cet ensemble centré autour de la salle de concert principal prévue pour 770 spectateurs. Consacrée à la musique classique, chaleureuse grâce à l'utilisation d'érable du Canada, la salle, de configuration traditionnelle, est surtout adaptée à la musique de chambre. L'ensemble comprend également des salles d'étude et de répétitions. Selon l'architecte, la silhouette originale du toit «s'éloigne autant que possible de la massivité habituelle des salles de concert.» Sa forme évoque abstraitement les montagnes avoisinantes, ou celle des toits des salles de sport conçues par Maki pour Fujisawa ou Tokyo. Par cette proximité avec la nature, et peut-être plus fortement encore que dans ses autres réalisations aux évocations de casques de samouraïs, Fumihiko Maki a créé ici un bâtiment authentiquement moderne, qui n'en possède pas moins une qualité intemporelle.

Kirishima Concert Hall, Aira, Kagoshima, Japan, 1993–94.

Kirishima Concert Hall, Aira, Kagoshima, Japan, 1993–94.

Salle de concert de Kirishima, Aira, Kagoshima, Japon, 1993–94.

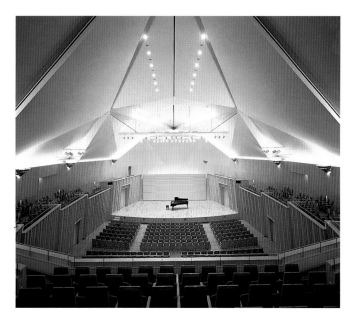

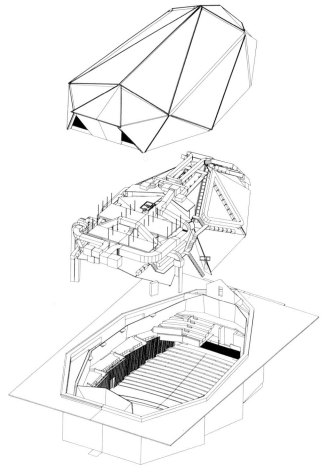

The spectacular roof of the Kirishima Concert Hall is
its most visible feature, covering the main concert hall.
As in some of the sports facilities designed by Maki,
the roof can be read as a metaphorical shell, but it also
brings to mind the form of neighboring mountains.

Das aufsehenerregende Dach der Kirishima Concert
Hall über der großen Konzerthalle. Wie bei einigen von
Makis Sportstätten kann auch dieses Dach als meta-
phorische Muschel gesehen werden; allerdings erinnert
es ebenso an die Formen der benachbarten Berge.

Le toit de l'auditorium de Kirishima est la caractéristique la plus forte de la salle principale. Comme dans
certains équipements de sport conçus par Maki, il peut
être assimilé à une coque métaphorique. Il évoque
également les montagnes des environs.

140 Fumihiko Maki: Kirishima Concert Hall, 1993–94

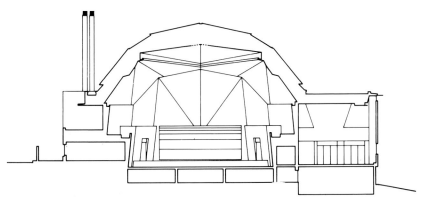

Pages 142/143: *Interior views and sections show the relatively simple nature of the structure, focused on the main concert hall. Maki's use of natural light makes the transition to the artificial lighting of the hall's interior as seen in this view of the ascent to the foyer from the entry hall.*

Seite 142/143: *Innenansichten und Querschnitte dokumentieren den relativ einfachen Aufbau der Konstruktion, der in der großen Konzerthalle seinen Höhepunkt findet. Wie in dieser Ansicht des Anstiegs von der Eingangshalle zum Foyer zu erkennen, schafft Maki durch die Verwendung von natürlichem Licht einen Übergang zur künstlichen Beleuchtung des Halleninneren.*

Pages 142/143: *Vues intérieures et coupes montrant la conception relativement simple du bâtiment, centrée sur la salle principale. La vue de la montée du foyer vers le hall d'entrée illustre la façon dont la lumière naturelle fait transition avec l'éclairage artificel, depuis l'intérieur du hall.*

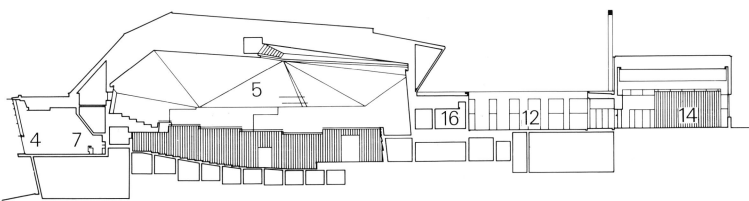

Fumihiko Maki: Kirishima Concert Hall, 1993–94 **143**

Isar Büro Park

Munich, Germany, 1993–1995

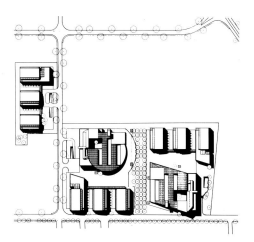

Fumihiko Maki's first built project in Europe, this office park, designed as a result of an international competition, is located in the Hallbergmoos area near Munich's new international airport. Completed in May 1995, the five-story, eleven building complex has a total floor area of 68,366 m². Two types of offices are offered, depending on whether the clients seek a large space or a small one. In the case of the large ones, the structures are designed around a central atrium intended to give employees a sense of unity, while the offices for smaller clients have more readily dividable units. Taking advantage of neighboring forest and meadow land, the complex offers various footpaths between the offices or the nearby town. Once again, the architect succeeds in creating very contemporary forms, which are not aggressive, but rather harmoniously related to the surrounding site. Maki has been involved in three projects in Germany over the past seven years: this low-rise office complex in Hallbergmoos; the Frankfurt Main Center (FMC), an enormous (300,000 m²) redevelopment project on a site once occupied by a yard for freight trains; and the Düsseldorf Buro Center Grafenberger Allee (BGA). In each case, the current economic slowdown in Germany has had a delaying effect on these projects.

Page 145: A view of Haus 1 as seen from Haus 5. One of the great strengths of Fumihiko Maki is his ability to make spectacular modern forms that are also highly functional and well designed.

Seite 145: Ein Blick auf Haus 1, von Haus 5 aus gesehen. Eine der Stärken Fumihiko Makis ist seine Fähigkeit, aufsehenerregende moderne Formen zu schaffen, die zugleich gut durchdacht und hochgradig funktionell sind.

Page 145: Vue de Haus 1, prise de Haus 5. L'une des grandes forces de Fumihiko Maki est sa capacité à imaginer des formes modernes spectaculaires qui n'en sont pas moins hautement fonctionnelles et parfaitement conçues.

Dieser Bürokomplex ist Fumihiko Makis erstes europäisches Projekt und das Ergebnis eines internationalen Wettbewerbs. Das im Münchener Hallbergmoos in der Nähe des neuen Flughafens gelegene Bauwerk wurde im Mai 1995 fertiggestellt und umfaßt elf fünfgeschossige Gebäude mit einer Gesamtfläche von 68 366 m². Zur Wahl stehen zwei verschiedene Bürotypen, je nachdem, ob der Kunde große oder eher kleine Geschäftsräume sucht. Die großen Büroräume erstrecken sich rund um ein zentrales Atrium, das den Angestellten das Gefühl von Gemeinsamkeit vermitteln soll, während die kleineren Räumlichkeiten sich durch leicht unterteilbare Büroelemente auszeichnen. Der Komplex bietet verschiedene Fußwege zwischen den Bürogebäuden und der nahelegenen Stadt an, die von der Nähe zur angrenzenden Wald- und Wiesenlandschaft profitieren. Wieder einmal gelang es dem Architekten, ein sehr zeitgenössisches Bauwerk zu entwerfen, das sich nicht aggressiv, sondern sehr harmonisch in die umliegende Landschaft einfügt. In den vergangenen sieben Jahren war Maki an drei Projekten in Deutschland beteiligt: dem hier beschriebenen Bürokomplex in Hallbergmoos; dem Frankfurt Main Center (FMC), einem gewaltigen (300 000 m²) Sanierungsprojekt auf dem ehemaligen Gelände eines Güterbahnhofs, und dem Bürocenter Grafenberger Allee (BGA) in Düsseldorf. In allen drei Fällen bewirkte die gegenwärtige Rezession in Deutschland eine deutliche Verzögerung der Arbeiten.

Premier projet réalisé en Europe par Fumihiko Maki, cet ensemble de bureaux, construit à l'issue d'un concours international, est situé dans le quartier de Halbergmoos, près du nouvel aéroport international de Munich. Achevé en mai 1995, cet ensemble de onze immeubles de cinq niveaux représente une surface totale de planchers de 68 366 m². Les bureaux sont de deux tailles différentes, selon les besoins des clients. Les grands bureaux sont organisés autour d'un atrium central conçu pour donner à leurs utilisateurs un sentiment d'unité, tandis que les petits sont plus facilement divisibles. A la limite des bois et des champs, ce complexe propose différents cheminements piétonniers entre les bureaux et la ville proche. Là encore, l'architecte a réussi à créer des formes très contemporaines qui ne sont pas pour autant agressives, mais harmonisées à leur environnement. Maki a réalisé trois projets en Allemagne au cours des sept dernières années: cet ensemble de bureaux d'Halbergmoos, le Frankfurt Main Center (FMC), énorme projet de restructuration sur un site jadis occupé par un gare de marchandises, et le Düsseldorf Büro Center Grafenberger Allee (BGA). Dans chacun de ces cas, la récession que connaît actuellement l'économie allemande a ralenti ces projets.

146 Fumihiko Maki: Isar Büro Park, 1993–95

Page 146: An elevation of the complex, and above a view of Haus 5. **Page 147 top:** A distant view shows the surrounding meadows. **Page 147 center:** The semien-closed courtyard give a campus-like quality according to the architect. **Page 147 bottom:** The stair hall in Haus 5.

Seite 146: Ein Aufriß des Komplexes und eine Ansicht von Haus 5. **Seite 147 oben:** Eine Gesamtansicht zeigt den Komplex inmitten der Landschaft. **Seite 147 Mitte:** Laut Architekt erinnert der teilweise umschlossene Innenhof an einen Universitätscampus. **Seite 147 unten:** Das Treppenhaus von Haus 5.

Page 146: Elévation de l'ensemble, et au dessus, vue de Haus 5. **Page 147 en haut:** Vue à distance avec les champs environnants. **Page 147 centre:** La cour semi-entourée crée une sorte d'atmosphère de campus. **Page 147 en bas:** La cage d'escalier-atrium de Haus 5.

Kazuyo Sejima

One of the most outstanding representatives of a new generation of Japanese architects who seem most interested in going beyond the conquests of early Modernism toward a kind of neo-Modernism, Kazuyo Sejima, born in 1956, worked for several years in the office of Toyo Ito before establishing her own practice in Tokyo in 1987. Like other young Japanese architects, her main achievements have come after the end of the so-called "Bubble" economy of the 1980s, imposing a bit more sobriety of style than might be the case with older designers. Although she still works out of very cramped offices, Sejima has obtained international recognition for buildings such as the Saishunkan Seiyaku Women's Dormitory in Kumamoto (1990–91), which was featured on the cover of the catalogue of the 1995 "Light Construction" exhibition organized by Terry Riley at New York's Museum of Modern Art. Kazuyo Sejima maintains that it is now no more difficult to be an architect as a woman in Japan than it is for a man.

Kazuyo Sejima gehört zu den herausragendsten Vertreterinnen einer neuen Generation japanischer Architekten, die sehr daran interessiert scheinen, die Errungenschaften der frühen Moderne hinter sich zu lassen und eine Art Neo-Moderne anzustreben. Sejima wurde 1956 geboren und arbeitete nahezu zehn Jahre im Büro von Toyo Ito, bevor sie 1987 ihr eigenes Büro in Tokio eröffnete. Wie viele junge japanische Architekten erzielte sie ihre größten Erfolge nach dem Ende der sogenannten »Seifenblasenökonomie« der 80er Jahre, das die junge Architektengeneration zu einem Stil nötigte, der häufig nüchterner wirkte als der der älteren Architektengeneration. Obwohl sie nach wie vor unter sehr beengten Verhältnissen arbeitet, erwarb Sejima internationales Ansehen für ihre Gebäude wie etwa das Saishunkan Seiyaku-Wohnheim in Kumamoto (1990–91), welches das Titelblatt des Ausstellungskatalogs »Light Construction« zierte – eine Ausstellung, die Terry Riley 1995 im New Yorker Museum of Modern Art organisierte. Kazuyo Sejima vertritt die Ansicht, daß es in Japan für eine Frau heutzutage nicht schwieriger ist, als Architekt zu arbeiten als für einen Mann.

L'une des plus brillantes représentantes de cette nouvelle génération d'architectes japonais qui s'intéressent à l'exploration des conquêtes du modernisme dans une approche néomoderniste, Kazuyo Sejima, née en 1956, a travaillé pendant presque dix ans dans l'agence de Toyo Ito, avant de créer son propre cabinet à Tokyo en 1987. Comme d'autres jeunes architectes japonaises, ses principales réussites sont postérieures à «l'économie de la bulle» des années 80, d'où une plus grande sobriété de style que chez ses aînés. Travaillant toujours dans sa petite agence encombrée, elle s'est fait reconnaître au niveau international grâce à des réalisations comme le Foyer pour femmes de Saishunkan Seiyaku à Kumamoto (1990–91), représenté sur la couverture du catalogue de l'exposition «Light Construction» organisée par Terry Riley au Museum of Modern Art de New York. Kazuyo Sejima pense qu'il n'est pas plus difficile pour une femme, d'exercer la profession d'architecte aujourd'hui au Japon, qu'à un homme.

Pachinko Parlor III, Hitachi, Ibaraki, Japan, 1995.
Pachinko Parlor III, Hitachi, Ibaraki, Japan, 1995.
Club de Pachinko III, Hitachi, Ibaraki, Japon, 1995.

Saishunkan Seiyaku Dormitory
Kumamoto, Kumamoto, Japan, 1990–1991

This is a 1,254 m² two-story dormitory for employees of a local business, the Saishunkan Company. Approximately eighty women are intended to live here during the first year of their employment. An emphasis was placed on communal living, with a large open, central space and twenty rooms for four persons each. The large living space is constituted by reinforced concrete slabs standing on round steel posts. Five towers rising from the bottom level, containing toilets, air-conditioning and ventilation equipment as well as plumbing, bear the horizontal loads of the structure, particularly in the case of an earthquake. According to Terry Riley, curator of the Museum of Modern Art's "Light Construction" show in which this project was included, "Sejima's division of the program into minimal private areas and larger communal ones is a typically Japanese use of space, emphasizing group identity and socialization. Her dormitory is also a contemporary expression of a traditional Japanese type, the soudou of the Zen monastery, in which the student's personal space is peripheral to a larger communal space."

Dieses 1254 m² große, zweigeschossige Wohnheim ist für die Angestellten eines örtlichen Unternehmens, der Saishunkan Company, gedacht. Etwa 80 Frauen sollen hier während des ersten Jahres ihrer Anstellung wohnen. Besonderer Wert wurde auf gemeinschaftliches Wohnen mit einem großen, zentralen Wohnraum und 20 Vierbettzimmern gelegt. Der große Wohnraum ist aus Stahlbetonplatten gefertigt, die auf runden Stahlpfosten ruhen. Fünf Türme enthalten Toiletten, Klimaanlage, Lüftungsschächte und Installationssysteme und bilden die horizontalen, lasttragenden Elemente des Bauwerks, insbesondere für den Fall eines Erdbebens. Terry Riley, der Leiter der Ausstellung »Light Construction« im New Yorker Museum of Modern Art, an der auch dieses Projekt teilnahm, erklärte: »Bei Sejimas Unterteilung des Gebäudes in minimale Privaträume und große Gemeinschaftsräume handelt es sich um eine typisch japanische Einstellung zum Raum, bei der Gruppenzugehörigkeit und soziale Kontakte im Vordergrund stehen. Darüber hinaus ist ihr Wohnheim eine zeitgenössische Ausdrucksform eines traditionellen japanischen Baustils, dem soudou der Zenklöster, in denen der den Mönchen privat zur Verfügung stehende Raum den großen Gemeinschaftsräumen untergeordnet ist.«

Ce foyer de deux niveaux et de 1254 m² est destiné aux employées d'une usine locale, la société Saishunkan. 80 femmes environ passent ici la première année de leur contrat. L'accent a été mis sur la vie communautaire, avec un vaste espace central ouvert, et 20 chambres de quatre personnes chacune. Le grand espace réservé à la vie en commun est en dalles de béton armé dressées sur des piliers cylindriques en acier. Cinq tours partent du niveau inférieur et contiennent les sanitaires, les installations d'air conditionné et de ventilation, la plomberie, et supportent les charges horizontales, disposition prévue pour atténuer les effets des tremblements de terre. Selon Terry Riley, commissaire de l'exposition du Museum of Modern Art de New York «Light Construction», dans laquelle figurait cette réalisation: «La répartition de l'espace en zones privées de dimensions réduites et d'espaces communs vastes est typiquement japonaise. Elle met l'accent sur l'identité de groupe et la socialisation.» Ce foyer est également l'expression contemporaine d'un type japonais traditionnel, le soudou des monastères Zen, dans lequel l'espace personnel des étudiants est périphérique à un vaste espace communautaire.»

Pages 150/151: Altering between opaque and translucent surfaces, Kazuyo Sejima gives this dormitory a facade that is very much in the current "neo-modern" style very popular amongst younger Japanese architects.

Seite 150/151: Durch den Wechsel zwischen opaken und transparenten Oberflächen verleiht Kazuyo Sejima diesem Wohnheim eine Fassade, die sehr stark dem unter jüngeren japanischen Architekten so beliebten »neomodernen« Baustil entspricht.

Pages 150/151: En alternant les surfaces opaques et transparentes, Kazuyo Sejima donne à ce foyer une façade de ce style «néomoderne» si populaire parmi la nouvelle génération d'architectes japonais.

Pages 152/153: *Plans and interior views emphasize the importance of the communal space, as opposed to the living quarters, which are aligned in two strips. Though the overall color scheme is muted, occasional touches of blue, yellow or red offer an artistic counterpoint.*

Seite 152/153: *Aufrisse und Innenansichten betonen die Bedeutung der Gemeinschaftsräume im Vergleich zu den Privaträumen, die in zwei langen Reihen angeordnet sind. Obwohl das allgemeine Farbschema gedämpft wirkt, setzen gelegentliche blaue, rote und gelbe Farbflächen einen künstlerischen Kontrapunkt.*

Pages 152/153: *Les plans et les vues intérieures mettent l'accent sur l'importance de l'espace communautaire, par rapport aux chambres alignées sur deux rangées. Si la coloration générale est estompée, des touches occasionnelles de bleu, jaune ou rouge apportent un contrepoint artistique.*

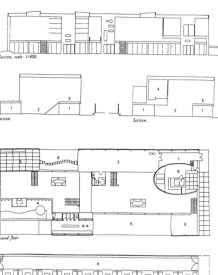

Section, scale: 1/400.

Section.

Section.

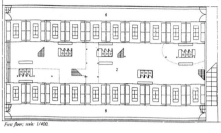

Second floor.

First floor; scale: 1/400.

Pachinko Parlor III

Hitachi, Ibaraki, Japan, 1995

This 800 m² project was built for the same client as two earlier pachinko parlors by Sejima. It is located on a 4,042 m² highway side lot. Although the basic plan is rectangular to accommodate the rows of pachinko machines, the structure is curved slightly to echo the curvature of the nearby road. Pachinko parlors with their garish neon signs are a typical fixture of the Japanese urban or even rural environment. It may be surprising that an architect as talented as Kazuyo Sejima would participate in a competition to build such structures, as she did in the case of her first project with this client. She says quite simply that she did so because she "didn't have much other work." When asked how she approached the already quite affirmed architectural vocabulary of this building type, she replies, "The usual signal for a pachinko parlor is bright neon lights. I tried to respect that aspect as much as possible at the same time as I transformed it. I tried to make the symbols more abstract." Perhaps unintentionally in this instance, because it is the nature of the client that requires it, Kazuyo Sejima is delving into the vocabulary of popular roadside architecture. While making it more "abstract," she is also enriching the range of her own creativity.

Pages 154/155: A very simple structure designed to meet the requirements of the rows of pachinko machines here takes on a modern perfection that is not fundamentally at odds with the nature of this roadside architecture.

Seite 154/155: Diese sehr simple Konstruktion, die entworfen wurde, um den Reihen von Pachinko-Maschinen genügend Platz zu bieten, zeigt einen hohen Grad moderner Perfektion, der dennoch nicht im Widerspruch zur Natur dieser Straßenarchitektur steht.

Pages 154/155: Cette construction très simple, dictée par l'organisation en rangées des machines de pachinko, atteint ici à une perfection moderne qui n'est pas fondamentalement opposée à la nature de cette architecture de bord de route.

Dieses 800 m² große Projekt, das sich auf einem 4042 m² großen Gelände neben einer Schnellstraße befindet, errichtete Sejima für den gleichen Auftraggeber wie ihre beiden früheren Pachinko-Spielhallen. Obwohl das Bauwerk im Grunde einen rechteckigen Grundriß besitzt, um die Reihen von Pachinkogeräten aufstellen zu können, verfügt es über eine leichte Krümmung, die die Kurvatur der nahegelegenen Straße aufnimmt. Pachinko-Spielhallen mit ihren grellen Neonlichtern sind nicht nur ein typisches Kennzeichen japanischer Stadtlandschaften, sondern auch der ländlichen Gegenden. Es mag verwundern, daß sich eine solch talentierte Architektin wie Kazuyo Sejima an einer Ausschreibung für derartige Baulichkeiten beteiligt – wie sie es bei ihrem ersten Projekt für diesen Auftraggeber tat. Dazu erklärt sie einfach, daß sie an der Ausschreibung teilnahm, weil sie »nicht viele Aufträge hatte«. Und auf die Frage, wie sie sich der relativ festgelegten Formensprache dieses Bautyps annäherte, antwortet sie: »Das übliche Kennzeichen einer Pachinko-Spielhalle sind grelle Neonlichter. Ich bemühte mich, diesen Aspekt weitestgehend zu respektieren und ihn gleichzeitig zu transformieren. Ich habe versucht, die Symbole und Zeichen abstrakter erscheinen zu lassen.« Wahrscheinlich unbewußt – denn die Natur des Auftrags erforderte es – griff Kazuyo Sejima in diesem Fall auf die Formensprache der verbreiteten Straßenarchitektur zurück, und während sie das Gebäude »abstrakter« erscheinen ließ, erweiterte sie gleichzeitig die Bandbreite ihrer eigenen Kreativität.

Ce projet de 800 m² a été édifié pour le même client que les deux clubs de pachinkos (i.e. des jeux électroniques, billards électriques, etc.) précédents conçus par Sejima. Il est situé sur un terrain de 4042 m² en bordure d'une route. Bien que le plan de base soit rectangulaire, pour faciliter l'installation des rangées de machines, la construction est en légère courbe, qui rappelle celle de la route avoisinante. Les clubs de pachinko, avec leurs enseignes au néon agressives sont typiques de l'environnement urbain et même rural japonais. Il peut sembler surprenant qu'une architecte aussi talentueuse que Kazuyo Sejima participe à un concours de ce genre, comme elle le fit lors du premier projet pour ce client. Elle explique très simplement qu'à l'époque «elle n'avait pas d'autre chantier.» Elle précise cependant son approche personnelle pour ce type de bâtiment: «L'enseigne classique des clubs de pachinko est le néon. J'ai essayé de respecter cet aspect, autant que possible, tout en le transformant, en essayant de rendre ce symbole plus abstrait.» Peut-être sans intention réelle dans ce cas précis, étroitement déterminé par les attentes du client, Kazujo Sejima explore le vocabulaire de l'architecture populaire des bords de route. Son travail pour le rendre plus «abstrait» a enrichi le spectre de sa propre créativité.

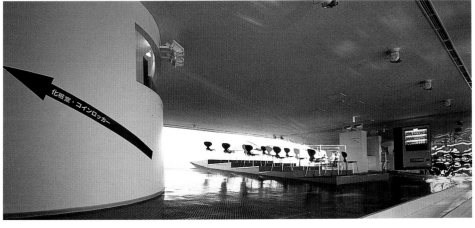

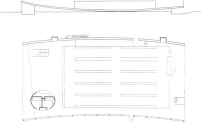

Pages 156/157: Although flashing neon lights are the hallmark of pachinko parlors all over Japan, Sejima has subverted them somewhat by making them a more subtle yet still integral part of the concept.

Seite 156/157: Obwohl in ganz Japan blinkende Neonlichter das typische Kennzeichen der Pachinko-Spielhallen sind, gelang es Sejima, sie zu transformieren und zu einem subtileren und dennoch integralen Teil ihres Gesamtkonzepts zu machen.

Pages 156/157: Les néons clignotant sont le signe d'identification des clubs de pachinko dans tout le Japon: Sejima a subtilement réussi à les intégrer dans son concept.

Kazuyo Sejima: Pachinko Parlor III, 1995 **157**

Shin Takamatsu

Born in 1948, Shin Takamatsu has been one of the most distinctive of contemporary Japanese architects, particularly well known for his anthropomorphic or mechanical imagery as expressed in such buildings as his masterful 1985–87 Kirin Plaza Osaka (Chuo, Osaka), or in the 1988–90 Syntax building (Sakyo-ku, Kyoto). Educated at Kyoto University, Takamatsu is still based in that city, where he set up his own practice in 1980. Many of his important structures, such as Origin I, II and III (Kamigyo, Kyoto, 1980–86) are located there. The powerful though somewhat eccentric designs of Takamatsu are naturally to be related to the speculative boom in private property in Japan in the 1980s. With the end of the so-called "Bubble Economy," Takamatsu has turned to a less overtly expressive style, as evidenced by the recent Kirin Headquarters (Chuo-ku, Tokyo, 1993–95), or the almost modernist Shoji Ueda Museum of Photography (Kishimoto-cho, Tottori, 1993–95). Though this change in style might be attributed to a maturation of the architect, it is also undoubtedly due to the change in the Japanese economy, where small private projects have become rare.

Der 1948 geborene Shin Takamatsu zählt zu den eigenwilligsten Vertretern moderner japanischer Architektur und ist insbesondere für seine anthropomorphe oder mechanische Formensprache bekannt, die sich in seinen Gebäuden wie dem Kirin Plaza Osaka (Chuo, Osaka, 1985–87) und dem Syntax Gebäude (Sakyo-ku, Kioto, 1988–90) zeigt. Nach seiner Ausbildung an der Kioto University blieb Takamatsu in dieser Stadt und gründete 1980 sein eigenes Architekturbüro. Hier in Kioto befinden sich auch zahlreiche seiner bedeutendsten Bauwerke, wie etwa Origin I, II und III (Kamigyo, Kioto, 1980–86). Seine kraftvollen, wenn auch etwas exzentrischen Entwürfe stehen in engem Zusammenhang mit dem Spekulationsboom im privaten Bausektor, den Japan während der 80er Jahre erlebte. Nach dem Ende der sogenannten »Seifenblasenökonomie« ging Takamatsu zu einem weniger expressiven Stil über, für den das vor kurzem fertiggestellte Kirin Headquarters (Chuo-ku, Tokio, 1993–95) und sein nahezu modernistisches Shoji Ueda Museum of Photography (Kishimoto-cho, Tottori, 1993–95) exemplarisch sind. Obwohl sein Stilwandel sicherlich mit der persönlichen Entwicklung des Architekten zusammenhing, spielten auch die Veränderungen in der japanischen Wirtschaft, aufgrund derer kleine Privatprojekte immer seltener wurden, eine wichtige Rolle.

Né en 1948, Shin Takamatsu a longtemps été l'un des architectes japonais les plus remarqués, en particulier pour son vocabulaire anthropomorphique ou mécaniste, exprimé dans des constructions comme le Kirin Plaza (Chuo, Osaka, 1985–87), ou l'immeuble Syntax (Sakyo-ku, Kyoto, 1988–90). Formé à l'Université de Kyoto, Takamatsu est demeuré dans cette ville, où il a fondé son agence en 1980, et édifié plusieurs de ses œuvres importantes comme Origin I, II, et III (Kamigyo, Kyoto, 1980–86). Ses projets puissants, assez excentriques, doivent beaucoup aux facilités offertes par la spéculation immobilière des années 80. Avec la fin de «l'économie de la bulle», Shin Takamatsu s'est tourné vers un style moins ouvertement provocant, comme le montre son récent siège social pour la brasserie Kirin (Chuo-ku, Tokyo, 1993–95), ou le presque moderniste Musée de la photographie Shoji Ueda (Kishimoto-cho, Tottori, 1993–95). Bien que cette évolution stylistique puisse être attribuée à sa maturité, elle correspond néanmoins à une situation économique nouvelle dans laquelle les petits projets privés se sont fait rares.

Kunibiki Messe, Matsue, Shimane, Japan, 1991–93.

Kunibiki Messe, Matsue, Shimane, Japan, 1991–93.

Kunibiki Messe, Matsue, Shimane, Japon, 1991–93.

Kunibiki Messe

Matsue, Shimane, Japan, 1991–1993

The word *kunibiki*, meaning "land-pulling," makes reference to one of the myths about the creation of Japan, in which the gods of Izumo are said to have brought many smaller islands together. This steel frame and reinforced concrete structure is divided into one basement, six stories and a one-story penthouse, with a total floor area of 15,916 m². Its facilities, intended as a stimulus for industrial activities in this prefecture, include an exposition hall with a capacity of 5,000 persons, multi-purpose halls for medium to small-scale events, an international conference hall and offices. The most spectacular space of the building is the 24 meter high public area on the third floor. Here cones of various sizes, including one housing a tea-ceremony room and covered with aluminum panels, recall some of the unusual forms for which Shin Takamatsu became famous in the 1980s, even if the rest of the building seems to have set aside his former vocabulary, based on extravagant machine-like forms, and to have taken on a much more "neo-modern" style.

Das Wort *kunibiki* bedeutet »das Zusammenziehen von Land« und bezieht sich auf eine der Sagen um die Entstehung Japans, derzufolge die Götter des Izumo-Stammes kleinere Inseln zu einer Landmasse zusammenfügten. Diese Stahlskelett- und Stahlbetonkonstruktion mit einer Gesamtfläche von 15 916 m² unterteilt sich in ein Untergeschoß, sechs Stockwerke sowie ein eingeschossiges Penthouse. Die als Stimulanz für die Wirtschaftsförderung dieser Präfektur geplante Einrichtung umfaßt eine Ausstellungshalle mit einer Kapazität von 5000 Besuchern, mehrere Mehrzweckhallen für mittlere bis kleine Veranstaltungen, einen internationalen Konferenzsaal sowie verschiedene Büroräume. Der beeindruckendste Raum des Gebäudes ist die 24 Meter hohe, öffentliche Halle im dritten Stock. Ihre diversen, mit Aluminiumpaneelen verkleideten Kegel in unterschiedlichen Größen, darunter einer, der Platz für eine traditionelle Teezeremonie bietet, erinnern an die ungewöhnlichen Formen, für die Shin Takamatsu während der 80er Jahre berühmt wurde – auch wenn der Rest des Gebäudes sich weit von seiner früheren Formensprache entfernt hat, die auf extravaganten maschinenartigen Formen beruhte und nun einem eher neo-modernen Stil gleicht.

Le terme de *kunibiki* signifie à peu près «travaux de terrassement» et fait référence à l'un des mythes de la création du Japon, selon lequel les dieux d'Izumo auraient réunis diverses petites îles. Cette construction à structure d'acier et béton armé se répartit en un sous-sol, six niveaux et une *penthouse*, pour une surface totale de 15 916 m². Elle comprend divers équipements de promotion des activités industrielle de cette préfecture: un hall d'exposition pouvant accueillir 5000 personnes, des halls polyvalents de taille moyenne ou petite, une salle de conférences internationales et des bureaux. La partie la plus spectaculaire est un espace public de 24 m de haut, situé au troisième étage. Des cônes de tailles diverses, recouverts de panneaux d'aluminium, dont l'un abrite un salon pour la cérémonie du thé, rappellent certaines des formes curieuses qui ont rendu Shin Takamatsu célèbre dans les années 80. Toute fois le reste du bâtiment ne relève pas de ce vocabulaire formel inspiré de machines imaginaires extravagantes, mais d'un style plus sagement néo-moderne.

Pages 160/161: As is usually the case, the very precise renderings of Shin Takamatsu correspond closely to his finished buildings. A shift toward a less mechanical vocabulary is seen in this structure, which includes essentially geometric forms.

Seite 160/161: Die präzisen Computergrafiken Shin Takamatsus entsprechen fast immer sehr genau den fertigen Gebäuden. In diesem Bauwerk, das im wesentlichen aus geometrischen Formen besteht, ist eine Veränderung hin zu einer weniger mechanischen Formensprache zu erkennen.

Pages 160/161: Comme souvent, le rendu des dessins de Shin Takamatsu correspond de très près à la construction finale. Ce bâtiment traduit un glissement d'un vocabulaire mécaniste vers des formes essentiellement géométriques.

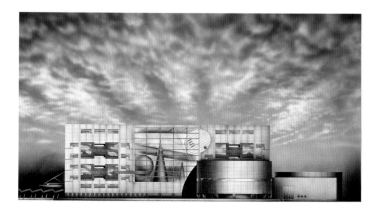

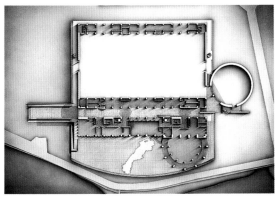

Pages 162/163: Within the 24 meter high central area,
a collection of cones, the largest of which encloses a tea
house, tubes and globes bring to mind an almost surre-
alist composition where scale no longer seems a perti-
nent concern.

Seite 162/163: Innerhalb der 24 Meter hohen Halle
befinden sich neben Röhren und Kugeln mehrere Kegel,
deren größter ein Teehaus beherbergt. Das Ganze
erinnert an eine surrealistische Komposition.

Pages 162/163: Dans la zone centrale de 24 m de haut,
un ensemble de cônes, de tubes et de sphères, crée une
composition presque surréaliste, qui échappe à toute
échelle rationnelle.

Shoei Yoh

Unlike many of his colleagues who prefer to work out of Tokyo, Shoei Yoh has remained in his native Fukuoka. This metropolis, located in Kyushu at the southern end of the Shinkansen train lines, has a reputation as an active commercial center, and a gateway to nearby Korea. After obtaining a degree in economics at Keio Gijuku University in Tokyo, Yoh studied Fine and Applied Arts at Wittenberg University in Springfield, Ohio. He created his firm, Shoei Yoh + Architects, in Fukuoka in 1970, specializing not only in architecture but also in industrial design. His background in design and interiors certainly had an influence on buildings like his 1980 Stainless-Steel House with Light Lattice (Nagasaki, Nagasaki), which shows a strongly neo-modernist flair as the post-modern period was drawing to a close. As he said about his own Glass House, "I started out with the precepts of modernism and ended up finding my Japanese roots in them." The same can be said in a different mode of his Oguni Dome (Oguni, Kumamoto, 1986). Here, the unusual wooden truss roof design may have presaged the bamboo lattice and concrete dome vault of his 1995 Uchino Community Center for Seniors & Children (Kaho, Fukuoka).

Im Gegensatz zu vielen seiner Kollegen, die gerne in Tokio leben und arbeiten, blieb Shoei Yoh seiner Heimat Fukuoka treu. Diese auf Kyushu gelegene Metropole am südlichen Ende der Shinkansen-Bahnlinie besitzt den Ruf eines aktiven Wirtschaftszentrums und gilt als Tor zum nahegelegenen Korea. Nachdem Yoh seinen Abschluß in Wirtschaftswissenschaft an der Keio Gijuku University in Tokio erhalten hatte, studierte er Freie und Angewandte Kunst an der Wittenberg University in Springfield, Ohio. 1970 gründete er sein eigenes Büro Shoei Yoh + Architects in Fukuoka, das sich nicht nur auf Architektur spezialisierte, sondern auch auf modernes Industriedesign. Seine Ausbildung als Designer und Innenarchitekt übte sicherlich großen Einfluß auf seine Gebäude aus, wie etwa das Stainless-Steel House with Light Lattice (Nagasaki, Nagasaki, 1980), das eine stark ausgeprägte neomoderne Ausstrahlung besitzt und zu einer Zeit entstand, als sich die Postmoderne gerade ihrem Ende zuneigte. Yoh urteilte über sein eigenes Glass House: »Ich begann mit den Regeln der Moderne und fand am Ende meine japanischen Wurzeln in ihnen.« Dies gilt ebenso – wenn auch in leicht abgewandelter Form – für seinen Oguni Dome (Oguni, Kumamoto, 1986), dessen ungewöhnliche Dachkonstruktion aus Holzbalken möglicherweise als Vorläufer des Bambusgitter-Betonkuppelgewölbes seines Uchino Community Center for Seniors & Children (Kaho, Fukuoka, 1995) diente.

A la différence de beaucoup de ses collègues qui préfèrent travailler à Tokyo, Shoei Yoh s'est installé dans sa ville natale de Fukuoka. Cette métropole de l'île de Kyushu, à l'extrémité de la ligne de chemin de fer du Shinkansen, est un centre commercial actif et la porte vers la Corée assez proche. Après avoir obtenu un diplôme de sciences économiques à l'Université Keio Gijuku de Tokyo, Yoh étudie les beaux arts et les arts appliqués à Wittenberg University de Springfield, Ohio. Il crée son agence, Shoei Yoh + Architects à Fujuoka en 1970, spécialisée à la fois en architecture et en design industriel. Sa formation en design et architecture intérieure a certainement influencé certaines de ses réalisations comme sa «Maison d'acier inoxydable en lattis léger» (Nagasaki, Nagasaki, 1980), marquée par une forte inspiration néomoderniste, à une époque de postmodernisme finissant. Au sujet de sa Maison de verre il a déclaré: «Je l'ai commencée avec les préceptes du modernisme en tête, et terminée en retrouvant mes racines japonaises.» On pourrait dire la même chose de son Dôme d'Oguni (Oguni, Kumamoto, 1986) dans lequel le curieux dessin du toit présage peut-être le lattis de bambou et les courbes du béton de son Foyer de personnes âgées et d'enfants (Kaho, Fukuoka, 1995).

Glass House, Itoshima, Fukuoka, Japan, 1984–91.

Glass House, Itoshima, Fukuoka, Japan, 1984–91.

Maison de verre, Itoshima, Fukuoka, Japon, 1984–91.

Glass House

Itoshima, Fukuoka, Japan, 1984–1991

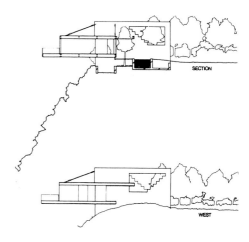

This house is almost literally suspended over a 140 meter drop in order to give it a 270° panoramic view of the Sea of Japan, looking toward the Korean Channel. As the architect says, "This Glass House between Sea and Sky isn't an ordinary house to dwell in but a sailing boat floating between sea and sky." Two 12 x 6 meter vertical concrete slabs are used to suspend 12 x 18 horizontal slabs staggered toward the sea to permit the house to project over the cliff side. Formerly part of a ranch, this spectacular site is located about 40 kilometers from the city of Fukuoka. There is a white marble terrace overlooking the sea on the north side of the building. The sheets of glass are joined together only by silicone despite the fact that the house must withstand very high winds. It might be said that this house represents the ultimate proof of a profound connection between the refined simplicity of traditional Japanese architecture and the equally unadorned geometric purity of the best modern architecture. This fundamental similarity may simply be due to the fact that the first modernists were inspired by Japan.

Dieses Haus hängt buchstäblich über einem 140 Meter hohen Abgrund und bietet einen 270°-Panoramablick über das japanische Meer und die Straße von Korea. Yoh erklärte dazu: »Das Glass House zwischen Himmel und Meer ist kein gewöhnliches Wohnhaus, sondern gleicht einem Segelboot, das zwischen Himmel und Meer schwebt.« Zwei 12 x 6 Meter große, verikale Betonplatten dienen zur Aufhängung von 12 x 18 Meter großen horizontalen, zum Meer hin gestaffelten Platten, die eine über das Kliff auskragende Lage des Hauses ermöglichen. Dieses ungewöhnliche, ehemals zu einer Farm gehörende Gelände liegt etwa 40 Kilometer außerhalb der Stadt Fukuoka. Eine weiße Marmorterrasse mit Blick auf das Meer schließt sich auf der Nordseite des Gebäudes an. Die Glasscheiben wurden ausschließlich mit Silikon verbunden – ungeachtet der Tatsache, daß das Haus heftigen Stürmen ausgesetzt ist. Man könnte sagen, daß dieses Haus den ultimativen Beweis einer profunden Verbindung zwischen der raffinierten Schlichtheit traditioneller japanischer Architektur und der gleichfalls klaren geometrischen Reinheit führender moderner Architektur darstellt. Diese fundamentale Übereinstimmung mag schlicht und einfach auf der Tatsache beruhen, daß sich die ersten Modernisten von Japan inspirieren ließen.

Cette maison, littéralement suspendue au dessus d'une falaise de 140 m de haut, offre une vue panoramique à 270° sur la mer du Japon, face au détroit de Corée. Comme le précise l'architecte: «Cette maison de verre n'est pas une maison ordinaire, mais plutôt un bateau voguant entre mer et ciel.» Deux dalles-murs verticales de béton de 12 x 6 m servent à suspendre des dalles horizontales de 12 x 18 m en surplomb au dessus de la mer qui permettent à la maison de se projeter au dessus de la falaise. Faisant naguère partie d'une exploitation agricole, ce site se trouve à 40 km de la ville de Fukuoka. Côté nord, une terrasse recouverte de marbre blanc donne sur la mer. Les panneaux de verre sont simplement rejointés aux silicones, bien que la maison doive résister à des vents très puissants. Elle est la preuve ultime d'un lien profonde entre la simplicité raffinée de l'architecture japonaise et la pureté géométrique, également sans ornement, du meilleur de l'architecture contemporaine. Cette similarité fondamentale est peut être due à ce que les premiers modernistes s'inspirèrent du Japon.

Pages 166–169: Glass furniture and polished marble floors, together with the uninterrupted glass surfaces, emphasize the feeling of continuity between sea, sky and architecture that Shoei Yoh sought in this simple design.

Seite 166–169: Glasmöbel und polierte Marmorböden sowie die ununterbrochenen Glasflächen unterstreichen das Gefühl der Kontinuität zwischen Meer, Himmel und Architektur, das Shoei Yoh mit diesem schlichten Entwurf zu erreichen suchte.

Pages 166–169: Des meubles de verre et des sols en marbre poli, ainsi que les surfaces de verre ininterrompues, accentuent le sentiment de continuité entre la mer, le ciel, et l'architecture, recherché par Shoei Yoh, dans ce projet tout de simplicité.

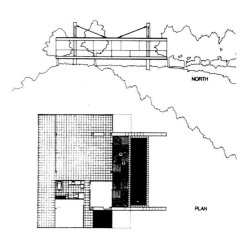

Biographies | Biographien

Tadao Ando Architect & Associates
5-23, Toyosaki 2-Chome, Kita-ku
Osaka 531, Japan

Tel: + 81 6 375 1148
Fax: + 81 6 374 6240

B2 Bokura Barbot
32, rue Pierre Sémard
75009 Paris, France

Tel: + 33 1 40 82 88 41
Fax: + 33 1 40 82 99 42

Tadao Ando

Born in Osaka in 1941, Tadao Ando was self-educated as an architect, largely through his travels in the United States, Europe and Africa (1962–69). He founded Tadao Ando Architect & Associates in Osaka in 1969. He has received the Alvar Aalto Medal, Finnish Association of Architects (1985); Medaille d'or, French Academy of Architecture (1989); the 1992 Carlsberg Prize; and the 1995 Pritzker Prize. He has taught at Yale (1987), Columbia (1988) and Harvard (1990). Notable buildings include: Rokko Housing, Kobe (1983–93); Church on the Water, Hokkaido (1988); Japan Pavilion Expo '92, Seville, Spain (1992); Forest of Tombs Museum, Kumamoto (1992); and the Suntory Museum, Osaka (1994). Current projects include new housing for Kobe and a large complex on the island of Awaji.

Tadao Ando wurde 1941 in Osaka geboren; seine Kenntnisse der Architektur eignete er sich als Autodidakt auf seinen ausgedehnten Reisen durch die Vereinigten Staaten, Europa und Afrika (1962–69) an. 1969 gründete er in Osaka sein Büro Tadao Ando Architect & Associates. 1985 erhielt Ando die Alvar Aalto Medaille der Finnischen Architektenvereinigung, 1989 die Medaille d'or der Französischen Akademie für Architektur, 1992 den Carlsberg Preis und 1995 den Pritzker Preis. Ando unterrichtete in Yale (1987), an der Columbia University (1988) und in Harvard (1990). Zu seinen bedeutendsten Bauten zählen: Rokko Wohnsiedlung, Kobe (1983–93); Church on the Water, Hokkaido (1988); der japanische Pavillon für die Expo '92 in Sevilla (1992); Forest of Tombs Museum, Kumamoto (1992); und das Suntory Museum, Osaka (1994). Zur Zeit beschäftigt er sich mit einem Wohnbauprojekt in Kobe und einem großen Komplex auf der Insel Awaji.

Né à Osaka en 1941, Tadao Ando est un architecte autodidacte, formé par ses voyages aux Etats-Unis, en Europe et en Afrique (1962–69). Il fonde Tadao Ando Architect & Associates à Osaka, en 1969. Il reçoit l'Alvar Aalto Medal de l'Association finnoise des architectes (1985); la médaille d'or de l'Académie française d'architecture (1989); le Prix Carlsberg (1992) et le prix Pritzker (1995). Il enseigne à Yale (1987), Columbia (1988) et Harvard (1990). Parmi ses œuvres les plus remarquables: l'immeuble de logements Rokko, Kobe (1983–93); l'Eglise sur l'eau, Hokkaido (1988); le pavillon japonais d'Expo '92 à Séville (1992); le Musée de la forêt des tombes, Kumamoto (1992); et le Musée Suntory, Osaka (1994). Il travaille actuellement à un nouveau projet d'immeuble de logements à Kobe, et à un important ensemble sur l'île d'Awaji.

Masakazu Bokura

Born in Tokyo in 1949, Masakazu Bokura received his degree in Architecture and Urbanism from Waseda University in Japan in 1976, and a second degree from the Ecole des Beaux-Arts, Paris (U.P. 6, 1979). He worked in the office of Michel Macary in Paris (1977–82). It was with M. Macary and then with I.M. Pei that he worked from 1982 to 1990 on the Grand Louvre project, before creating his own firm, Bokura & Associés, in 1990, and his current firm, B2 Bokura Barbot, in 1992. He teaches at the Ecole Spéciale d'Architecture (ESA) in Paris. Recent projects include an apartment for a Japanese fashion designer, Paris (1990), and a boutique for Jil Sander, Paris (1992). Current work includes the Consulat General of Japan (Strasbourg) and a new housing project in Kobe, Japan.

Masakazu Bokura wurde 1949 in Tokio geboren und erhielt 1976 seinen Abschluß in Architektur und Stadtplanung an der Waseda University sowie einen zweiten Abschluß an der Ecole des Beaux-Arts in Paris (U.P.6, 1979). Zwischen 1977 und 1982 war er für Macary in Paris tätig. Zusammenarbeit mit Macary und später mit I.M. Pei (1982–90) am Grand Louvre-Projekt, bevor er 1990 sein eigenes Büro Bokura & Associates und 1992 seine jetzige Firma B2 Bokura Barbot gründete. Masakazu Bokura lehrt an der Ecole Spéciale d'Architecture (ESA) in Paris. Zu seinen vor kurzem fertiggestellten Bauwerken gehören ein Appartement für einen japanischen Modedesigner, Paris (1990); und eine Boutique für Jil Sander, Paris (1992); zur Zeit beschäftigt er sich mit dem Bau des japanischen Generalkonsulats in Straßburg und einem neuen Wohnbauprojekt in Kobe (Japan).

Né à Tokyo en 1949, Masakazu Bokura est diplômé en architecture et urbanisme de l'Université japonaise Waseda en 1976, et de l'Ecole des Beaux-Arts de Paris, U.P.6 (1979). Il travaille dans l'agence de Michel Macary à Paris (1977–82). Avec M. Macary et I.M. Pei, il intervient sur le projet du Grand Louvre (1982–1990), avant de créer sa propre agence, Bokura & Associés en 1990, aujourd'hui B2 Bokura Barbot en 1992. Il enseigne à l'Ecole Spéciale d'Architecture (ESA) à Paris. Parmi ses récents projets, l'appartement parisien d'un créateur de mode japonais, Paris (1990); et une boutique pour Jil Sander, Paris (1992). Il travaille actuellement sur le consulat général du Japon à Strasbourg, et un projet d'immeuble d'habitation à Kobe, au Japon.

170 Biographies | Biographien

Atelier φ
Daikanyama Edge 5F, 28-10, Sarugaku-cho
Shibuya-ku
Tokyo 150, Japan

Tel: + 81 33 464 8670
Fax: + 81 33 464 8612

Itsuko Hasegawa, Architect
1-9-7 Yushima Bunkyo-ku
Tokyo 113, Japan

Tel: + 81 33 818 5470
Fax: + 81 33 818 2244

Arata Isozaki & Associates
Nogizaka Atelier
9-6-17 Akasaka, Minato-ku
Tokyo 107, Japan

Tel: + 81 33 405 1526
Fax: + 81 33 475 5265

Hiroshi Hara

Born in Kawasaki, Japan in 1936, Hiroshi Hara received his BA from the University of Tokyo (1959), his MA in 1961, and his Ph.D. from the same institution in 1964, before becoming an associate professor at the University's Faculty of Architecture. Though his first work dates from the early 1960s, he began his collaboration with Atelier φ in 1970. Notable structures include numerous private houses, such as his own residence, Hara House, Machida, Tokyo (1973–74). He participated in the 1982 International Competition for the Parc de la Villette, Paris, and built the Yamato International Building, Ota-ku, Tokyo (1985–86); the Iida City Museum, Iida, Nagano (1986–88); and the Sotetsu Culture Center, Yokohama, Kanagawa (1988–90). Recent work includes the Umeda Sky City (Kita-ku, Osaka 1988–93) and the Kyoto JR Station (Shimogyo, Kyoto, 1991–97).

Hara wurde 1936 in Kawasaki (Japan) geboren; er erhielt 1959 seinen Bachelor of Architecture an der University of Tokyo, 1961 seinen Master of Architecture und promovierte 1964, ebenfalls an der University of Tokyo. Anschließend war er als außerordentlicher Professor am gleichen Institut tätig. Obwohl seine ersten Bauten aus den frühen 60er Jahren stammen, begann er seine Zusammenarbeit mit dem Atelier φ erst 1970. Zu seinen bedeutendsten Bauwerken gehören zahlreiche Privathäuser – u.a. sein eigenes Domizil, Hara House, Machida, Tokio (1973–74). 1982 nahm er an der internationalen Ausschreibung für den Parc de la Villette in Paris teil; anschließend errichtete er das Yamato International Building, Ota-ku, Tokio (1985–86); das Iida City Museum, Iida, Nagano (1986–88); und das Sotetsu Culture Center in Yokohama, Kanagawa (1988–90). Zu seinen aktuellen Projekten zählen: Umeda Sky City, Kita-ku, Osaka (1988–93); und die Kyoto JR Station, Shimogyo, Kioto (1991–97).

Né à Kawasaki, Japon, en 1936, Hiroshi Hara a passé son BA en architecture à l'Université de Tokyo en 1959, son MA en 1961, et son doctorat en 1964, avant de devenir professeur associé de la faculté d'architecture. Ses premières œuvres datent du début des années 60, et il collabore avec l'Atelier φ en 1970. Il construit de nombreuses résidences privées dont sa propre maison, à Machida, Tokyo (1973–74). Il participe au concours international pour le Parc de la Villette en 1982; construit le Yamato International Building, Ota-ku, Tokyo (1985–86); le Musée municipal d'Iida, Iida, Nagano (1986–88); et le centre culturel Sotetsu, Yokohama, Kanagawa (1988–93). Parmi ses œuvres récentes, l'Umeda Sky City, Kita-ku, Osaka (1988–93); et la gare JR de Kyoto, Shimogyo, Kyoto (1991–97).

Itsuko Hasegawa

Itsuko Hasegawa was born in Shizuoka Prefecture in 1941. She graduated from Kanto Gakuin University in Yokohama in 1964. After working in the atelier of Kiyonori Kikutake (1964–69), she was a research student in the Department of Architecture of the Tokyo. Institute of Technology. She was subsequently an assistant of Kazuo Shinohara in the same school (1971–78) before creating Itsuko Hasegawa Atelier (1979) in Tokyo. Her built work includes houses in Nerima (1986); Kumamoto (1986); and Higashitamagawa (1987). In more recent years, she has built on a larger scale: Shonandai Cultural Center, Fujisawa, Kanagawa (1987–90); Oshima-machi Picture Book Museum, Imizu, Toyama (1992–94); and the Sumida Culture Factory, Sumida, Tokyo (1991–94). She was the runner up in the 1993 competition for the new Cardiff Bay Opera House.

Itsuko Hasegawa wurde 1941 in der Präfektur Shizuoka geboren und schloß 1964 ihr Studium an der Kanto Gakuin University in Yokohama ab. Nach ihrer Tätigkeit im Atelier von Kiyonori Kikutake (1964–69) arbeitete sie als wissenschaftliche Hilfskraft in der Abteilung für Architektur am Tokyo Institute of Technology. Im Anschluß daran war sie als Assistentin Kazuo Shinoharas am gleichen Institut tätig (1971–78) und gründete 1979 ihr eigenes Büro Itsuko Hasegawa Atelier. Zu ihren fertiggestellten Bauten zählen u.a. verschiedene Häuser in Nerima (1986), Kumamoto (1986) und Higashitamagawa (1987). In den letzten Jahren hat sie vermehrt in größerem Maßstab gearbeitet: Shonandai Cultural Center, Fujisawa, Kanagawa (1987–90); Oshima-machi Picture Book Museum, Imizu, Toyama (1992–94); und die Sumida Culture Factory, Sumida, Tokio (1991–94); Bei der Ausschreibung für das neue Cardiff Bay Opera House 1993 belegte sie den zweiten Platz.

Itsuko Hasegawa naît à Shizuoka, en 1941, et étudie à l'Université Kanto Gatuin de Yokohama. Après avoir travaillé dans l'atelier de Kiyonori Kikutake (1964–69), elle fait des recherches au département d'architecture de l'Institut de Technologie de Tokyo, puis devient assistante de Kazuo Shihonara (1971–78), avant de créer Itsuko Hasegawa Atelier à Tokyo, en 1979. Son œuvre construite comprend des maisons à Nerima (1986), Kumamoto (1987), et Higashitamagawa (1987). Elle s'est récemment lancée dans des réalisation plus importantes: le Centre culturel Shonandai, Fujisawa, Kanagawa (1987–91); le musée du livre d'images Oshima-machi, Imizu, Toyama (1992–94); et l'Atelier culturel Sumida, Sumida, Tokyo (1991–94). Elle été selectionnée pour le nouvel opéra de Cardiff.

Arata Isozaki

Born in Oita City on the Island of Kyushu in 1931, Arata Isozaki graduated from the Architectural Faculty of the University of Tokyo in 1954 and established Arata Isozaki & Associates in 1963, having worked in the office of Kenzo Tange. Winner of the 1986 Royal Institute of British Architects Gold Medal, he has been a juror of major competitions such as that held in 1988 for the new Kansai International Airport. Notable buildings include: the Museum of Modern Art, Gunma (1971–74); the Tsukuba Center Building, Tsukuba (1978–83); the Museum of Contemporary Art, Los Angeles (1981–86); Art Tower Mito, Mito (1986–90); Team Disney Building, Florida (1990–94); B-con Plaza, Oita (1991–95). Current projects include Higashi Shizuoka Plaza Cultural Complex, Shizuoka, and Ohio's Center of Science and Industry (COSI), Columbus, Ohio.

Arata Isozaki wurde 1931 in Oita auf der Insel Kuyushu geboren. Er schloß 1954 sein Studium an der Fakultät für Architektur der University of Tokyo ab und gründete 1963 – nach seiner Tätigkeit für Kenzo Tange – sein eigenes Architekturbüro, Isozaki & Associates. 1986 gewann er die Goldmedaille des Royal Institute of British Architects und war danach als Jurymitglied bei verschiedenen bedeutenden Ausschreibungen tätig, u.a. dem 1988 ausgeschriebenen Wettbewerb für den neuen Kansai International Airport. Zu seinen wichtigsten Bauten gehören: Museum of Modern Art, Gunma (1971–74); Tsukuba Center Building, Tsukuba (1978–83); Museum of Contemporary Art, Los Angeles (1981–86); Art Tower Mito, Mito (1986–90); Team Disney Building, Florida (1990–94); B-con Plaza, Oita (1991–94). Seine gegenwärtigen Projekte umfassen: Higashi Shizuoka Plaza Cultural Complex, Shizuoka; Columbus Ohio Center of Science and Industry (COSI), Columbus, Ohio.

Né à Oita, sur l'île de Kyushu en 1931, Arata Isozaki passe son diplôme à la faculté d'architecture de Tokyo en 1954, et fonde Arata Isozaki & Associates en 1963, après avoir travaillé chez Kenzo Tange. Titulaire de la médaille d'or du Royal Institute of British Architects en 1986, il est juré dans de nombreux concours internationaux comme celui de 1988 pour l'aéroport international de Kansai. Parmi ses réalisations: le Musée d'art moderne, Gunma (1971–74); le Centre Tsukuba, Tsukuba (1978–83); The Museum of Contemporary Art, Los Angeles (1981–86); la Tour d'art de Mito, Mito (1986–90); l'immeuble Team Disney, Floride (1990–94); B-con Plaza, Oita (1991–95). Il travaille actuellement à divers projets dont le complexe culturel Higashi Shizuoka Plaza, Shizuoka; l'Ohio's Center of Science and Industry (COSI), Columbus, Ohio.

Toyo Ito & Associates
Fujiya Bldg. 19-4 1-Chome, Shibuya, Shibuya-ku
Tokyo 150, Japan

Tel: + 81 33 409 5822
Fax: + 81 33 409 5969

Maki & Associates
3-6-2 Nihonbashi, Chuo-ku
Tokyo 103, Japan

Tel: + 81 33 274 6681
Fax: + 81 33 273 4871

Kazuyo Sejima
601, 2-4-4 Ebisu Koyo Heights
Ebisu-Minami, Shibuya-ku
Tokyo 150, Japan

Tel: + 81 33 711 1092
Fax: +81 33 711 0699

Toyo Ito

Born in 1941 in Seoul, Korea, Toyo Ito graduated from the University of Tokyo in 1965, and worked in the office of Kiyonori Kikutake until 1969. He created his own office in 1971, assuming the name of Toyo Ito Architect & Associates in 1979. His completed work includes the Silver Hut Residence, Tokyo (1984); Tower of the Winds, Yokohama, Kanagawa (1986); Yatsushiro Municipal Museum, Yatsushiro, Kumamoto (1989–91); and the Elderly People's Home (1992–94) and Fire Station (1992–95), both located in the same city on the island of Kyushu. He participated in the Shanghai Luijiazui Center Area International Planning and Urban Design Consultation in 1992, and has built a Public Kindergarten (Eckenheim, Frankfurt, Germany, 1988–91).

Toyo Ito wurde 1941 in Seoul (Korea) geboren; er schloß 1965 sein Studium an der University of Tokyo ab und arbeitete bis 1969 im Büro von Kiyonori Kikutake. 1971 gründete er sein eigenes Büro, das seit 1979 unter dem Namen Toyo Ito Architect and Associates firmiert. Zu seinen fertiggestellten Bauwerken gehören u.a.: Silver Hut Residence, Tokio (1984); Tower of the Winds, Yokohama, Kanagawa (1986); Yatsushiro Municipal Museum, Yatsushiro, Kumamoto (1989–91) sowie das Altenheim (1992–94) und die Feuerwache von Yatsushiro (1992–95) auf der Insel Kyushu. Ito nahm 1992 an der Shanghai Luijiazui Center Area International Planning and Urban Design Consultation teil und errichtete zwischen 1988 und 1991 einen städtischen Kindergarten in Frankfurt-Eckenheim.

Né en 1941 à Séoul, Corée, Toyo Ito est diplômé de l'Université de Tokyo en 1965, et travaille dans l'agence de Kiyonori Kikutake jusqu'en 1969. Il crée sa propre agence en 1971, prenant le nom de Toyo Ito Architect & Associates en 1979. Parmi ses œuvres figurent la résidence "Hutte d'argent", Tokyo (1984); la Tour des vents, Yokohama, Kanagawa (1986); le Musée municipal, Yatsushiro, Kumamoto (1989–91); le Foyer de personnes âgées (1992–94); et la caserne des pompiers (1992–95) de Yatsushiro sur l'île de Kyushu. Il a participé à la consultation internationale d'urbanisme sur le quartier central Luijiazui de Shanghai en 1992, et a construit un jardin public pour enfants, Eckenheim, Francfort, Allemagne (1988–91).

Fumihiko Maki

Born in Tokyo in 1928, Fumihiko Maki received his B. Arch. degree from the University of Tokyo in 1952, and M. Arch. degrees from the Cranbrook Academy of Art (1953) and the Harvard Graduate School of Design (1954). He worked for Skidmore, Owings and Merrill in New York (1954–55) and Sert Jackson and Associates in Cambridge, Massachusets (1955–58) before creating his own firm, Maki and Associates, in Tokyo in 1965. Notable buildings include: Fujisawa Municipal Gymnasium, Fujisawa, Kanagawa (1984); Spiral, Minato-ku, Tokyo (1985); National Museum of Modern Art, Sakyo-ku, Kyoto (1986); Tepia, Minato-ku, Tokyo (1989); Tokyo Metropolitan Gymnasium, Shibuya, Tokyo (1990); Center for the Arts Yerba Buena Gardens, San Francisco, California (1991–93). Current projects include Nippon Convention Center Makuhari Messe Phase II, Chiba, Chiba (1997 completion).

Fumihiko Maki, geb. 1928 (Tokio), 1952 B. Arch an der University of Tokyo, 1953 M. Arch an der Cranbrook Academy of Art, studierte 1954 an der Harvard Graduate School of Design. Er war für Skidmore, Owings and Merill in New York sowie für Sert Jackson and Associates in Cambridge, Massachusetts tätig, bevor er 1965 sein Büro Maki & Associates in Tokio gründete. Bedeutende Bauten: Fujisawa Municipal Gymnasium, Kanagawa (1984); Spiral, Minato-ku, Tokio (1985); National Museum of Modern Art, Sakyo-ku, Kioto (1986); Tepia, Minato-ku, Tokio (1989); Tokyo Metropolitan Gymnasium, Shibuya, Tokio (1990); Center for the Arts, Yerba Buena Gardens, San Francisco, Kalifornien (1991–93). Zur Zeit arbeitet er an Phase II des Nippon Convention Center Makuhari Messe, Chiba, Chiba (Fertigstellung voraussichtlich 1997).

Né à Tokyo en 1928, Fumihiko Maki passe son B. Arch. à l'Université de Tokyo en 1952, et son M. Arch. à la Cranbrook Academy of Art (1953) et à l'Harvard Graduate School of Design (1954). Il travaille pour Skidmore, Owings and Merrill à New York (1954–55), et Sert Jackson and Associates à Cambridge, Massachusetts (1955–58), avant de créer Maki and Associates, à Tokyo (1965). Parmi ses réalisations: le gymnase municipal de Fujisawa, Kanagawa (1984); Spiral, Minato-ku, Tokyo (1985); Musée national d'art moderne, Sakyo-ku, Kyoto (1986); Tepia, Minato-ku, Tokyo (1989); le gymnase métropolitain de Tokyo, Shibuya, Tokyo (1990); le Centre for the Arts Yerba Buena Gardens, San Francisco, Californie (1991–93). Il travaille actuellement à la Phase II (extension) du Centre de Congrès nippon de Makuhari, Chiba, Chiba (achevé en 1997).

Kazuyo Sejima

Born in Ibaraki Prefecture in 1956, Kazuyo Sejima received her M. Arch. degree from Japan Women's University in 1981 and went to work in the office of Toyo Ito the same year. She established Kazuyo Sejima and Associates in Tokyo in 1987. She has been a visiting lecturer at Japan Women's University and at Waseda University since 1994. Her built work includes the Saishunkan Seiyaku Women's Dormitory in Kumamoto, Kumamoto (1990–91); Pachinko Parlor I, Hitachi, Ibaraki (1992–93); Pachinko Parlor II, Nakamachi, Ibaraki (1993); Villa in the Forest, Tateshina, Nagano (1993–94); Chofu Station Police Box, Tokyo (1993–94); Pachinko Parlor III, Hitachi Ibaraki (1995). She is currently participating in the design of apartment units in Gifu, and a Multimedia Artists Studio in the same city.

Kazuyo Sejima wurde 1956 in der Präfektur Ibaraki geboren; sie erhielt 1981 ihren Master of Architecture an der Japan Women's University und nahm noch im gleichen Jahr ihre Tätigkeit im Büro von Toyo Ito auf. 1987 gründete sie Kazuyo Sejima and Associates in Tokio und ist seit 1994 als Gastdozentin für die Japan Women's University und die Waseda University tätig. Zu ihren bedeutendsten Bauten zählen: Saishunkan Seiyaku-Wohnheim in Kumamoto, Kumamoto (1909–91); Pachinko Parlor I, Hitachi, Ibaraki (1992–93); Pachinko Parlor II, Nakamachi, Ibaraki (1993); Villa in the Forest, Tateshina, Nagano (1993–94); Chofu Station Police Box, Tokio (1993–94); Pachinko Parlor III, Hitachi, Ibaraki (1995). Zur Zeit arbeitet sie am Entwurf für ein Appartementhaus und ein Multimedia Artists Studio (beide in Gifu).

Née dans la préfecture d'Ibaraki en 1956, Kazuyo Sejima passe sa maîtrise d'architecture à l'Université des Femmes du Japon en 1981, et travaille immédiatement pour l'agence de Toyo Ito. Elle crée Kazuyo Sejima and Associates à Tokyo en 1987. Elle est lectrice invitée à l'Université des Femmes et à l'Université Waseda depuis 1994. Parmi ses réalisations: le foyer pour femmes Saishunkan Seiyaku à Kumamoto, Kumamoto (1990–91); le club de pachinko I, Hitachi, Ibaraki (1992–93); le club de pachinko II, Nakamachi, Ibaraki (1993); la Villa dans la forêt, Tateshina, Nagano (1993–94); le poste de police de Chofu, Tokyo (1993–94); le club de pachinko III, Hitachi, Ibaraki (1995). Elle travaille actuellement sur des immeubles d'appartements à Gifu, et à un studio d'artistes multimédia dans la même ville.

Shin Takamatsu
43-6 Uchihata-Cho
Takeda Fushimi-ku
Kyoto 612 Japan

Tel: + 81 75 621 6002
Fax: + 81 75 621 6079

Shoei Yoh + Architects
1-12-30 Heiwa
Minami-ku, Fukuoka-shi
815 Japan

Tel: + 81 92 521 4782
Fax: + 81 92 521 6718

Shin Takamatsu

Born in Shimane Prefecture in 1948, Shin Takamatsu graduated from Kyoto University in 1971 and from the Graduate School of the same institution in 1979. He created his own office in Kyoto in 1980, and has taught at Kyoto Technical University and at the Osaka University of Arts. Profiting amply from the building boom of the 1980s, Takamatsu completed a large number of structures, including Origin I, II and III, Kamigyo, Kyoto (1980–86); the Kirin Plaza Osaka, Chuo, Osaka (1985–87); and Syntax, Sakyo-ku, Kyoto (1988–90). In his more recent, less mechanical style, Takamatsu has completed the Kirin Headquarters, Chuo-ku, Tokyo (1993–95); the Shoji Ueda Museum of Photography, Kishimoto-cho, Tottori (1993–95); and the Nagasaki Port Terminal Building, Motofune-cho, Nagasaki (1994–95).

Shin Takamatsu wurde 1948 in der Präfektur Shimane geboren; er erhielt 1971 seinen Abschluß an der Kyoto University und schloß 1979 sein Postgraduierten-Studium an der gleichen Universität ab. 1980 gründete er sein eigenes Büro in Kioto; außerdem unterrichtete er an der Kyoto Technical University und der Osaka University of Arts. Dank des Baubooms der 80er Jahre errichtete Takamatsu zahlreiche Gebäude, u.a. Origin I, II und III, Kamigyo, Kioto (1980–86); Kirin Plaza Osaka, Chuo, Osaka (1985–87); und Syntax, Sakyo-ku, Kioto (1988–90), während er die folgenden Bauwerke in einem neueren, weniger mechanisch geprägten Stil fertigstellte: Kirin Headquarters, Chuo-ku, Tokio (1993–95); Shoji Ueda Museum of Photography, Kishimoto-cho, Tottori (1993–95); und das Nagasaki Port Terminal Building, Motofune-cho, Nagasaki (1994–95).

Né dans la préfecture de Shimane en 1948, Shin Takamatsu est diplômé en architecture de l'Université de Tokyo en 1971 et de l'Ecole supérieure de la même institution en 1979. Il crée son agence à Kyoto en 1980 et enseigne à l'Université technique de Kyoto et à l'Université des arts d'Osaka. Profitant amplement de l'explosion dans le domaine de la construction des années 80, il construit beaucoup, dont Origin I, II et III, Kamigyo, Kyoto (1980–86); le Kirin Plaza, Chuo, Osaka (1985–87); et l'immeuble Syntax, Sakyo-Ku, Kyoto (1988–90). Dans son style plus récent, moins mécaniste, Takamatsu a récemment achevé le siège social de Kirin, Chuo-ku, Tokyo (1993–95); le Musée de photographie Shoji Ueda, Kishimoto-cho, Tottori (1993–95); et les bâtiments du terminal du port de Nagasaki, Motofune-cho, Nagasaki (1994–95).

Shoei Yoh

Born in 1940 in Kumamoto City, Shoei Yoh received a degree in economics from Keio Gijuku University, Tokyo (1962) and studied Fine and Applied Arts at Wittenberg University in Springfield, Ohio (1964). Self-trained as an architect, he opened Shoei Yoh + Architects in Fukuoka in 1970, and gained a local reputation in industrial and interior design. His Stainless-Steel House with Light Lattice, Nagasaki, Nagasaki (1980), was widely published. More recent work, such as his Kanada Children Training House, Tagawa, Fukuoka (1994) and his Uchino Community Center for Seniors & Children, Kaho, Fukuoka (1995), shows his flair for spectacular forms. Shoei Yoh is a Professor of Architecture and Urban Design at the Graduate School of Keio University.

Shoei Yoh wurde 1940 in Kumamoto City geboren; er erhielt 1962 seinen Abschluß in Wirtschaftswissenschaft an der Keio Gijuku University in Tokio und studierte Freie und Angewandte Kunst an der Wittenberg University in Springfield, Ohio (1964). Als Autodidakt im Bereich Architektur öffnete er 1970 sein eigenes Büro Shoei Yoh + Architects in Fukuoka und erwarb sich den Ruf eines fähigen Industriedesigners und Innenarchitekten. Sein Stainless-Steel House with Light Lattice, Nagasaki, Nagasaki (1980) fand große Beachtung. Dagegen dokumentieren seine vor kurzem fertiggestellten Bauten – das Kanada Children Training House Tagawa, Fukuoka (1994) und das Uchino Community Center for Seniors & Children, Kaho, Fukuoka (1995) – seine Begeisterung für aufsehenerregende Formen. Shoei Yoh ist Professor für Architektur und Stadtplanung an der Graduate School der Keio University.

Né en 1940 à Kumamoto City, Shoei Yoh passe un diplôme de sciences économiques à l'Université Keio Gijuku de Tokyo (1962), et étudie les beaux-arts et les arts appliqués à Wittenberg University à Springfield, Ohio (1964). Architecte autodidacte, il ouvre l'agence Shoei Yoh + Architects à Fukuoka en 1970, et se fait une réputation de designer industriel et d'architecte d'intérieur. Sa "Maison d'acier inoxydable en lattis léger", Nagasaki, Nagasaki (1980) est largement commentée. Des réalisations plus récentes comme son Centre de formation pour enfants Kanada, Tagawa, Fukuoka (1994), et son Centre communautaire pour personnes âgées et enfants Uchino, Kaho, Fukuoka (1995) montrent son goût pour des formes spectaculaires. Shoei Yoh est professeur d'architecture et d'urbanisme à l'Ecole supérieure de l'Université Keio.

Bibliography | Bibliographie

"Tadao Ando". *GA Architect 8.*
A.D.A. Edita, Tokyo, 1987.

"Tadao Ando". *GA Architect 12.*
A.D.A. Edita, Tokyo, 1993.

"Tadao Ando". *El Croquis, 44 + 58.*
El Croquis Editorial, 1994.

"Tadao Ando". *GA Document Extra 01.*
A.D.A. Edita, Tokyo, 1995.

Banham, Reyner and Hiroyuki Suzuki:
Contemporary Architecture of Japan, 1958–1984.
Architectural Press, London, 1985.

Bognar, Botond: *The New Japanese Architecture.*
Rizzoli, New York, 1990.

Frampton, Kenneth: *Tadao Ando.*
The Museum of Modern Art, New York, 1991.

"Hiroshi Hara". *GA Architect 13.*
A.D.A. Edita, Tokyo, 1993.

"Hiroshi Hara". SD, *Space Design* n° 9401.
Tokyo, 1994.

Itsuko Hasegawa. Architectural Monographs
n° 31, Academy Editions, Ernst & Sohn, London,
1993.

Isozaki, Arata: *Katsura: A Model for Post-
Modern Architecture.* in: Katsura Villa – Space
and Form. Iwanami Shoten Publishers, Tokyo,
1983.

Isozaki, Arata: *Architecture 1960–1990.*
The Museum of Contemporary Art, Los Angeles,
Rizzoli, New York, 1991.

"Arata Isozaki", *GA Document* Extra 05.
A.D.A. Edita, Tokyo, 1996.

"Toyo Ito". *JA Library,* n° 2. The Japan Architect
Co., Ltd., Tokyo, 1993.

"Toyo Ito". *El Croquis* 71. El Croquis Editorial,
1995.

JA, N°2, 1991–2, The Japan Architect Co., Ltd.,
Tokyo, 1991.

JA, N°5, 1992–1, The Japan Architect Co., Ltd.,
Tokyo, 1992.

JA, N°7, 1992–3, The Japan Architect Co., Ltd.,
Tokyo, 1992.

JA, N°19, 1995–3, The Japan Architect Co., Ltd.,
Tokyo, 1995.

JA, N°20, Winter 1995, The Japan Architect Co.,
Ltd., Tokyo, 1995.

Japan '94, GA Document 39, A.D.A. Edita,
Tokyo, 1994.

"Fumihiko Maki". *JA* n° 16. Winter 1994,
The Japan Architect Co., Ltd., Tokyo, 1994.

Riley, Terence: *Light Construction.* Museum
of Modern Art, New York, 1995.

Kazuo Shinohara. Introduction by Irmtraud
Schaarschmidt-Richter, Ernst & Sohn, Berlin,
1995.

"Shin Takamatsu". *GA Architect* 9. A.D.A. Edita,
Tokyo, 1990

"Shin Takamatsu". *JA Library,* n° 1. The Japan
Architect Co., Ltd., Tokyo, 1993.

Tokyo, Form and Spirit. Walker Art Center, Harry
N. Abrams, New York, 1986.

Umeda Sky Bldg, Sekisui House, Ltd,
Osaka, 1994.

Wright, Frank Lloyd: *An Autobiography.* Duell,
Sloan and Pearce, New York, 1943.

Index

Ando, Tadao 18, 19, 28, **28**, 29–32, 45, 46, 47, 49–53, **53**, 54, **54**, 55, **55**, **56**, **65**, 66, 67, **67–68**, 69, **69–73**, 74, **75–78**, 79, **79–81**, 99, 118, 170
Arakawa, Shusaku 110, **112**

Böckmann, Wilhelm 22, 23
Bokura, Masakazu 6, 7, 56, 57, 58, **58**, 59, **82**, 83, **83**, 84, **84**, 85, **85–89**, 170
Botta, Mario 118, 134, **135**, **137**
Breuer, Marcel 79, **79**

Conder, Josiah 20, 21, **22**, 23
Cook, Peter 36, 37, 38

Diller, Elisabeth 36, 37, 38
Diller & Scofidio 36, 37, 38

Eisenman, Peter 13, 14, 37, 38, 39
Ende, Hermann 22, 23
Erickson, Arthur 16, 17

Gregotti, Vittorio 16, 17

Hadid, Zaha 49, 50
Hara, Hiroshi 31, 32, 39–42, **42**, 43–45, **45**, 46, 65, **90**, 91, **91**, 92, **92–98**, 99, **100–101**, 118, 171
Hasegawa, Itsuko 30, 31, 47, 48, **48**, **49**, 50, 59, 63, 65, **102**, 103, **103**, 104, **105–107**, 171
Hawley, Christine 36, 37, 38
Holl, Steven 13, 14
Hollein, Hans 118

Ishii, Kazuhiro 20, 21, 114
Isozaki, Arata **2**, 14, 15, 16, 24, 25, 28, 29–32, 35, 36, 37, **37**, 38, **38**, 39, 40, 57, 58, 59, 65, 83, 92, **108**, 109, **109**, 110, **110–113**, 114, **114–117**, 118, **118–120**, 121, **121–125**, 127, 171

Ito, Toyo 20, 21, 30, 31, 32, 36, 37, 45, 46, **46**, 47, 48, 59–63, 65, 83, 103, **126**, 127, **127**, 128, **128–131**, 149, 172

Kikutake, Kiyonori 28, 29, 30, 45–48, 103, 172
Koolhaas, Rem 39, 40
Kuma, Kengo 20, 21
Kurokawa, Kisho 29–32, 39, 40, 42, 99, 118

Lampugnani, Vittorio 118
Le Corbusier 22, 23, 24, 41, 42, 43, 46, 47, 48, 53, 54

Macary, Michel 170
Maekawa, Kunio 22–25, 27
Maki, Fumihiko 16, 17, 31, 32, **32**, 33, **33**, 34, **34**, 35, 36, 39, **40–41**, 65, 114, **132**, 133, **133**, 134, **135–138**, 139, **140–143**, 144, **144–147**, 172
Meier, Richard 118
Mies van der Rohe, Ludwig 49, 50
Miyawaki, Aiko 37, 38, 39, 110, **113**

Nervi, Pier Luigi 79, **79**
Noguchi, Isamu 27, 28, 29, **29**, 79, 114
Nouvel, Jean 39, 40

Okazaki, Kazuo 110, **111**

Pei, Ieoh Ming 16, 17, 83
Pelli, Cesar 16, 17
Piano, Renzo 39, 40
Polshek, James Steward 134
Portzamparc, Christian de 13, 14, 118
Prattz, Gustav 24, 25

Quoniam, Laure 84, **87**

Riley, Terry 57, 60, 150

Rogers, Richard 39, 40
Rossi, Aldo 13, 14

Sakakura Associates 114
Sant'Elia, Antonio 43, 44
Schwarz, Martha 36, 37, 38
Sejima, Kazuyo 20, 21, 36, 37, 38, 57–61, **61**, 62, 63, 65, **148**, 149, **149**, 150, **150–153**, 154, **154–157**, 172
Shinohara, Kazuo 29, 30, **30**, 31, **31**, 36, 37, 45, 47, 48, 103, 118, 127, 171
Skidmore, Owongs and Merill 32, 33, 133, 172
Soami 13
Starck, Philippe 12, 13, 14
Stirling, James 99, 118

Takamatsu, Shin 55, 56, **57**, 59, 65, 114, **158**, 159, **159**, 160, **160**, 161, **162–163**, 173
Takahashi, Akiko 36, 37, 38
Tange, Kenzo **13**, 24, 25, **25**, **26**, 27–32, 43, 44
Taut, Bruno 23, 24, 25
Teshigahara, Hiroshi 28, **28**, 29, 30
Teshigahara, Sofu 24, 25, 28, 29
Tschumi, Bernard 99
Tsuchiya, Kimio 6, **6**, 7

Viñoly, Rafael 16, 17, **17**

Watanabe, Makoto Sei 13, 14, **15**, **21**
Waters, Thomas 20, 21, 23
Wright, Frank Lloyd 22, 23

Yoh, Shoei 49, 50, **51**, 65, **164**, 165, **165**, 166, **166**, 167, **168–169**, 173

Credits | Fotonachweis | Crédits photographiques

l. = left | links | à gauche
r. = right | rechts | à droite
t. = top | oben | ci-dessus
c.= center | Mitte | centre
b. = bottom | unten | ci-dessous

2	© Arata Isozaki
6	© Photo: Tadasu Yamamoto
7	© Photo: Alfred Wolf
9 t.	© Photo: Arnaud Carpentier
9 c.	© Photo: Alfred Wolf
10	13 t.	© Photo: Arnaud Carpentier
13 b.	© Photo: Osamu Murai
15	© Photo: Arnaud Carpentier
17	© Photo: Masashi Kudo
18 t.	© Photo: Patrick Robert	Sygma
18 b.	© Photo: Bunyo Ishikawa	Sygma
21	© Photo: Arnaud Carpentier
22	25	© Photo: Alfred Wolf
26	© Photo: Osamu Murai
28	29	© Photo: Alfred Wolf
30	31	© Photo: Arnaud Carpentier
32 t.	© Photo: Toshiharu Kitajima
32 b.	© Photo: Fumihiko Maki
33	© Photo: Toshiharu Kitajima
34	© Maki and Associates
37	© Photo: Arnaud Carpentier
38	© Arata Isozaki
40–41 t.	© Kisho Kurokawa
41	© Photo: Tomio Ohashi
42	© Photo: Shigeru Ono
45	© Photo: Antonio Martinelli
46 t.	© Photo: Toyo Ito & Associates
46 c.	© Toyo Ito & Associates
48	© Photo: Shuji Yamada
49	© Photo: Arnaud Carpentier
51	© Photo: Satoshi Asakawa
53	© Photo: Shinkenchiku-sha
54	© Photo: Dieter Leistner	Architekton
55	© Tadao Ando
57	© Photo: Arnaud Carpentier
58 t.	© Masakazu Bokura
58 b.	© Photo: B² Bokura Barbot
61	© Photo: Kazuyo Sejima & Associates
62	© Photo: Arnaud Carpentier
66	© Photo: Shinkenchiku-sha
67	© Photo: Mitsuru Mizuta
68–71	© Photo: Shinkenchiku-sha
72 t.	© Tadao Ando
72 b.	73	© Photo: Tomio Ohashi
75 t.	© Photo: Mitsuo Matsuoka
75 b.	© Tadao Ando
76 l.	© Photo: Shinkenchiku-sha
76 r.	© Tadao Ando
77	© Photo: Shinkenchiku-sha
78	© Photo: Stéphane Couturier	Archipress
79	© Photo: Tadao Ando
80 l.	© Tadao Ando

80 r.	© Photo: Tadao Ando
81	© Photo: Stéphane Couturier	Archipress
82–84	© Photo: B² Bokura Barbot
85 t.	© Photo: B² Bokura Barbot
85 b.	© Masakazu Bokura
86 t.	© Photo: B² Bokura Barbot
86–87	© Photo: B² Bokura Barbot
87 t.	© Masakazu Bokura
87 c.	© Photo: B² Bokura Barbot
88–89	© Photo: B² Bokura Barbot
90	© Photo: Antonio Martinelli
91	© Hiroshi Hara
92	© Photo: Antonio Martinelli
93	© Photo: Tomio Ohashi
94–95	© Photo: Antonio Martinelli
95 t.	© Hiroshi Hara
95 b.	© Photo: Antonio Martinelli
96–97	© Photo: Antonio Martinelli
98	© Photo: Tomio Ohashi
100	101 t.	© Hiroshi Hara
101 b.	© Photo: Tomio Ohashi
102	© Photo: Mitsumasa Fujitsuka
103	© Photo: Arnaud Carpentier
105	© Photo: Mitsumasa Fujitsuka
106	© Itsuko Hasegawa
106	107	© Photo: Taisuke Ogawa
108	© Photo: Katsuaki Furudate
109	© Photo: Eiichiro Sakata
110	© Photo: Shinkenchiku-sha
111–113	© Photo: Katsuaki Furudate
113 b.	© Arata Isozaki
114	© Arata Isozaki
115	© Photo: Katsuaki Furudate
116 t.l.	© Arata Isozaki
116–117	© Photo: Katsuaki Furudate
118	119	© Arata Isozaki
120	© Photo: Katsuaki Furudate
121	122 t.	© Arata Isozaki
122 c.	© Photo: Manel Armengol
122 b.	© Photo: Katsuaki Furudate
123	© Photo: Manel Armengol
124	© Photo: Katsuaki Furudate
125 l.	© Arata Isozaki
125 t.	© Hisao Suzuki	Archivo Eye
125 b.	© Photo: Manel Armengol
126	© Photo: Tomio Ohashi
127	© Photo: Nacása & Partners inc.
128	129	© Photo: Tomio Ohashi
130 l.	© Photo: Tomio Ohashi
130 r.	b.	© Toyo Ito
131	© Photo: Tomio Ohashi
132	© Photo: Richard Barnes

133	© Maki and Associates
135 t.l.	© Maki and Associates
135 b.l.	© Photo: Richard Barnes
135 t.r.	© Photo: Paul Peck. Robinson Mills + Williams
135 b.r.	© Photo: Richard Barnes
136–137	© Photo: Paul Peck. Robinson Mills + Williams
138	© Photo: Toshiharu Kitajima
140 t.l.	© Photo: Toshiharu Kitajima
140 b.l.	© Maki and Associates
140–142	© Photo: Toshiharu Kitajima
143 t.	© Maki and Associates
143 c.	© Photo: Toshiharu Kitajima
143 b.	144	© Maki and Associates
145	© Maki and Associates	Photo: Matteo Piazza
146–147	© Maki and Associates	Photo: Matteo Piazza
146 b.	© Maki and Associates
147	© Photo: Shinkenchiku-sha
148	© Photo: Kozo Takayama	Nacása & Partners inc.
149	© Photo: Nacása & Partners inc.
150	© Photo: Tomio Ohashi
151	© Photo: Shinkenchiku-sha
152 r.	© Kazuyo Sejima
152 l.	© Photo: Shinkenchiku-sha
153	154	© Photo: Shinkenchiku-sha
155	© Photo: Kozo Takayama	Nacása & Partners inc.
156–157	© Photo: Kozo Takayama	Nacása & Partners inc.
157 t.	© Photo: Kozo Takayama	Nacása & Partners inc.
157 c.	© Kazuyo Sejima
157 b.	© Photo: Kozo Takayama	Nacása & Partners inc.
158	© Photo: Nacása & Partners
159	© Photo: Arnaud Carpentier
160	© Shin Takamatsu
161 t.	© Photo: Toshiyuki Kobayashi
161 b.l.	© Shin Takamatsu
161 b.r.	© Photo: Nacása & Partners inc.
162 t.	© Photo: Nacása & Partners inc.
162 b.	© Photo: Katsuaki Furudate
162–163	© Photo: Nacása & Partners inc.
164	165	© Photo: Satoshi Asakawa
166	© Shoei Yoh
167–169	© Photo: Satoshi Asakawa

The publisher and author wish to thank each of the architects and photographers for their kind assistance.